MIDWAY

MIDWAY

HUGH BICHENO

CASSELL&CO

HILLS

Men
cc

**Previous page:
William Leonard
of VF-3 takes off
on combat air
patrol, morning
of 4 June**

To Kay and Clear Lake Curia for their friendship and guidance

Cassell & Co
The Orion Publishing Group
Orion House
5 Upper St Martin's Lane
London WC2H 9EA

A catalogue record for this book is available
from the British Library

ISBN 0-304-35715-4

2721 3403 ³/₀₃

Designed by Goldust Design
Printed and bound in Spain

CONTENTS

LIST OF MAPS

FOREWORD

Although the battle of Midway was not the first major action waged primarily by carrier-based aircraft (that honour goes to the Coral Sea, fought in May 1942) it was a carrier battle on a far larger scale, which inflicted lasting damage on the Imperial Japanese Navy. In the process it set the pattern for much of what followed in the Pacific War, although it would have taken a sharp-eyed observer to discern that at the time. Midway is, understandably enough, a much-described battle, but Hugh Bicheno (whose other contribution to this series is the similarly much-chronicled Gettysburg) has approached it in a way which throws new light onto familiar events.

Firstly, he emphasises that war often embodies a cultural as well as physical clash between opponents. Indeed, there is a strong case for saying that, at the beginning of the 21st Century, when military theorists frequently write about 'asymmetric warfare', potentially the most disturbing asymmetry is not a technical imbalance between the contending parties, but a cultural asymmetry which may enable one side to sustain a long war with heavy casualties while the other is conditioned to demand quick, cheap victory. There was a profound cultural asymmetry in the Pacific War, and its currents run far deeper than apparent similarities between the Imperial Japanese Navy and its western opponents (from whom it had borrowed much in the first years of its young life) would suggest. Hugh Bicheno quotes the assertion of Commander Mitsuo Fuchida, leader of the attack on Pearl Harbor on 7 December 1941, that cultural factors were 'the root cause of Japan's defeat, not alone in the battle of Midway but in the entire war...' The US Navy tended to regard its men and machines as interchangeable parts and battle as a management exercise, while for the Japanese battle was an art, with will and elan its key instruments.

Although there were weaknesses in the American approach, we have only to compare the blinding glimpses of the obvious in the Japanese after-action report with the measured analysis of the American to see at least one of its strengths.

Commanders were both prisoners and directors of the forces they led. Fleet Admiral Isoroku Yamamoto, the Japanese commander, had lived in the United States and was well aware of the marked disparity between American and Japanese economic strength, but his attempt to seek an early decision based on technical and numerical superiority was marred by a plan that, as Hugh Bicheno puts it, 'combined maximum dispersion with less than the minimum reconnaissance.' In sharp contrast, Admiral Chester Nimitz, Yamamoto's opponent, was provided with accurate intelligence gleaned from the interception of Japanese radio traffic and the cracking of its ciphers. This gave him just enough information to form a firm judgement of Yamamoto's intentions, and it speaks much for Nimitz's clarity of vision and moral courage that, despite bickering within his intelligence community and considerable nervousness in high places, he pressed ahead with a deployment which was to enable his aircrew to win the battle.

The weapons used in the battle reflected culture as well as technology. Yamamoto had suggested that battleships were as useful in modern war as a samurai sword, and in 1936 had complained that they were 'a matter of faith, not reality.' However, it was precisely because of the importance accorded to such symbolism that his fleet contained these monsters, and that his staff planned, almost in defiance of tactical reality, to use them in the role for which they had been built. There were, however, areas where the Japanese had a clear technological edge. Their 'Long Lance' torpedo (its very name another example of cultural symbolism) had more than three times the effective range of its American counterpart and a reliable firing mechanism. In contrast, US torpedoes often failed to detonate on impact, and the aircraft that dropped them had to fly low and slow to do so. The Japanese also had a clear lead in fighter design. Their Zero consistently outperformed its opponents, leading an experienced US fighter pilot to observe that the Grumman F4F 'is pitifully inferior in *climb, manoeuvrability* and *speed.*' This time culture worked against the Americans, who were reluctant to accept 'the unpalatable truth of non-derivative Japanese technical superiority.'

Next, Hugh Bicheno emphasises the dangerous absence of what he terms 'creative dissent' in the Japanese staff. Like courtiers across the ages, Yamamoto's staff sought to anticipate their patron's wishes, and in the process managed to create a deeply flawed plan, and proceeded to use the threat of their master's resignation to force it past the Naval General Staff. He goes on to unpick the complex patchwork quilt of luck which enfolded the participants, and concludes that although on the whole fortune favoured the Americans, bad luck trickled into 'a cascade of poor Japanese decisions made with a carelessness bordering on frivolity' to swamp their plan.

For all the long-term effects of national or service culture, and the more immediate consequences of technology and tactics, battles are ultimately lost and won by the men who fight them, and in the pages that follow there are brave men aplenty, at sea, in the air and on the ground. Ensign Albert Earnest brought his torpedo bomber home after a long flight with his turret gunner dead and his radioman unconscious, his controls wrecked and over seventy hits on his aircraft. USS *Hornet's* torpedo-bomber squadron under Lieutenant Commander John Waldron was a total loss, its planes hacked from the sky by the Zeros protecting the Japanese carrier *Akagi*: a brother officer described the unit's annihilation as 'a death in the immediate family.' Rear Admiral Yamaguchi and Captain Kaku chose to go down with *Hiryu*, having ordered their reluctant officers to leave them and making grim jokes about how they would use the ship's payroll to buy themselves a better billet in hell. There were visions of sheer horror: an America airman saw the stricken *Akagi* 'like a haystack in flames' and most of the eight hundred men who died aboard *Kaga* perished in a conflagration deep within her. There were flashes of chivalry: an American pilot could not bring himself to machine-gun men in the water. But there were also bursts of gratuitous savagery: after three American aircrew were rescued from the sea by Japanese warships one was beheaded and the other two tied to oil-drums full of water and pushed over the side alive. Much about Midway was new, but much too was as old and cruel as war itself.

RICHARD HOLMES

COMMAND TREE – US NAVY

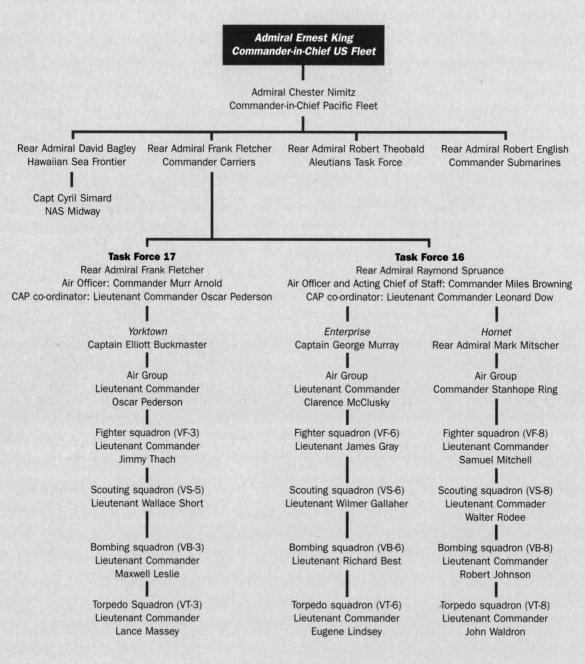

Admiral Ernest King
Commander-in-Chief US Fleet

Admiral Chester Nimitz
Commander-in-Chief Pacific Fleet

Rear Admiral David Bagley
Hawaiian Sea Frontier

Rear Admiral Frank Fletcher
Commander Carriers

Rear Admiral Robert Theobald
Aleutians Task Force

Rear Admiral Robert English
Commander Submarines

Capt Cyril Simard
NAS Midway

Task Force 17
Rear Admiral Frank Fletcher
Air Officer: Commander Murr Arnold
CAP co-ordinator: Lieutenant Commander Oscar Pederson

Task Force 16
Rear Admiral Raymond Spruance
Air Officer and Acting Chief of Staff: Commander Miles Browning
CAP co-ordinator: Lieutenant Commander Leonard Dow

Yorktown
Captain Elliott Buckmaster

Enterprise
Captain George Murray

Hornet
Rear Admiral Mark Mitscher

Air Group
Lieutenant Commander
Oscar Pederson

Air Group
Lieutenant Commander
Clarence McClusky

Air Group
Commander Stanhope Ring

Fighter squadron (VF-3)
Lieutenant Commander
Jimmy Thach

Fighter squadron (VF-6)
Lieutenant James Gray

Fighter squadron (VF-8)
Lieutenant Commander
Samuel Mitchell

Scouting squadron (VS-5)
Lieutenant Wallace Short

Scouting squadron (VS-6)
Lieutenant Wilmer Gallaher

Scouting squadron (VS-8)
Lieutenant Commader
Walter Rodee

Bombing squadron (VB-3)
Lieutenant Commander
Maxwell Leslie

Bombing squadron (VB-6)
Lieutenant Richard Best

Bombing squadron (VB-8)
Lieutenant Commander
Robert Johnson

Torpedo Squadron (VT-3)
Lieutenant Commander
Lance Massey

Torpedo squadron (VT-6)
Lieutenant Commander
Eugene Lindsey

Torpedo squadron (VT-8)
Lieutenant Commander
John Waldron

COMMAND TREE – IMPERIAL JAPANESE NAVY

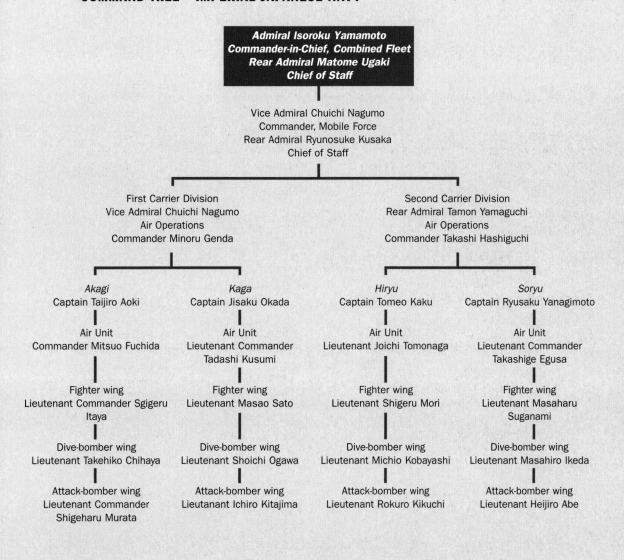

Admiral Isoroku Yamamoto
Commander-in-Chief, Combined Fleet
Rear Admiral Matome Ugaki
Chief of Staff

Vice Admiral Chuichi Nagumo
Commander, Mobile Force
Rear Admiral Ryunosuke Kusaka
Chief of Staff

First Carrier Division
Vice Admiral Chuichi Nagumo
Air Operations
Commander Minoru Genda

Second Carrier Division
Rear Admiral Tamon Yamaguchi
Air Operations
Commander Takashi Hashiguchi

Akagi
Captain Taijiro Aoki

Air Unit
Commander Mitsuo Fuchida

Fighter wing
Lieutenant Commander Sgigeru Itaya

Dive-bomber wing
Lieutenant Takehiko Chihaya

Attack-bomber wing
Lieutenant Commander Shigeharu Murata

Kaga
Captain Jisaku Okada

Air Unit
Lieutenant Commander Tadashi Kusumi

Fighter wing
Lieutenant Masao Sato

Dive-bomber wing
Lieutenant Shoichi Ogawa

Attack-bomber wing
Lieutenant Ichiro Kitajima

Hiryu
Captain Tomeo Kaku

Air Unit
Lieutenant Joichi Tomonaga

Fighter wing
Lieutenant Shigeru Mori

Dive-bomber wing
Lieutenant Michio Kobayashi

Attack-bomber wing
Lieutenant Rokuro Kikuchi

Soryu
Captain Ryusaku Yanagimoto

Air Unit
Lieutenant Commander Takashige Egusa

Fighter wing
Lieutenant Masaharu Suganami

Dive-bomber wing
Lieutenant Masahiro Ikeda

Attack-bomber wing
Lieutenant Heijiro Abe

CHRONOLOGY

The International Date Line runs between Midway and Wake. All events on the Japanese side of it are dated a day ahead of simultaneous US events until 3 June, when Midway time applies.

1941

7 Dec IJN Mobile Force/First Air Fleet attacks Pearl Harbor.

10 Dec HMS *Prince of Wales* and *Repulse* sunk. Surrender of Guam.

11 Dec First Japanese assault on Wake repelled.

17 Dec President Roosevelt dismisses Kimmel, Commander-in-Chief Pacific Fleet (CinCPac).

23 Dec Surrender of Wake following recall of Kimmel's relief effort.

25 Dec Surrender of Hong Kong.

31 Dec King formally takes over as Commander-in-Chief US Fleet (CinCUS), Nimitz as CinCPac.

1942

11 Jan *Saratoga* torpedoed southwest of Hawaii, returns to USA for repairs.

14 Jan Combined Fleet Chief of Staff Ugaki's draft of future operations includes Midway.

25 Jan Chief Staff Officer Kuroshima ignores Ugaki's project in favour of a Burma/India advance.

1 Feb *Enterprise* raids Kwajalein and Wotje, *Yorktown* raids Jaluit and Makin.

15 Feb Surrender of Singapore – end of British resistance in Malaya.

19 Feb Mobile Force wrecks port of Darwin, northern Australia.

20 Feb *Lexington* in air battle off Bougainville.

24 Feb *Enterprise* raids Wake.

27–28 Feb Battle of the Java Sea – annihilation of Allied East Indies fleet.

4 Mar *Enterprise* raids Marcus.

9 Mar Surrender of Java – end of Dutch resistance in the East Indies.

10 Mar *Lexington* and *Yorktown* raid Lae and Salamua, New Guinea.

12 Mar Offices of CinCUS and Chief of Naval Operations merged, King hereafter CominCh.

28 Mar Combined Fleet Staff begins detailed work on Midway operation (MI).

5 Apr Naval General Staff reluctantly approves MI in principle.

5–9 Apr Indian Ocean – Mobile Force sinks HMS *Dorsetshire*, *Cornwall*, *Hermes* and *Vampire*.

18 Apr *Hornet* with *Enterprise* escorting launches Doolittle raid on Japan.

22/23 Apr Mobile Force returns to Japan.

30 Apr Midget submarine Special Duty Forces sortie from Japan for Australia and Madagascar.

1-4 May Preliminary MI war games on board *Yamato*.

5 May Imperial GHQ Navy Order No. 18

authorizes MI/Aleutians operation.

6 May Surrender of Corregidor – end of US resistance in the Philippines.

7–11 May Battle of the Coral Sea – *Shoho* and *Lexington* sunk, *Yorktown* and *Shokaku* damaged.

20 May Yamamoto issues final orders for MI. Occupation Force sorties from Japan to Saipan.

22 May Pacific COMINT stations confirm Midway is 'AF' in Japanese naval code.
Half of Midway's aviation fuel tanks destroyed by accident.

24 May Final MI war games aboard *Yamato*.

25 May Hypo (Hawaii COMINT station) deciphers timing for attack on Aleutians and Midway.

26 May Fifth Fleet (Aleutians Main Force) sorties from Ominato, northern Japan. *Enterprise* and *Hornet* (TF 16) return to Pearl Harbor. Spruance replaces ill Halsey.

27 May Japanese Navy Day (anniversary of battle of Tsushima). IJN ciphers changed. Mobile Force sorties from Hiroshima, part Aleutians Invasion Force from Ominato.

28 May Fletcher and *Yorktown* (TF 17) return to Pearl Harbor, intensive repair of Coral Sea battle damage begins. Nimitz briefs Fletcher and Spruance, latter sorties with TF 16.

29 May First and Second Fleets (Midway)

sortie from Hiroshima, part Aleutians Invasion Force from Ominato, Midway Occupation and Support Forces from Guam/Saipan.

29/30 May *I-123* finds *Thornton* at French Frigate Shoals, Operation 'K' postponed.

30 May Japanese note long report from US submarine on course of Midway Occupation Force.
Yorktown repairs completed. Fletcher sorties with TF 17.

30/31 May Midget submarines sink a freighter, cripple HMS *Ramillies* at Diego Suarez, Madagascar, sink a floating barracks in Sidney harbour.

31 May Operation K cancelled. TF 1 (Pye, battleships) sorties from San Francisco.

1 June Tokyo reports increased US high-priority radio traffic, RDF indications of task forces at sea near Hawaii and the Aleutians. *I-168* and Wake report increased air patrols |from Midway.
TF 11 (*Saratoga*) sorties from San Diego, California.

2 June TF 16 and TF 17 meet at Point Luck at 1600.

3 June Japanese submarine screens take up positions, two days behind schedule.

3 JUNE

0500 TF 8 (Theobald, cruisers) assembles in mid ocean east of the Aleutians

0700 Second Carrier Strike Force attacks Dutch Harbor (Aleutians).

0904 Minesweeper Group from Wake spotted by PBY (Lyle).

0925 Occupation Force spotted by PBY (Reid).

1500 First Fleet divides, Aleutians Support Force heads north-east, Main Force towards Midway.

1640 Six B-17s attack occupation force.

Unknown Tokyo reports RDF indications of US task force in the vicinity of Midway, received by the main force but not by the mobile force.

4 JUNE

0130 PBY-5As make torpedo attack on occupation force, *Akebono Maru* hit.

0300 Nagumo orders rapid advance to bombardment range by Kurita's four heavy cruisers.

0430–35 Japanese carriers launch A/S \patrols followed by Midway attack force. *Akagi*, *Kaga* and *Haruna* launch search aircraft 1, 2 and 7. *Chikuma* launches search aircraft 5.

0437 Dawn.

0438 *Chikuma* launches search aircraft 6.

0442 *Tone* launches search aircraft 3.

0500 *Tone* launches search aircraft 4.

0532 PBY (Ady) reports sighting 'many carriers'.

0544 PBY (Chase) reports 'many aircraft heading Midway'.

0552 Ady reports two carriers and battleships.

0600 All Midway aircraft ordered into the air.

0607 Fletcher orders TF 16 to close and attack when targets confirmed.

0630–0705 Air raid on Midway.

Tomonaga signals second attack needed.

0700 TF16 begins to launch strike aircraft.

0705 Midway Avengers attack *Hiryu*.

0710 Midway Marauders attack *Akagi*.

0715 Nagumo orders attack aircraft re-armed with land bombs.

0728 *Tone* #4 search aircraft reports large surface force.

0745 Nagumo halts change over, requests clarification from *Tone* #4.

0750 Periscopes (*Grouper* and *Nautilus*) strafed, surface units detached to attack.

0805–15 Midway Dauntlesses (SDB) attack *Hiryu*.

0805 TF 16 completes launch of strike aircraft.

0815–20 Midway B-17s near-miss *Soryu*, *Kaga* and *Hiryu*.

0820 *Tone* #4 reports force 'appears to include a carrier'.

0820–30 Midway Vindicators attack *Haruna*.

0835 Nagumo orders Midway strike recovered before launching against enemy task force.

0840 *Yorktown* launches strike aircraft.

0855 *Tone* #4 search aircraft reports 'ten enemy torpedo planes heading toward you'.

0917 Recovery of Midway strike complete, Mobile Force turns north.

0920 *Hornet* torpedo bombers (VT-8, Waldron) attack *Soryu*.

0930 *Arashi* breaks off attack on *Nautilus*, races back towards Mobile Force.

0940 *Enterprise* torpedo bombers (VT-6, Lindsey) attack *Kaga*.

0955 *Enterprise* SDBs (VS-6/VB-6, McClusky) parallel line of *Arashi*'s wake.

1002 McClusky sights carriers.

1005 *Yorktown* group (VT-3, Massey, VB-3, Leslie, VF-3, Thach) sights carriers.

1015 VT-3 attacks *Hiryu*. VF-3 engages Japanese CAP.

1022-1027 VS-6/VB-6 wreck *Kaga* and *Akagi*. VB-3 wrecks *Soryu*.

1050 Nagumo shifts flag to *Nagara*, signals Yamamoto that three carriers lost. *Hiryu* launches dive bombers (Kobayashi).

1220 Yamamoto orders concentration of Midway forces.

1230 *Yorktown* hit by dive bombers.

1310 Yamamoto orders suspension of Midway and Aleutians occupations.

1324 Fletcher transfers flag to *Astoria*.

1330 *Hiryu* launches torpedo bombers (Tomonaga).

1400 *Nautilus* fires three torpedoes at *Kaga* hulk.

1440 *Yorktown* hit by torpedo bombers.

1445 *Yorktown* scout aircraft (VS-5, Adams) locates *Hiryu* group.

1705–10 VS-6/VB-6/VB-3 wreck *Hiryu*.

1720 VS-8/VB-8 from *Hornet* attack *Tone*.

1710–1830 B-17s attack Mobile Force

1730 Yamamoto reinstates Aleutians operation.

1915 Yamamoto orders a general advance.

1915–25 *Soryu* and *Kaga* sink.

2255 Yamamoto puts Kondo (Second Fleet) in command over Nagumo.

5 JUNE

0020 Bombardment of Midway by heavy cruisers cancelled.

0125 *I-168* shells Midway.

0215 *Tambor* seen on the surface, *Mikuma* and *Mogami* collide during evasive action.

0255 Yamamoto cancels occupation of Midway.

0500 *Akagi* scuttled. *Makigumo* torpedoes *Hiryu*.

0810 6 Midway SDBs attack cruisers.

0840 6 Midway Vindicators attack, Fleming's aircraft crashes into *Mikuma*.

0850 B-17s attack cruisers.

0900 *Hiryu* sinks.

1635–1845 *Tanikaze* attacked by seven B-17s and forty-two SDBs. One SDB and two B-17s lost.

Night Yamamoto orders reinforcement of northern force.

6 JUNE

0950 *Hornet* SDBs and fighters hit both cruisers and *Asashio*. Two SDBs lost.

1230 *Enterprise/Yorktown* SDBs hit *Mogami*, wreck *Mikuma*.

1240 B-17s attack *Grayling*, report sinking a cruiser in fifteen minutes.

1335 *I-168* torpedoes *Hammann* (sinks immediately) and *Yorktown* (sinks at dawn the next day).

1445 Second *Hornet* strike hits *Arashio*, devastates *Mikuma* (sinks at nightfall).

AFTERMATH

7 Jun General Tinker lost in failed LB-30 raid on Wake. Article in the Chicago *Tribune* implies Japanese code broken.

11 Jun Japanese press announces a great victory.

12 Jun US Army announces its bombers won the battle.

The masterless Japanese samurai Miyamoto Musashi (1584–1645) was probably the deadliest practitioner of single combat of all time. Between the ages of thirteen and twenty-nine he is reputed to have killed sixty men in duels, becoming so skilled that he eventually dispensed with swords and used whatever came to hand. He subsequently retired to teach and paint, and at the end of his life wrote a brief treatise in which he scorned those who overemphasized weapons and tactics because 'once we are talking about the art of the advantages, it cannot be limited to swordsmanship alone'. The killing stroke followed not merely from the will to conquer but from high seriousness, itself the product of a cultured nature, mental and physical austerity, rigorous training and cold-eyed self-knowledge, without which the mental leap of 'becoming the enemy' was impossible. For Musashi, the field of battle was in the mind and the battle of

Midway, fought nearly three centuries after his death, was won and lost in that arena.

More than the details of who, what and where, this is the biggest challenge for a historian, whose duty it is to assess the actions of men by their own standards and by those of their moment in time. As with *Gettysburg*, my previous contribution to this series, my purpose here is to explore the practical constraints and human variables in the formulation and execution of key decisions in a much-chronicled battle, as far as possible in terms of the reasonable – or unreasonable – expectations of the protagonists. One thing is unarguable: what for convenience we call 'luck' seemed to have worked so overwhelmingly in favour of the Americans that Gordon Prange and his posthumous collaborators can be forgiven for calling it *Miracle at Midway*. Although I dispute this in the chapter 'Point Luck', it was precisely the suggestion of divine favour that made it so encouraging for the Americans and so disheartening for the Japanese, who left far more to chance than they needed to.

Also, as Winston Churchill wrote, 'at one stroke, the dominant position of Japan in the Pacific was reversed … the qualities of the United States Navy and Air Force and the American race shone forth in splendour.' This was ultimately what the war was about and the reason why it was waged with such appalling ferocity. Unable to resist making the chapter 'Midway', the midpoint of the book, at the place where theory and planning give way to action, I have therefore entitled this introduction 'Start', but this is not solely semantic whimsy. It really does all begin with the social factors that created a time or mood for war, when hatred dared speak its name, until the urge to put basic assumptions about racial and cultural superiority to the test became irresistible.

Military history tends to support the hypothesis that God is on the side of the big battalions, but in an evenly matched battle such as Midway the outcome may hinge on any of a thousand personal decisions. Consideration must therefore be given to what we today call the 'default' mind-set of those involved. Rudyard Kipling wrote 'Oh East is East, and West is West, and never the twain shall meet' as a preamble to the less-quoted observation, 'But there is neither East nor West, border, nor breed, nor birth, when two strong men stand face to face, though they come from the end of the earth.' Nonetheless how they then attempt to kill each other will owe much to the vital myths and the institutional frameworks that sustain them. This in turn will be reflected in the weapons they employ, and I deal with these linked themes in the chapters 'Mind', and 'Machinery'. Commander Mitsuo Fuchida, leader of the attack on Pearl Harbor that began the Pacific War on 7 December 1941, was in no doubt the outcome at Midway was the product of cultural factors:

> ... the root cause of Japan's defeat, not alone in the Battle of Midway but in the entire war, lies deep in the Japanese national character. There is an irrationality and impulsiveness about our people, which results in actions that are haphazard and often contradictory ... Indecisive and vacillating, we succumb readily to conceit, which in turn makes us disdainful of others ... Our want of rationality often leads us to confuse reality and desire, and thus to do things without careful planning.[1]

One must, of course, be wary of such explanations – this is a fair indictment of humanity at large. A great deal of thought and technical proficiency went into the preparation for war, and the attack on Pearl Harbor itself was meticulously planned and thoroughly rehearsed. Breast-beating about collective blame is often employed to dilute individual responsibility and if we are to select one reason above all why the Americans prevailed at Midway, it is that easy victories had left officers like Fuchida more than half persuaded the United States Navy (USN) was a paper tiger. But while we can excuse the young staff and operations personnel of the Japanese Combined Fleet for overconfidence, this does not extend to the senior officers, whose job it was to moderate their enthusiasm. The principal responsibility remaining at the highest command levels is to ensure that all subordinate commanders work together to achieve decisive concentration somewhere on the field of battle, and at Midway the overall Japanese commander signally failed to do so.

Isoroku Yamamoto

In the chapter 'Cleverness' I discuss the genesis and development of the fundamentally flawed undertaking known to the Japanese as 'Operation MI'. Directly or indirectly, it reflected the thinking of the eight-fingered Admiral Isoroku Yamamoto (Isoroku means 'fifty-six', his father's age when he was born in 1884), a samurai's son who bore the name of one of the founders of the Imperial Japanese Navy (IJN). His opponent was the nine-fingered Admiral Chester Nimitz (whose father died before he was born in 1885), of German immigrant stock from the barely moist hill country of Texas, who acted with a singleness of purpose applauded in the chapter 'Intelligence'.

Underlying it all was the fact that between 1941 and 1942 the Japanese militarists sincerely believed the notoriously henpecked and materialistic American male was no warrior, and their hope for salvation was that the United States would fold when the crunch came. That belief was shattered by the bravery of the American pilots at Midway, and the related hope was dispersed by the knowledge that they had not only been outfought but also unequivocally outwitted. We now know the crucial role played by communications intelligence (COMINT), but at the time it seemed to the Japanese the obscure Nimitz, not the great Yamamoto, had succeeded in getting into his opponent's mind to 'become the enemy'.

Operation MI ran counter to the decades-old IJN doctrine, which assumed the USN would charge across the Pacific, suffering attrition from submarines and night attacks, to a climactic confrontation between the battle fleets in Far Eastern waters. Having lived in the United States, Yamamoto was more acutely aware than most of the disproportion between the US and Japan's economic strength, and used his personal authority to impose a departure from orthodoxy on the Naval General Staff. He was right to seek an early conclusion based on temporary numerical and technical superiority, but thence to a plan that frittered away the overwhelming force at his disposal was very much more than a slip 'twixt strategic cup and operational lip, and one that demands a fuller explanation than it has received. Walter Lord called it an *Incredible Victory*, but I argue that it was an avoidable defeat, born of the intellectual arrogance that has caused many clever men to fail the test of war. Nor should we forget that Yamamoto was an inveterate gambler who had an 'infallible' system to win at roulette, and that casinos maintain hospitality suites for such as he because the longer they play, the more certain it is the house will win.

Yamamoto's innermost thoughts on the subject died with him less than a year later, but the planning was nominally the responsibility of his chief of staff, Rear Admiral Matome Ugaki, who kept a voluminous personal diary. One can open it at random and find some stunningly inconsequential remark or adolescent maundering about death, **Chester Nimitz** but the following entry, written on 7 May 1942 after the loss of the brand new light aircraft carrier *Shoho* during the battle of the Coral Sea, is representative:

> A dream of great success has been shattered. There is an opponent in a war, so one cannot progress just as one wishes. When we expect enemy raids, can we not employ the forces in a little more unified way? After all, not a little should be attributed to the insufficiency of air reconnaissance. We should keep this in mind.[2]

Indeed he should have, but instead he presided over the development of a plan that combined maximum dispersion with less than the minimum reconnaissance, then overrode well-founded doubts expressed by the uneasy subordinate commanders of the Combined Fleet and even cheated during the war games held to test it. But Ugaki's lack of high seriousness was not unusual – the men who took Japan to war were uniformed bureaucrats who were highly conscious that if they did not, they could no longer justify the

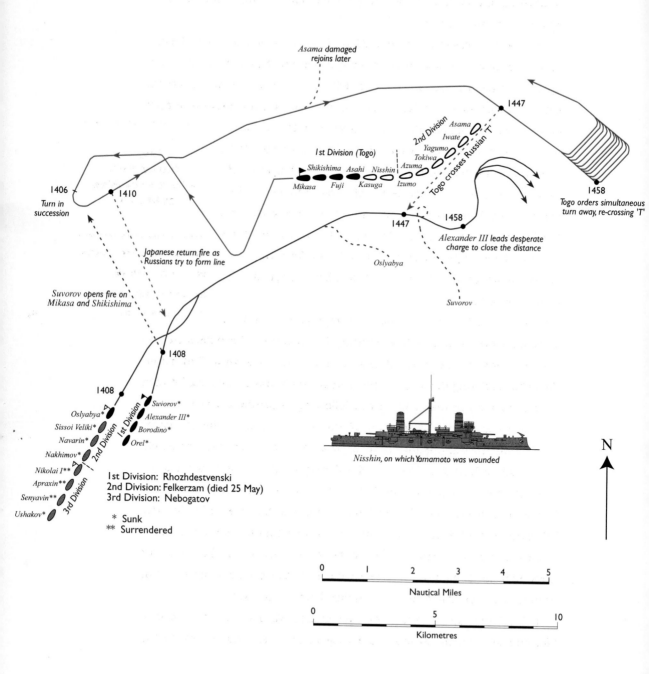

Asama damaged
rejoins later

1st Division (Togo)

Shikishima   Asahi   Nisshin
2nd Division

Asama
Iwate
Yagumo
Tokiwa
Azuma

Mikasa   Fuji   Kasuga   Izumo

Togo crosses Russian 'T'

1447

1447

1458

1458

Togo orders simultaneous
turn away, re-crossing 'T'

1406

Turn in
succession

1410

Alexander III leads desperate
charge to close the distance

Japanese return fire as
Russians try to form line

Oslyabya

Suvorov

Suvorov opens fire on
Mikasa and *Shikishima*

1408

1408

*Oslyabya**
*Sissoi Veliki**
*Navarin**
*Nakhimov**
*Nikolai I***
*Apraxin***
*Senyavin***
*Ushakov**

1st Division

2nd Division

3rd Division

*Suvorov**
*Alexander III**
*Borodino**
*Orel**

Nisshin, on which Yamamoto was wounded

1st Division: Rhozhdestvenski
2nd Division: Felkerzam (died 25 May)
3rd Division: Nebogatov

  * Sunk
** Surrendered

N

0   1   2   3   4   5
Nautical Miles

0   5   10
Kilometres

smothering proportion of Japan's gross national product they had been appropriating for decades.

This was the reason given in 1931 by Fleet Admiral Heihachiro Togo to undermine navy resistance to the military adventure the army was embarking upon in China, which all knew carried with it the risk of a naval war with the United States. 'The Naval General Staff has been presenting operational plans every year to the Emperor', he said. 'If we were to say that we were not able to carry out operations against the United States, it would mean that we had been lying to the Emperor.' His words were later cited by Navy Minister Admiral Koshiro Oikawa to explain why he did not throw the navy's weight into the balance against war in October 1941, when the Army Minister (later Prime Minister) General Hideki Tojo said, 'I am at a crossroads as to which path to take. I have not yet decided which it is to be'.[3]

Map 1
Crossing the 'T'
– Battle of Tsushima,
27 May 1905

Warships, nowhere near to scale

● First class battleship

◖ Coastal defence battleship

◌ Armoured cruiser

It would be difficult to overstate the importance of Admiral Togo in the events we shall be examining. He opened the Russo-Japanese War with a surprise attack on the Russian Pacific Fleet at anchor in Port Arthur (Manchuria) during the night of 8/9 February 1904, and all but closed it with the annihilation of their Baltic Fleet, following its painful Odyssey halfway around the world, at Tsushima on 27 May 1905. The latter, the first major fleet action since the battle of Trafalgar a century earlier, was immensely influential. At Jutland in 1916, the Royal Navy sought to duplicate the tactic of 'crossing the T' employed by Togo to achieve a decisive concentration of firepower on the head of the Russian columns, and the dream of a climactic battle beguiled admirals all over the world throughout the battleship era. In Japan Togo's prestige was so great that he was entrusted with the tutelage of Hirohito from 1914 until 1924, when the Crown Prince was appointed Regent because of the mental illness of his father, Emperor Taisho.[4]

At Tsushima, an explosion on the cruiser *Nisshin* severely wounded Midshipman Isoroku Takano and among many other injuries severed the index and second finger of his left hand (his future opponent Nimitz lost his ring finger to machinery in 1915). In 1916 the thirty-two year old Isoroku was adopted by an heirless family with the professionally advantageous name of Yamamoto. Admiral Gombei Yamamoto was the architect of the modern IJN, future Navy Minister and Prime Minister, and his namesake rose to command the third-largest fleet in the world.

Sailors and gamblers alike are generally omen-conscious and superstitious, and the attack on Pearl Harbor was launched with Togo's battle ensign flying at the mast of Admiral Chuichi Nagumo's flagship aircraft carrier, *Akagi*. It also seems likely that the preparations for Operation MI were fatally rushed to get it under way on Navy Day, the anniversary of Tsushima. It is not difficult to imagine what the hard-headed Togo would have done to an officer who let himself be influenced by such considerations.

In geopolitical terms, the Japanese defeat of the powerful Russian Empire was of an order of magnitude more remarkable than their defeat of moribund Manchu China in the Sino-Japanese War of 1894–95, also begun without a formal declaration of war, from which they obtained the cession of Formosa (Taiwan). The latter conflict was akin to the *coup de grâce* administered to the remains of the Spanish Empire by the Americans in their 'splendid little war' of 1898–1899, which netted them Guam and the Philippines. These conquests marked the eruption onto the world stage of vigorous new players, and together they planted the seeds of the Pacific War.

There was a closer overlap between what is broadly known as the 'expansion of Europe' and the muscle-flexing of the United States and Japan than is generally appreciated. The Dutch did not complete their centuries-long conquest of the East Indies until 1913, seven years after the American suppression of the Filipino Revolt, and the Japanese were, with some justification, indignant at being condemned during the 1930s for behaving little worse than their critics had done only slightly earlier.[5]

The difference lay not so much in the genocidal nature of the war they waged against China as in the fact that it offended the long-standing US

'Open Door' policy of strong opposition to treaties and territorial concessions that gave favoured access to other countries. Exhausted by one World War and mesmerized by the approach of another, the European powers could do little. But trade with the United States was vital to the Japanese and in 1939 the Americans revoked the commercial treaty of 1911 between the two countries. Through 1940 and 1941 the export of strategic materials was progressively cut off until, on 22 July 1941, the United States froze all Japanese assets and declared a trade embargo. The Dutch government-in-exile and the British felt compelled to join in because by that time their hopes for victory over Nazi Germany in Europe depended on getting the United States involved.

The embargo was an act of war bar the shooting but it was not backed by a deterrent Allied military presence in the Far East. Instead it depended on the Japanese surrendering without a fight, something so unlikely that theories have flourished ever since about President Franklin Roosevelt sacrificing the US Pacific Fleet in a Machiavellian ploy to rouse an indifferent nation to go to war. But the war he was trying to provoke was with Germany and although Adolf Hitler declared war on the United States three days after the attack on Pearl Harbor, Roosevelt could not have predicted such a satisfactory outcome. Underlying all of the excuses, the main reason why the Americans were taken by surprise was because they could not bring themselves to take the Japanese as seriously as they should have.

Myth also has it that a formal declaration of war was delayed by bureaucratic fumbling at the Japanese Embassy in Washington until after the attack on Pearl Harbor began, but to use a contemporary American phrase, the Japanese had no intention of 'giving a sucker an even bet'. As in 1894 and 1904, too much depended on gaining an early upper hand for such quaint niceties to be considered. Pearl Harbor stirred the United States to righteous wrath, but it was going to do so with or without a prior declaration of war.

The Japanese leaders did not anticipate how annihilating the American reaction would be, but the main reason why they embarked upon a wider war

RUSSIAN
EMPIRE

Mongolia
(occupied by Russia 1921)

Manchukuo
(occupied by Japan 1932)

*Sea of
Japan*

Korea
(annexed 1908)

CHINESE
EMPIRE

*Yellow
Sea*

Tsushima Straits

JAPANESE EMPIRE

Tokyo
*(Perry, Putiatin
1853)*

*East
China
Sea*

Ryukyu Islands • Okinawa

UNITED STATES EMPIR

• Iwo Jima

• Marcus

Taiwan
(from China 1895)

Hong Kong
(from China 1842)

FRENCH EMPIRE

Hainan

*South
China
Sea*

Manila •

Philippine Islands
(conquered 1898-1906)

Mariana
Islands

• Saipan

• Guam

Ma

GERMAN EMPIRE
(seized by Japan 1914)

Eniwetok •

• Saigon

• Yap

• Palau

• Truk

Caroline Islands

BRITISH
EMPIRE

Malaya

• Singapore

Brunei •

Sarawak

Borneo

Celebes

Sumatra

*Conquest not
completed
before 1913*

Java

DUTCH EMPIRE

Timor

Dutch
New
Guinea

Papua
New
Guinea

New
Britain

New Ireland

Solomon Islands

Coral Sea

Australia

110°   120°   130°   140°   150°   160°

P A C I F I C

Midway ●

Hawaiian Islands
(annexed 1898)

● Oahu

Hawaii

Johnston ●

O C E A N

Wotje ●

ds

ajalein

Jaluit ●

Gilbert Islands

● Makin

Tarawa ●

u

● Ocean

Fiji Islands

170°   180°   170°   160°

50°
40°
30°
20°
10°
0°
10°

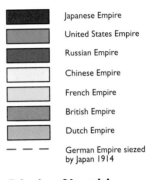

Map 2
Crowded empires:
The Far East to 1932

■	Japanese Empire
■	United States Empire
■	Russian Empire
☐	Chinese Empire
■	French Empire
■	British Empire
■	Dutch Empire
– – –	German Empire siezed by Japan 1914

Episodes of Imperial Expansion

1839-42 First Opium War, Britain v. China

1841 Sir James Brooke becomes Rajah of Sarawak

1853 Armed representatives of Russia & USA end three centuries ofJapanese self-isolation

1856-60 Second Opium War, Britain v. China

1858-95 French conquest of Vietnam and Laos

1879 Japan annexes the Ryukyu Islands from China

1886 Britain annexes Burma

1894-95 Sino-Japanese War

1901-02 Boxer Rebellion, military intervention in China by Britain, USA, Germany, Russia and Japan

1904-05 Russo-Japanese War, mainly fought in China

1914 Japan captures German Pacific islands

1921-25 Russia makes Mongolia a Soviet Republic

1932 Japan occupies Manchuria (Manchukuo)

was because their decision-making had become a frankly pathological process. It was dominated by inter-service rivalry and a realistic expectation among generals and admirals that they would be assassinated by ultranationalist junior officers should they be suspected of holding less than extremist views. How they got into that situation owed much to the psychological phenomenon observed by Britain's Field Marshal Lord Slim, who commented that in contrast to their tactical flexibility, Japanese officers would not adapt to changed operational circumstances. He attributed this to 'a lack of moral, as distinct from physical courage. They were not prepared to admit that they had made a mistake, that their plans had misfired and needed recasting'.

This is not a uniquely Japanese characteristic, but the fact remains that there was only one occasion during their long slide to ruin when a member of the ruling élite in Japan dared to suggest, even elliptically, that a humble peace would be preferable to the proud uncertainty of war. On 5 September 1941, at the end of the Imperial Conference where a deadline for the final decision was set, Hirohito caused short-lived consternation by reading a poem written by his grandfather, Emperor Meiji:

All the seas in every quarter are
   as brothers to one another.
Why, then, do the winds and waves of strife rage
   so turbulently throughout the world?

Once battle was joined, everything hinged on whether or not the United States had the stomach for a long war. If it did, Japan must lose because it could never hope to compel surrender. Yamamoto declared that peace could only be dictated on the lawn of the White House, not as the expression of intent that US propaganda ascribed to it but to ridicule the idea that outright victory was a possibility. However he was also impatient with those who pinned their hopes on Germany defeating Russia and Britain – something that seemed very likely between 1941 and 1942. Here institutional and national pride overrode strategic coherence, for the next best thing to the

White House lawn was definitely to confront the Americans with the prospect of a two-ocean war. The Japanese would have been better advised to stab Russia in the back than to kick the United States in the groin. The Siberian Army, withdrawn from the Manchurian front thanks to accurate intelligence on Japan's intentions from the Russian agent Richard Sorge in Tokyo, turned back the German advance on Moscow in late 1941.

But an attack on Russia would have given the army pre-eminence and the first call on national resources, so the IJN insisted on a strike southwards, enclosed in an argument of perfect circularity. In order to be able to wage war against the US and European empires, they said, war must be embarked upon to seize the oil and other raw materials of the US and European imperial holdings, as well as the ships to transport them to refineries and factories in Japan. This would, assuming no major fleet action in the meantime, postpone the coming of the economic crunch to mid-1944. But after mid-1943 the US warship-building programme provoked by Japan would begin to swamp the IJN, so a major fleet action had to be fought before then. Operation MI was intended to bring this about, but the most it could hope to achieve was to force the USN back to its own west coast and to buy time for the Japanese to consolidate their conquests and build up their Pacific island bastions.

They would not be able to hold them for very long, however, because the increased expenditure and liabilities of intensive ocean-wide operations would accelerate their oil and transportation crisis. Thus while the only hope of avoiding defeat was to protract the war until American public opinion turned against it, there was no prospect of doing this without significantly reducing Japan's ability to wage a protracted war – a classic 'no-win' situation. ● Furthermore those who depend on factors beyond their control, such as enemy morale or an opponent doing exactly what is expected of him, do not win wars. Operation MI embodied these errors because it attempted to resolve the contradictions in Japanese strategy and, beyond material considerations, Midway was the turning point in the Pacific because it laid bare the moral and intellectual bankruptcy of those who took Japan to war.

Thirty-six years earlier, Inazo Nitobe's introduction to the West of *Bushido* declared, 'the state built upon the rock of Honour and fortified by the same is fast falling into the hands of quibbling lawyers and gibbering politicians armed with the logic-chopping engines of war.' He had it precisely the wrong way around. It was when the self-appointed guardians of national honour pushed aside the civilians that the Japanese state went off the rails. Classes and sections of society commonly convince themselves that their own and the national interest are one and the same, but had the pseudo-samurai who directed Japan's energies to war nurtured any genuine respect for ancestral teachings, they would have remembered that twenty-three centuries earlier Sun-tzu declared the highest expression of *The Art of War* was to win without fighting. Their successors, quibbling lawyers and gibbering politicians to a man, have proved how right he was.

I n 1946 the US occupation authorities in Japan were given the text of an
eight-hour 'Monologue' dictated by Emperor Hirohito, which resurfaced
only after his death in 1989. General Douglas MacArthur suppressed the
document because it revealed that the emperor was closely involved in the
conspiracy to wage aggressive war, for which MacArthur intended to hang the
leading Japanese militarists, and he needed Hirohito to provide a core of
institutional continuity. Recent analyses by *hen na gaijin* ('peculiar outside
persons' who believe they understand the Japanese[1]) agree that Hirohito
could have stopped the drive for war had he been prepared to risk the survival
of the monarchy. This makes it all the more notable that at a time when it
would have been prudent to express regret about, for example, the 10 million
'outside persons' killed during the brutal war of aggression the Japanese call
the 'China Incident', he still blamed Western racism for the war. 'When we

look for the causes of the Greater East Asia War,' he told the stenographer, 'they lie in the past, in the peace treaty after the First World War. The proposal of racial equality [as one of the founding principles of the League of Nations] put forward by Japan was not something the Allies would accept.'

In July 1943, a so-called 'Greater East Asia War Enquiry Commission' published a report that identified ABCD (American, British, Chinese, Dutch) encirclement of Japan as the proximate reason for the war. 'The arrogant Anglo-Saxons, ever covetous of securing world hegemony according to the principle of the white man's burden, thus dared to take recourse to measures designed to stifle Nippon to death. It is small wonder that Nippon had to rise to arms.' Omitting to mention that this came about in response to the intensification of the China Incident from July 1937, the report portrayed the wider war as the result of two deep currents in US history – westward expansion and racism – running into the barrier posed by the Japanese Empire, standard bearer for the coloured races of the world. This is the view of today's moral-equivalence school of revisionism in the West and, barring the awkward fact that the main Japanese grievance was being included among the coloured people they themselves despise, it is a fair interpretation of the undercurrents at work.[2]

The ruling ideology in the United States for much of the twentieth century was Progressivism, one of the milder manifestations of Social Darwinism. Briefly, this is the belief that one is rich and powerful because God ordained it, dressed in pseudo-scientific clothing very loosely derived from the process of natural selection outlined by Charles Darwin. This came together with the older and unashamedly imperialist creed known as Manifest Destiny during the 1901 to 1909 presidency of Theodore Roosevelt. It was unfortunate that these ideas were current in technologically dominant Western culture when Japan emerged from its centuries-long hibernation in the mid-nineteenth century, because along with the technology the Japanese absorbed the mortal insult of being regarded as racially inferior by people whom they regarded as evil-smelling barbarians. The result was that modernization and a particularly nasty brand of reactive, violently assertive nationalism went hand-in-hand.

The 1919 diplomatic rebuff Hirohito thought emblematic was only one of many twists of the knife. The ones that concern us most are the Washington and London Naval Arms Limitation Treaties of 1922 and 1930, which established a ratio of 5:5:3 among British, US and Japanese capital ships and heavy cruisers (light cruisers and destroyers were 10:10:7 and there was parity in submarines). Given British and US naval commitments elsewhere, these ratios tacitly conceded predominance in the Far East to the IJN. But the Japanese did not see it that way and picked at the scab of the perceived insult until, between 1934 and 1936, they wrecked negotiations to renew the treaties. Although planning and stockpiling in violation of the treaties was well advanced, giving them a two-year head start, the ensuing naval arms race was one the Japanese always knew they could not win. The IJN was annihilated (see the 'Sunk' column in **Appendix A**) by the application of about 25 per cent of US military power, and those who took Japan to war against the US and European empires in 1941 were well aware that this would be the inevitable outcome of any except a relatively short conflict.

Military men are no more inclined than the rest of humanity to walking away from a bad investment. But militarists (uniformed or civilian) are notoriously averse to cutting their losses because they are so wedded to the aesthetics of the military way that it becomes a substitute for policy rather than an adjunct to it. This was the change that had come about between 1905 when, despite winning resounding victories on land and sea, the Japanese had the wisdom to accept an unsatisfactory peace settlement rather than continue an unsustainable war with Russia, and 1941 when, rather than withdrawing from their unwinnable war in China, they broadened it by attacking the US, British and Dutch empires. There was also a grave risk that civil war would follow a decision to back down and the 'Monologue' contains strong hints that Hirohito calculated his dynasty could better survive a military defeat.

He was probably right, as he was about the underlying ethos of the war. Defeat by the Japanese was more humiliating and aroused greater hatred

CHINA

INDIA

BURMA

THAILAND

FRENCH
INDO-CHINA

Taiwan

Hong Kong
26.12.41

10.12.41

Hanoi

Hainan

Rangoon

Bangkok

Manila
6.05.42

Philippines
12.12.41

8.12.41

Cam
Ranh

Saigon

8.12.41

*Carrier raids
early April 1942*

19.12.41

8.12.41

Brunei

15.12.41

Malaya

Sarawak

10.01.42

11.01.42

23.12.41

Celebes

Singapore
15.02.42

24.01.42

Sumatra

Borneo

24.01.42

30.01.42

14.02.42

Java Sea

8.02.42

INDIAN

28.02.42

28.02.42

OCEAN

Batavia
9.03.42 Java

19.02.42

20.02.42

Timor

Carrier
19.02.

D

AUSTRAL

90°   100°   110°   120°   130°

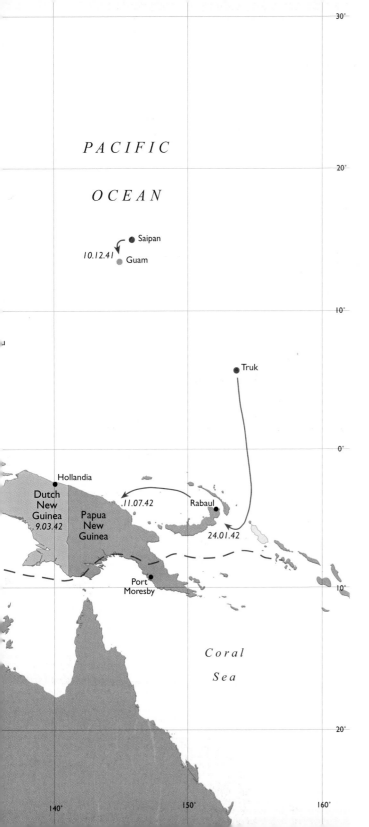

**Map 3
The Japanese offensive
1941–42**

Simplified scheme of the
initial Japanese advance in
South East Asia and the East
Indies from 8th Dec (7th at
Pearl Harbor) until shortly
after the Battle of Midway

████████ Areas controlled
prior to 8th
December

24.01.42 ──▶ Invasion or strike
(with date)

— — — Perimeter of
Japanese
dominance
July 1942

PACIFIC

OCEAN

● Saipan

10.12.41 ● Guam

● Truk

Hollandia

Dutch
New
Guinea
9.03.42

.11.07.42   Rabaul ●

Papua
New
Guinea

24.01.42

Port
Moresby

Coral

Sea

because they had previously been so despised. The head of the British Foreign Office referred to them as 'yellow dwarf slaves' in his private diary, while the US ambassador to Tokyo thought they were either insects in thrall to the hive Emperor or mindless sheep. When these buck-toothed, near-sighted, pint-sized monkeys (as the US Army's *Infantry Journal* put it) sank or disabled every US and British battleship in the Pacific area during three days in December 1941 and then swung through the trees of Malaya (according to a celebrated cartoon in London's *Punch* magazine) to force the surrender of three times their number of British Empire soldiers at Singapore, the shock to Caucasian self-esteem was profound. It was meant to be – there can be little doubt that a visceral desire to wipe the patronizing smirk from white faces played an important part in the Japanese decision to go to war and damn the consequences.

Many *hen na gaijin* of the period believed the Japanese eschewed deductive analysis in favour of instinct, intuition and 'feelings', something that would be applauded today but was judged infantile at that time. 'Half devil and half child', wrote Rudyard Kipling in 1899, when urging the Americans to take up the white man's burden in the Philippines, which they did by herding the Filipinos into concentration camps and killing about 200,000 of them. Worthy of note is that while this was going on, American commentators castigated the British for doing the same on a minor scale to the white Boers in South Africa. It was not infantile of the Japanese, therefore, to resent being condemned by the Anglo-Saxons for actions that were morally indisting-uishable from their own in similar circumstances.

If there was a failure of deductive analysis in the confrontation between Japan and the Western powers, it lay in a gross underestimation by the latter of basic Japanese premises. These included the sanctity of the Emperor and his consequent right to rule over all peoples, a belief that markets as well as raw materials must be physically controlled by the metropolitan power, and a duellist's concept of personal honour. The Japanese vision of the world may have been borderline psychotic, but within it the reasoning was logical – thus

Emperor Hirohito about to add to the white man's burden. Caricature published after Pearl Harbor, when Caucasians stopped thinking the Japanese were amusing.

the war against China was intended to keep it divided and weak by destroying the authority of the modernising Kuomintang, and did so.

Diplomacy is largely the application of a double standard and ultimately treaties without the sword are just words, but if you do not wish to use the sword it is as well not create a situation in which another will feel compelled to draw his. If the United States was not actively seeking a war with Japan in 1941 – and its unpreparedness argues forcefully that it was not – the crowning illogicality was to demand that the Japanese should abandon policies they saw as essential for national survival and to put them in a position from which there was no face-saving way of retreat.

The tyranny of the guiding question 'what will people say?' was, and remains, stronger in Japan than in most other societies. Although pride is somewhat looked down upon, renown, shame, dishonour and, especially, 'face' or appearance in the eyes of the world, are terms of everyday Japanese discourse. The strongest warning against a particular course of action is 'don't do it, you will look bad'. This is not as alien to Western culture as some have portrayed it and has much in common with the code of the Spanish *caballero* and the English gentleman. Like the samurai, they were ruthless in war and cultivated in peace, valuing self-control over all other qualities and able to advance collective aspirations without sacrificing an individualistic conduct of their own lives.

Japanese uniqueness lay in the fact that the samurai class, formally abolished in 1876, was subsumed into the new authority structure and its values were transferred not only to the new officer class, but also to the civilian bureaucracy. In 1881, former samurai numbered a little over 5 per cent of the population but held over 40 per cent of official posts, and also supplied most of the teachers for the new elementary schools that virtually defined modern Japanese culture.

They had nonetheless lost social status and were in economic decline relative to the previously despised merchant class. As the history of Europe since the French Revolution illustrates so clearly, there is nothing more unprincipled and savage than the less dynamic element of the middle class when its status boundaries are eroding. The modern history of the old continent has been dominated by this phenomenon in various guises, and by attempts to appease it by expanding the bureaucracy to satisfy people whose aspiration is to be immune from social and economic uncertainty. This could not work in Japan because the class in question made a cult of the 'way of the warrior', thus at least part of the reason why evidently aggressive Japanese policies were expressed in terms of self-defence was that those who formulated them were not fighting to win, but to avoid losing.

In the United States any outbreak of lower-class activism was suppressed by the civil power employing all means, legal and illegal, thereby reducing the fear and perception of government weakness that wafted paramilitary parties to power elsewhere. Despite a tendency to elect successful generals to the presidency, the US was the least militaristic imperial power in world history. This was partly because a rejection of standing armed forces was an important part of its founding mythology, but mainly because of the ample, easily conquered *lebensraum* within the North American continent and the absence of any serious external military threat. But under Theodore Roosevelt, a nominal Republican, the political élite began to assert itself more forcefully at home and abroad. Having slipped from the hands of the Republicans, whose natural constituency it offended, the Progressive torch was picked up by the Democrats between 1913 and 1921 under the profoundly racist Woodrow Wilson. Wilson was also anxious to extend federal patronage in order to enable the Democratic Party to become 'the party of government', an ambition finally realised during the long presidency of Franklin Roosevelt from 1932 to 1945. It was a social transformation from above, directed by a class that, with the sole exception of Theodore Roosevelt's remarkable personal heroism during the war with Spain, derived no part of its authority from past or present military prowess.

Entry into the US military academies was effected by political patronage and represented a social step up for most cadets. Weapons systems were not the locomotive of technological advance that they were in Japan, but mastery of complicated machinery conveyed considerable prestige. Naval officers in particular were technocrats who could have earned more as civilians, but were grateful to their society for the opportunity that it had given them and believed they owed it a debt of service. This, coupled with the signature 'can do' spirit of the whole people, gave the US military a readiness to embark upon major enterprises unfettered by tradition or any thought of ultimate failure. But if there was nothing defensive about their attitude to military power, it coexisted with a compelling vision of the United States as the shining 'City On The Hill'. When we consider what was going on elsewhere in the world it is not easy to dismiss this vision as mere nationalist conceit, and it gave US politicians and military commanders the uncomplicated moral authority to demand that their enemies submit unconditionally.

Although a powerful navy was central to the security concerns of Japan, an island nation totally dependant on overseas trade, to a self-sufficient continental power like the United States it was the purest expression of a desire to project its power beyond its borders. The 'Blue Water Navy' was the

Val dive bomber pulling up after attacking Battleship Row, Pearl Harbor.

creation of Theodore Roosevelt and the apple of Franklin Roosevelt's eye, and from the beginning US war plans for both oceans were expansionist. War Plan Red assumed that any war with Britain would start with an invasion of Canada to which the Royal Navy would have to respond, putting itself at a disadvantage in American waters. But since Canada would obviously declare itself neutral well in advance of any such conflict, that scenario was never more than a wistful pipe dream. By contrast, War Plan Orange went through dozens of permutations and refinements because it was no less obvious that any war with Japan would be for dominance in the Far East, with the Philippines playing the role of Canada in a scenario that would oblige the US Navy to cross the ocean and do battle on its enemy's doorstep.

Japanese planning worked on precisely the same assumption, perhaps not surprising when we consider that holy writ for both navies were the works of

Captain Alfred Mahan. *The Interest of America in Sea Power, Present and Future* (1897) may well have been the most successful piece of special institutional pleading ever written, captivating Theodore Roosevelt and laying the keel for the Blue Water Navy. The allegedly eternal verities Mahan derived from his study of the Royal Navy between 1669 and 1815, set out in his two 'Influence of Sea Power' volumes, also left an indelible mark on naval thinking despite – or rather because of – their grossly overstated case for large and expensive fleets as the determinants of international power. Of particular interest to us here is that from the beginning the rock around which US planning swirled uneasily was the one upon which the Japanese were to base their hopes for victory.

> There was no question that US wealth could support a war indefinitely or that the obedient Japanese would fight as long as their leaders demanded. The prime uncertainty was whether the American public would tolerate a lengthy war, say of a year or two years' duration, for goals not vital to national survival. Mahan was certain it would not. The perception of a fickle society with a short attention span and no stomach for hardships led him and others to recommend strategies of rapid offensive movement.[4]

This perception also weighed heavily on Nimitz in 1942 and less than three months after becoming Commander-in-Chief Pacific Fleet he wrote rather sadly to his wife, 'I will be lucky to last six months. The public may demand action and results faster than I can produce'. The darling of the press was Vice Admiral William 'Bull' Halsey, commander of the carrier groups, whose robust motto was, 'Kill Japs, kill more Japs'. Among the many paradoxes that came together at Midway was that by taking out the US battle fleet at Pearl Harbor, Yamamoto disgraced the Halseyian Admiral Husband Kimmel and gave his successor a breathing space *vis-à-vis* a press and public thirsting for revenge. Although a charge to the Philippines was no longer planned, had the Pacific Fleet still been intact it is unlikely the government could have resisted popular demands for a relief expedition when US empire forces unexpectedly held out until May 1942. Pearl Harbor thus set the stage for Midway, not only because it failed to destroy fuel stocks or because the US carriers were not in port to share the battleships' fate, but because it rendered moot decades of planning on both sides for a climactic battle in Far Eastern waters.

Developments elsewhere had already forced the USN to reconsider. The Rainbow Five Plan relegated Japan to second place in recognition of the catastrophic possibility that Britain might succumb to Hitler and that part, or all, of the Royal Navy might fall under German control, to join what was left of the once powerful Italian and French fleets. The 'beat-Germany-first' policy advocated by Admiral Harold Stark, Chief of Naval Operations from August 1939 to March 1942, continued to define US strategy, despite Pearl Harbor. Fleet dispositions in August to September 1941 also reflect the fruition of the Japanese warship-building programme of 1936, including the new fleet aircraft carriers *Shokaku* and *Zuikaku*, while the US programme that would in time more than treble the size of the fleet still lagged two years behind.

Type	US Pacific (Asiatic)	IJN	US Atlantic
Battleships	9	10	6
Aircraft carriers	3	8	4
Heavy cruisers	8 (1)	18	5
Light cruisers	8 (1)	20	8
Destroyers	45 (13)	112	81
Submarines	33 (17)	65	63

Thus the USN was not in a position to seek a climactic battle in the Pacific before Pearl Harbor, still less so after it and during 1942, even when three of its less damaged battleships had been rehabilitated to join four brought back from the Atlantic, along with the aircraft carrier *Yorktown*. These were later joined by *Hornet*, leaving *Wasp* to assist the Royal Navy in the Mediterranean and little *Ranger* alone on the Atlantic coast. The odds worsened after the large carrier *Saratoga* was torpedoed off Hawaii in January 1942, putting her out of action for five months, while her sister ship *Lexington* was lost in the Coral Sea in May, following shattering Allied naval defeats off Java. Despite this the USN did not feel defeated, something the IJN planners failed to evaluate correctly. They assumed this cascade of losses would have made their opponents wary and hesitant to give battle, and it was above all because of this failure of appreciation that Operation MI went so badly awry.

On paper the Japanese should have been able to roll over the Americans at any time between Pearl Harbor and Midway, so why did they not? We have touched on some of the reasons, but there was also something oddly tentative about their approach to a battle with the USN. Thus Nagumo flinched from finishing the job at Pearl Harbor and refused to attack Midway on his way home, and the admirals in the Java and Coral Sea battles did not follow through as vigorously as doctrine dictated they should. It is as though at the deep level of childhood imprinting the Americans were the still the devils their mothers had warned them would come to get them if they misbehaved. Now they had – and they did.

For the Americans, Pearl Harbor was akin to the last time that they had suffered defeat at the hands of what Kipling called 'lesser breeds without the law', at Little Big Horn in 1876, a wake-up call followed by the implacable persecution and total subjugation of the offending party. On both occasions a froth of self-righteous indignation served to shield politicians from the blame that should have accrued to them for their failure to match means to ends. If it is a stretch to compare Nimitz with Major General Nelson Miles, who methodically mopped up the Plains Indians, the parallel is more exact between Miles's boss, General William 'War is All Hell' Sherman, and Admiral Ernest King, Commander-in-Chief of the US Fleet during World War II. King put his stamp on a navy that was growing so fast that it would have escaped the control of a lesser man (see **Appendix C**), but also proudly proclaimed himself a ruthless son-of-a-bitch, an assessment with which posterity has not been inclined to disagree.

The first attempt to recover the initiative was to be a raid on Wake, seized by the Japanese in December 1941 and a source of shame to the USN after a relief effort ordered by Kimmel fell victim to the command void following his dismissal. That raid never took place because *Lexington* was recalled after a submarine sank her oiler, but on 1 February 1942 two task forces under the command of Halsey, on *Enterprise*, with Rear Admiral Frank Fletcher on *Yorktown*, made simultaneous attacks on Japanese bases in the Marshall Islands and the northernmost of the Gilbert Islands.

Map 4

US carrier raids

→ *Enterprise*
→ *Hornet*
→ *Lexington*
→ *Yorktown*

Halsey approached to within 40 miles and then divided his force, sending the bombers against the main Japanese base at Kwajalein while his fighters, in combination with a cruiser group, attacked nearby Maloelap and Wotje. He was lucky to get away with it and had a hair-raising introduction to the 'Nell' bombers (see the next chapter), including an attempt by the strike leader to crash his burning aircraft on the crowded deck of *Enterprise* that came close enough to clip the tail off a Dauntless bomber. *Yorktown*'s raid on Jaluit and Makin was bedevilled by bad weather and achieved little, but considerable damage had been inflicted overall and the carriers received a rapturous welcome when they returned to Pearl.

Morale-boosting aside, at Kwajalein Rear Admiral Yuckicki Yashiro became the first Japanese flag officer to be killed in the war and his Naval Academy classmate Ugaki brooded 'we must admit that this is the best way to make us look ridiculous. Opportunism is one of their characteristics. They took advantage of the situation when we were busy fighting in the south and west, and attained their objective of restraining our southward advance in addition to the actual damage.' Hit-and-run raids continued with Halsey and *Enterprise* paying a visit to Wake on 24 February 1942 and then speeding away, only to double back and hit Marcus on 4 March. As Ugaki observed, the damage that these raids did was less important than the fact that they distracted Japanese resources from the advance on New Guinea, eventually to be put on hold while the Combined Fleet turned its attention to regaining the initiative in the central Pacific.

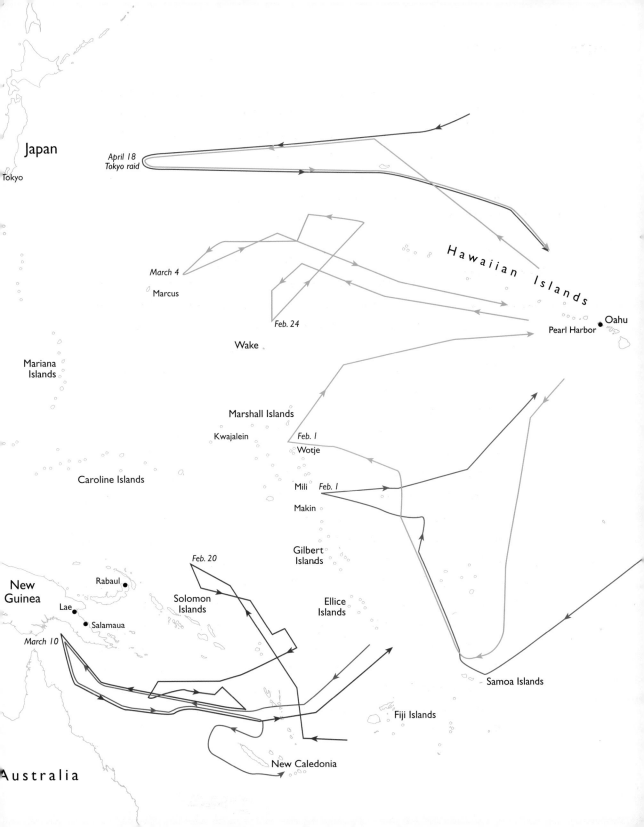

Japan

Tokyo

April 18
Tokyo raid

H a w a i i a n   I s l a n d s

March 4

Marcus

Feb. 24

Wake

Oahu

Pearl Harbor

Mariana
Islands

Marshall Islands

Kwajalein

Feb. 1
Wotje

Caroline Islands

Mili   *Feb. 1*

Makin

Gilbert
Islands

Ellice
Islands

Samoa Islands

New
Guinea

Rabaul

Lae

Salamaua

Solomon
Islands

Feb. 20

March 10

Fiji Islands

New Caledonia

Australia

Japanese strike leader attempts to 'body crash' on *Lexington*, 20 Feb 1942

Lexington's raid behind the Gilberts on 20 February 1942 made less of an impact, partly because it was detected before it could launch an attack on the important Japanese base at Rabaul on New Britain, and partly because it came in the midst of sweeping Japanese successes in the East Indies. Nonetheless it came as a shock to the Japanese after their easy success against HMS *Prince of Wales* and *Repulse* in December 1941 that only two of the seventeen new 'Betty' bombers sent against this task force returned, and that no hits were obtained. Had the bombers been escorted and carrying torpedoes *Lexington* might not have been so lucky, but in the event she was only straddled by bombs, and once again the strike leader attempted what the Japanese called a 'body crash' in his crippled aircraft. He was one of five kills credited to Lieutenant Edward O'Hare, the first US 'ace' of the war, for which he was awarded the Medal of Honor in a ceremony at the White House on 21 April 1942, thereby missing the battle of the Coral Sea during which carrier torpedo bombers mortally wounded his ship.[5]

These early raids were also invaluable training exercises, during which the US carriers and their Air Groups learned the strengths and limitations of their

A USAAC B-25 takes off from USS *Hornet* on the Doolittle Raid, 18 April 1942

weapons and systems, and evolved procedures to make the best of what they had. At the time that we are considering the USN was greatly outnumbered and, as we shall see in the next chapter, was outclassed in many categories of weapons systems. By all rights it should have been on the defensive, but instead it acted as though defeat was not an option, stinging the Japanese into trying to prove otherwise. The famous 18 April raid on Tokyo by US Army medium bombers launched from *Hornet* and led by Lieutenant Colonel James Doolittle was simply the icing on the cake, because the carrier raids had already persuaded the planners of the Combined Fleet to seek a decision in the central Pacific.

Whether or not the engines of war had the logic-chopping effect that Nitobe ascribed to them, there was no lack of coherence in the Japanese approach to them. At Midway, with the critical exception of radar, there was no category in which IJN weaponry was not at least of equal quality. Commander Minoru Genda, First Air Fleet Operations Officer, was asked during the preliminary war-gaming of Operation MI whether he considered there were sufficient fighters to protect Japanese carriers from enemy air attack as well as escorting their own bombers against Midway. He answered with the poetic idiom 'one touch of an armoured sleeve', roughly meaning 'we'll blow them away'.

So they did, even though Genda himself was stricken with pneumonia and unable to direct operations with his usual acuity. It took an almost unimaginably adverse sequence of events to tip the balance against the

Japanese who, until the US dive bombers arrived over their carriers unopposed, had shot down or evaded everything the enemy could throw at them. How they were exposed to such a worst-case scenario is the subject of later chapters – our purpose here is to examine the technical side of the symbiotic relationship among weapons, doctrine, operations and tactics.

Militarists are often enamoured of outward forms, but the Japanese were totally focused on their essential function. The word 'machinery' encompasses administrative arrangements as well as weapons and although there was considerable duplication of effort by the two armed forces, each practised something akin to the 'just in time' procurement of modern manufacturing. As the Japanese saw it, they were beset on all sides by hugely more numerous and potentially more powerful enemies, so they were obliged to extract the utmost fighting power from their own relatively limited population and resources. Criticism of the IJN machine focuses on its failure to provide sufficient weapons and trained personnel for the prolonged battle of attrition with the USA that developed, but, knowing they could not win that sort of war, why would they prepare for it? Instead they developed weapons with a range and hitting power that reflected the absolute priority they ascribed to operational and tactical surprise, what today we call a 'first strike' capability. ◦

There are no excuses for the American and British failure to deploy a credible deterrent, compounded by the assumptions of racial and cultural superiority that made them discount evidence of Japanese technical proficiency. The 'little yellow men' could not have resolved the problems that caused the British to abandon experiments with pure oxygen in torpedoes (eliminating the wake of exhaust nitrogen and permitting greatly increased range for the same bulk and weight), therefore the oxygen generators on Japanese ships must serve some other purpose. The huge binoculars on their 'pagoda' bridges were simply proof of their bad eyesight, which also implied they must be poor pilots, so the technical specifications for the 'Zero' fighter (obtained from the no less yellow Chinese and therefore suspect) were nothing to be alarmed about. Allied counterstrike capability was limited to the B-17

Flying Fortresses based at Clark Field outside Manila, in the Philippines, which the US Army chief of staff General George Marshall told journalists in November 1941 would be used to fire bomb Japan's paper cities. The Japanese, therefore, systematically eliminated them during the first days of the war.

One much commented on illogicality was that after sinking or disabling all the Allied battleships in the Pacific theatre the Japanese made no use of theirs, but since they were intended solely to fight others of their kind this was not as strange as it seems. Although no navy entered World War II institutionally convinced that aircraft had rendered battleships obsolete, much the strongest statement of wisdom made well before the event by any important naval officer came from Yamamoto. When arguing against the 1936 decision to construct the *Yamato* class, he compared battleships to 'elaborate religious scrolls which old people hang in their homes – a matter of faith, not reality'.

Nonetheless, there they were large numbers when war broke out and some use had to be made of them. US battleships eventually justified their existence by acting as floating anti-aircraft and shore bombardment batteries, but in Operation MI the Combined Fleet staff tried to find a use for them in the role for which they were designed. Yamamoto also commented that they were as useful in modern warfare as a samurai sword, but they were no less potent

Elaborate religious scroll *Yamato* **at full speed**

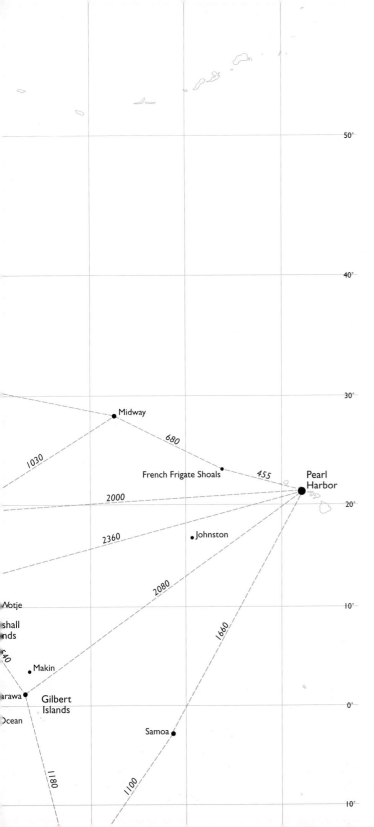

Map 5
Pacific theatre and
aircraft ranges

Maximum Aircraft Radii – Comparative Table

Emily	1945
Betty	1630
Catalina	1350
Mavis	1295
Nell	1180
Avenger	850
Zero	840
Kate	540
Marauder	500
Vindicator	475
Buffalo	420
Dauntless	415
Val	400
Wildcat	330

(Great Circle distances in nautical miles)

50°

40°

30°

Midway

680

1030

French Frigate Shoals

455

Pearl
Harbor

2000

20°

2360

Johnston

2080

10°

Notje

1660

shall
nds

40

Makin

arawa

Gilbert
Islands

0°

Ocean

Samoa

1180

1100

10°

**B-26 Marauder
with modified
torpedo (note
the fins), Alaska
1942**

symbols of the desire to close with the enemy and do him terrible damage that made Japanese military culture so formidable.

Although it installed heavier guns in larger numbers in all classes of warship, the IJN made an exceptional commitment to torpedoes. Alone among the major navies it conducted frequent live firings against warship hulks, so its torpedoes were not only better, but also considerably more dependable than those of other navies. In the chart below they are compared to their British and German as well as the US equivalents, in order to underline how absolutely superior the Japanese ship and submarine torpedoes were, although their airborne version was less so, apart from the high speed and variable height from which it could be dropped. The maximum expressions of torpedo warfare were the light cruisers *Oi* and *Kitakami*, rebuilt between 1940 and 1941 to carry ten quadruple torpedo launchers, but it is fair to say that Japanese naval aviation was built around the airborne torpedo. The range of their patrol and long-range strike aircraft was central to the planning of Operation MI, which intended to seize Midway and rapidly turn it into a forward air base to support the ensuing naval battle and to harass Hawaii.

At this stage of its development, the US airborne torpedo had many vices and few, if any virtues. Its stubbiness made it inherently less stable through the water, making its very long range doubly redundant, but its worst feature was the low altitude and speed at which it had to be dropped. This doomed the gallant US torpedo bombers at Midway quite as much as the failure of coordination that obliged them to attack alone. Some untried modifications were made to the torpedoes carried by the B-26 Marauder medium bombers at Midway to allow for their higher stalling speed, but it is significant that a lumbering Catalina made the only successful torpedo attack, the first ever at night, hitting the tanker *Akebono Maru* in the bow after a point-blank release at wave top level in the early morning of 4 June1942.

However, as *Nautilus* was to discover twelve hours later when she fired a salvo of torpedoes at the burning hulk of *Kaga*, there was no guarantee that even a perfect hit would be followed by a detonation: after the warhead of one of her torpedoes broke off on impact, the propulsion section floated up to serve as a life raft for some doubly fortunate Japanese sailors. German and US torpedoes suffered from identical problems with depth maintenance, failure of the magnetic pistol and malfunction of the impact striker, which helped spare Britain from being strangled by the U-boats between 1940 and 1942 and delayed the full effect of unrestricted submarine warfare against Japan until the problems of the US torpedo were finally corrected in late 1943. It is an intriguing thought that as part of its generally war-losing espionage activities, the German *Abwehr* may have inflicted flawed US torpedo technology on the *Kriegsmarine*.[1]

The comparative aircraft tables in this chapter use maximum performance figures and should be read bearing in mind that payload, climb rate, ceiling, range and speed were all closely interrelated, thus maximum range could only be obtained 'clean' and at cruising speed, etc. The trade-offs could be extreme – the Grumman Wildcat, for example, had a supercharger to boost performance, but this reduced its effective combat radius to around 200 miles. Japanese wing design was better, which gave their aircraft superior overall handling characteristics, and they chose not to install self-sealing tanks or armour, buying yet better performance at the expense of aircrew survivability in accordance with their uncompromising commitment to attack. For the single-engined aircraft in particular, defensive armament was only marginally effective, the gunner's main contribution to survival being the running commentary that permitted his pilot to take timely evasive action.

Every Japanese weapon had a type designation that identified the year in which it went into production according to their calendar, which counted from the founding of the Japanese Empire in 660 BC. Thus the Christian year 1940 was the Japanese 2600, and the superb Mitsubishi A6M fighter was the Type 0, with the model or variant numbers in parentheses. The nicknames ('Val', 'Kate', etc.) in English did not come into use until after Midway, but I employ them here for the same reason that they were introduced: to simplify aircraft identification. For US aircraft the first numeral is the model number followed by variant numbers and letters. The combinations of letters preceding the model numeral are functional: B – bomber; D – dive; F – fighter; P – patrol; S – scout; T – torpedo; Y – flying boat. The reader will also note the letters 'V' or 'VM' turning up in US aircraft and squadron designations, which simply mean 'fixed-wing aircraft' in service with the Navy and the Marines respectively.

The following comparison of the carrier bombers employed at Midway illustrates the pace of technological progress during the years before the war. Although the Avenger's similarity to its Grumman stable mate, the rotund Wildcat fighter, sometimes led an unwary Japanese fighter to approach from behind and into range of its rear turret, the self-defending bomber concept that it embodied was a chimera. All were dual-purpose or 'attack' bombers, as the Japanese called them, and a Kate dropped the modified 16-inch shell that detonated the magazine of the moored battleship *Arizona* at Pearl Harbor. However, three days later a swarm of Nells and Bettys only managed one bomb hit on the *Repulse* and none on the *Prince of Wales* until they slowed the vessels down with torpedoes. High-level bombing against ships under way

Torpedoes[2]

Surface ship

	Japanese	US	German	British
Name	Type 93 (1)*	Mark 15	G7a T1	Mark IX
Range/max. speed (yd/kt)	22,000/50	6,000/45	6,560/44	11,000/41
Max. range/speed (yd/kt)	43,700/38	15,000/27	15,300/30	15,000/35
Warhead (lb)	1,080	825	661	725
Propulsion	O_2/kerosene	Air/alcohol	Air/decalin	Air/shale oil
Diameter (in)	24	21	21	21
Length (in)	354	288	276	287
Weight (lb)	5,952	3,841	3,369	3,732

*Known as the 'Long Lance'.

Submarine

	Japanese	US	German	British
Name	Type 95 (1)	Mark 14	G7e T2	Mark VIII
Range/max. speed (yd/kt)	9,850/51	4,500/46	–	5,000/46
Max. range/speed (yd/kt)	13,100/47	9,000/31	5,470/30	7,000/41
Warhead (lb)	893	643	661	805
Propulsion	O_2/kerosene	Air/alcohol	Electric	Air/shale oil
Diameter (in)	21	21	21	21
Length (in)	282	246	276	259
Weight (lb)	3,671	3,280	3,534	3,452

Airborne

	Japanese	US	German	British
Name	Type 91 (2)	Mark 13	F5b	Mark XII
Range/max. speed (yd/kt)	2,200/43	6,300/34	2,200/40	1,500/40
Warhead (lb)	452	600	551	388
Propulsion	Air/kerosene	Air/alcohol	Air/decalin	Air/shale oil
Diameter (in)	17.7	22.4	17.7	17.7
Length (in)	216	161	203	195
Weight	1,841	2,216	1,790	1,548
Drop speed (kt)	260	110	150	150
Drop height (ft)	33-165	50	100-130	200

Air delivery systems[3]
Flying boats

	Kawanishi H6K4	Consolidated PBY-5	Kawanishi H8K1
Name	Type 97 'Mavis'	'Catalina'*	Type 2 'Emily'
Design year	1935-36	1934	1939-40
Power (hp)	1,000 x 4	1,200 x 2	1,530 x 4
Climb (ft/min)	1,170	620	1,130
Ceiling (ft)	31,500	18,000	25,000
Max. radius (nm)	1,295	1,350	1,945
Max. speed (mph)	210	150	290
Max. payload (lb)	3,500 (external)	4,000 (external)	3,500 (external)
Guns	20mm x 1, .303 x 4	.50 x 2, .30 x 2	20mm x 3, .303 x 3
Crew	8	7-9	10

*The heavier amphibian (5A) went into production in 1939. Speed/range/payload intervariables were extreme but both types could remain airborne for more than twenty-four hours at very low speed.

Land-based bombers

	Mitsubishi G3M2	Martin B-26-B	Mitsubishi G4M1
Name	Type 96 (22) 'Nell'	Marauder	Type 1 (11) 'Betty'
Design year	1933-34	1939	1937-38
Power (hp)	1,075 x 2	1,920 x 2	1,530 x 2
Climb (ft/min)	1,185	1,200	1,275
Ceiling (ft)	30,000	23,500	29,000
Max. radius (nm)	1,180	500	1,630
Max. speed (mph)	230	285	265
Max. payload (lb)	1,750 (external)	5,200 (internal)*	1,750 (internal)
Guns	20mm x 1, .303 x 4	.50 x 4, .30 x 2	20mm x 1, .303 x 4
Crew	5-7	7	7

*Modified to carry one 2,216-pound torpedo externally.

Carrier bombers

	Douglas TBD-1	Nakajima B5N2 (97)	Grumman TBF-1
Name	Devastator	Type 97 (11) 'Kate'	Avenger
Design year	1934	1936	1940
Power (hp)	850	1,000	1,700
Climb (ft/min)	720	1,300	1,430
Ceiling (ft)	19,700	27,100	22,600
Max. radius (nm)*	220/350	265/540	380/850
Max. speed (mph)	200	235	260
Max. payload (lb)	2,200 (external)	1,780 (external)	2,200 (internal)
Guns	.30 x 2	.303 x 1	.50 x 1, .30 x 2
Crew	2 (3 as bomber)	3	3

*With torpedo/with 1,000-pound bombs – 'Kate' and Avenger could carry auxiliary tanks with the latter.

required simultaneous bombing by a tight formation and although US Army Flying Fortresses dropped some 322 bombs at Midway, they were not trained for the task and, despite strident claims to the contrary, managed only a relatively small number of near misses.

Attack bombers were basically range enhancers for torpedoes and shells, but dive bombing offered a new, intermediate strike possibility, combining the high-level approach of the marginally effective level bomber with the close-range delivery of the deadly but extremely vulnerable torpedo bomber, sacrificing bomb velocity for a reduction in the target's manoeuvring time. It demanded a tough aircraft and a robust, nerveless pilot to dive at an angle of about 70° to a five-G pullout, and required some means to limit velocity and maintain control during the descent. The bombs carried on the centre line by the USN dive bombers at Midway were either 1,000 or 500-pound semi armour-piercing (30 per cent explosive), and with the latter some Dauntlesses in scouting configuration also carried two 100-pound bombs under the wings. The Vals carried 551-pound semi armour-piercing (40 per cent) or 532-pound 'land bombs' (53 per cent) on the centre line and could also carry a 132-pound bomb under each wing, although they did not in this battle.[4]

Dive bombers

	Vought SB2U-3	Aichi D3A1*	Douglas SBD-3
Name	Vindicator	Type 99 (11) Val	Dauntless
Design year	1934	1937	1938
Power (hp)	825	1,000	1,350
Climb (ft/min)	1,070	1,500	1,200
Ceiling (ft)	23,600	30,000	25,200
Max. radius (nm)	475	400	415
Max. speed (mph)	240	240	250
Max. payload (lb)	1,000	815	1,200
Guns	.50 x 2	.303 x 3	.30 x 2, .50 x 2
Crew	2	2	2

*Like the German Junkers 87 'Stuka', the Val had fixed, spatted wheels.

The fabric-covered Vindicator with which the Marines were equipped on Midway had no effective dive-braking mechanism and could attack at no better than 35°, and although they received some of the more robust Dauntlesses ten days before the battle they were not trained to use them properly. On board *Akagi* when the Marines attacked, Fuchida noted that so-called 'glide-bombing' was an unconscionable waste of brave men's lives. Although the Val sacrificed payload for greater agility and, clean, was supposed to be able to hold its own against fighters, as with the attack bombers there was little hope for any of these types in such a contest, so the greater punch of the Dauntless made it the better weapons system. Given the chronic unreliability of its torpedoes, this was just as well for the USN in the carrier battles of 1942.

Known as 'the Barge', 'Clunk' or 'the Beast' by its crews, the Dauntless was the star performer at Midway, blessed to find no high combat air patrol (CAP) over the enemy carriers, whose ochre decks were packed with fully fuelled and armed aircraft, their hangars littered with loose bombs and their fuel lines undrained. Any US carrier caught in a similar situation would have suffered the same fate, but with the early warning provided by radar and the lessons learned from the loss of *Lexington* in the Coral Sea, that was not going to happen. When counterattacking Vals reached *Yorktown* most of her aircraft were in the air, ordnance was properly stored and her fuel lines had been purged with carbon dioxide. Thanks to an early interception by US fighters, the Japanese dive bombers were not numerous enough, nor were their bombs sufficiently powerful, to wreck the carrier without assistance from her own stores.

American fire-control systems were the best in the world even before they began to integrate radar, but the 5-inch dual-purpose gun proved a disappointment in the AA role at Midway, while the 20mm cannon and .50 calibre machine guns lacked the range to down aircraft before they released their missiles. The 1.1-inch (27.9mm) guns were more effective, but they had a slower rate of fire and smaller magazine than the IJN's 25mm, with which its ships were more liberally equipped. On 4 June 1942 the quadruple 1.1-inch guns on *Yorktown* hacked two Vals apart when they were diving directly at her, and the next day the AA gunners on the destroyer *Tanikaze*, despite violent

manoeuvring to dodge the attentions of forty-two dive bombers and twelve B-17s, managed to shoot down one of the former and may have caused the loss of two of the latter. Gunnery does not get much better, but it was not enough and, especially for the carriers, the fighter CAP was indispensable.

Fighter pilots on both sides thought little of AA fire, although few took this as far as the Zero pilot who flew inverted over Midway's Eastern Island and got shot down for his pains, while at least one fighter pilot on each side was brought down by the gunners of his own fleet (*Soryu*'s Lieutenant Iyozo Fujita, who had just shot down three torpedo bombers, and Ensign Milton Tootle of

1.1-inch battery on *Yorktown*, hit by a bomb from a Val it had just destroyed

Yorktown, who was denied the chance). Naval aviators, with some justification, regard themselves as the finest pilots in the world, and the carrier fighter pilots were in no doubt that they were the *crème de la crème*. But the two comparably élite groups developed sharply divergent battle tactics and it was the Japanese fighter pilots who took the more individualistic approach, reflected in the outstanding agility of the aircraft they flew.

Fighters

	Brewster F2A-2	Mitsubishi A6M2	Grumman F4F-4
Name	Buffalo	Type 0 (21) 'Zeke'	Wildcat
Design year	1936	1938-39	1936
Power (hp)	1,200	950	1,200
Climb (ft/min)	2,290	2,625	2,083
Ceiling (ft)	33,200	32,800	34,800
Max. radius (nm)	420	500/840*	330
Max. speed (mph)	320	330	317
Guns	.50 x 4	.303 x 2, 20mm x 2	.50 x 6
Crew	1	1	1

*The Zero commonly flew with an auxiliary drop tank, developed but not yet in service for the Wildcat.

Although the Mitsubishi A6M was later officially designated 'Zeke', for most it will always be the dreaded 'Zero', the world's premier fighter at all save high altitude during 1941–42. As one who flew a captured example drily wrote, 'the aircraft's obvious weakness was an inability to absorb punishment from heavy calibre guns, but it did not expect to reckon with many of these.'[5] The US fighters were both designed in accordance with the same Bureau of Aeronautics (BuAer) specifications and the Buffalo was the US Navy's first choice. Production difficulties at Brewster let Grumman back into the picture and although the poor showing by the Buffalo at Midway and elsewhere during the first months of the war led to it being withdrawn from front-line service, the Wildcat did no better in the hands of average pilots. As noted earlier, the practical range of the Grumman F4F-4 was limited, and it carried only a limited amount of ammunition for each of its six .50-inch wing guns.

Even when flown by the very best it was barely able to hold its own, and Lieutenant Commander John 'Jimmy' Thach of *Yorktown* fighter group, did not mince his words in his after-battle report of 4 June 1942:

> Any success our fighter pilots may have against the Japanese zero fighter is <u>not</u> due to the performance of the airplane we fly but is the result of the comparatively poor marksmanship of the Japanese, stupid mistakes made by a few of their pilots and superior marksmanship and team work of some of our pilots. The only way we can ever bring our guns to bear on the zero fighter is to trick them into recovering in front of an F4F or shoot them when they are preoccupied in firing at one of our own planes. The F4F airplane is pitifully inferior in <u>climb</u>, <u>manoeuvrability</u> and <u>speed</u>. The writer has flown the F4F airplane without armor and leak proof tanks. Removal of their vital protection does not improve the performance of the F4F sufficiently to come anywhere near the performance of the zero fighter.

As well as modestly understating the degree to which Japanese errors were forced upon them by his own skill and leadership, Thach's assessment was a career-risking accusation that BuAer (in 1936 under the direction of none other than Ernest King) had foisted a turkey on the US Navy, and also refuted the face-saving excuse that its inferior performance was a trade-off for better pilot protection. One would have thought that the unequivocal verdict of the premier USN fighter pilot was definitive, but a reluctance to accept the unpalatable truth of non-derivative Japanese technical superiority still lingers.[6]

The Zero design emerged after close consultation with fighter pilots, drawing on their extensive combat experience over China, who demanded performance and the unique arrangement of nose-mounted .303s with ample tracer ammunition, used to 'lock on' to a target before firing the 20mm cannon mounted in the wings. Thach did not mention and may not have been aware of the most remarkable characteristic of the Zero, the long range that enabled it to conduct dynamic bomber-escort duty to the furthest targets and to spend more than twice as long as the F4F-4 on CAP. It was this that led

Hiryu on trials,
June 1939

Yorktown with
Catalina overhead,
4 June 1942

Genda to speak of 'one touch of an armoured sleeve' – one touch more, or rather better CAP discipline and the employment of all of the Zeros on board the Japanese carriers, and they might have won.

Appendices A and **B** show the similar solutions the USN and IJN found to the 1922 Washington Treaty limitations. Of the carriers, the first-generation *Akagi* and *Kaga* were large, converted capital ship hulls that would otherwise have been scrapped, as were the sunk *Lexington* and absent *Saratoga*, while the second-generation *Hiryu* was very similar to *Hornet* (both a bit larger than their sister ships to make use of every ton allowed under the treaty) and *Soryu* to both *Enterprise* and *Yorktown*. At Midway, the Japanese lacked the third-generation *Zuikaku* and *Shokaku*, which were recovering from battle damage in the Coral Sea, while the first of the comparable US *Essex* class was still on the slips. In many ways the carriers in both navies represented a continuation of the battlecruiser fallacy, sacrificing protection for speed and hitting power,

Opposite:
A Grumman
Avenger in flight
Inset: A Douglas
Dauntless

while their wooden decks made them extremely vulnerable to plunging fire.

Neither fleet distinguished itself in either submarine or anti-submarine operations at Midway. The Japanese were unable to kill the huge *Nautilus*, despite several attempts, and the Americans fared no better against the *I-168*, although both submarines only managed to fire on already crippled ships whose escorts were preoccupied with rescue operations. Against this must be set the fact that Nagumo was more concerned with flying off anti-submarine patrols in the morning of 4 June than with the long-range scouts that might have detected the US carriers earlier, while submarine sightings meant he could not pay undivided attention to the aerial dimension. The moment generally held to have decided the battle came when Lieutenant Commander Clarence McClusky led the *Enterprise* dive bombers to follow the line given by the wake of the destroyer *Arashi*, racing back towards the Mobile Force after attacking *Nautilus*. Finally, the sight of *Tambor* on the surface caused Vice Admiral Takeo Kurita to order the abrupt change of course in which the heavy cruiser *Mogami* rammed her sister ship *Mikuma*, leading to the destruction of the latter and the near loss of the former. These were important, if indirect, contributions to the outcome.

"I am looking forward to dictating peace to the United States in the White House at Washington"

— *ADMIRAL YAMAMOTO*

4

CLEVERNESS

The term 'inter-service rivalry' does not do justice to the relationship between the Japanese Army and the IJN – they loathed each other to the point at which they found it difficult to conceal their satisfaction when the other suffered a defeat. After living under daily threat of assassination by the secret police while Navy Vice Minister between 1936 and 1939, Yamamoto hated the Army with greater passion than most and this was one of the strands that came together in Operation MI. Another was that the IJN was itself riven by factions and the authority of senior officers was often more apparent than real. This was partly because they needed a following within the service to retire as fleet admirals with full pay and perquisites, and partly because the independent appointment of chiefs of staff tended to isolate their nominal commanders. The great exception was Yamamoto, but even he was obliged to accept the appointment of Ugaki as Combined Fleet

What do YOU say, AMERICA?

Chief of Staff in April 1941, despite his objection that Ugaki lacked the personality for the job. He was right and Ugaki was marginalized, as we can see from his rather pathetic diary entry at the time of the first US carrier raid.

> There have already been several cases that eventually turned out adversely because of my indecision. In spite of my feeling some apprehension, or contrary judgements, I refrained from giving my decisions in order to save the face of the staff officers who drafted the idea or after having been forced to give in to their strong one-sided arguments. ... Intuition, instinct, or sixth sense, even when it is right, tends to be ignored when many people or insensitive people are consulted. ... This intuition cannot be simply called instinct or presentiment. This, of course, owes much to talent, but its function will not be complete unless based on full knowledge of the enemy as well as ourselves – and everything in the universe.

The result was a dangerous absence of creative dissent at the top of the Combined Fleet and, in common with most men whose opinions are generally disregarded, when Ugaki could get one of his ideas accepted he over-invested in it. Thus his contribution to Pearl Harbor was an attempt to penetrate the anchorage with midget submarines, which he insisted against the evidence had been a great success and sought to repeat elsewhere. While he generally looked to the junior staff officers who were personally closer to Yamamoto for indications of what the great man wanted, the genesis of Operation MI was an outline he drew up in mid January 1942 and passed to Senior Staff Officer Captain Kameto Kuroshima. Kuroshima initially ignored it in favour of a projected advance on the Burma/Indian Ocean front, but after the army rejected this Ugaki's idea was taken up, and from that moment he acted as though it were a miraculous conception.

As courtiers have done throughout the ages, Yamamoto's staff were anxious to win the favour of their patron by anticipating his wishes. In addition to his known desire to have as little to do with joint Army-Navy operations as possible, when he assumed command of the Combined Fleet in 1939 he declared that naval operations in the Pacific would involve 'capturing an island, then building an airfield in as short a time as possible – within a week or so – moving up air units, and using them to gain air and surface control over the next stretch of ocean'. Staff Torpedo Officer Commander Takayasu Arima later confessed, 'The C-in-C was actually opposed to Midway … It was the staff officers who insisted that the plan for the Midway operation, which they themselves had come up with after a lot of hard work, represented the C-in-C's own wishes.' While the suggestion that the staff officers imposed it on Yamamoto is absurd, and was certainly an attempt to shield his memory from blame, it rings true as an explanation of how Operation MI came into being and acquired momentum.

The key figure was Kuroshima, known as 'the God of Operations', a shaman-like individual who devised plans in flashes of inspiration that came to him while meditating naked in his sealed cabin, drinking heavily, chain-smoking and burning incense. The unkempt, even unhygienic warrior-monk is a potent Japanese folk figure (Musashi never bathed and, not surprisingly, never married), and Kuroshima may have been encouraged in his eccentricity by the effect it had on the superstitious Yamamoto, himself not much given to linear thought. Kuroshima, not Ugaki, submitted the Pearl Harbor plan to the Naval General Staff (NGS) in October 1941 and also conveyed Yamamoto's threat to resign if it were not approved, but only as an operation to cover the Pacific flank of the attack by combined forces on the Philippines, Malaya and the Dutch East Indies. After this first phase was complete, the NGS did not contemplate further deliberate action against the US Pacific Fleet and the omnibus Combined Fleet Operation Order of 5 November 1941 listed the following 'to be rapidly occupied or destroyed as soon as the war situation permits: (1) Areas of Eastern New Guinea, New Britain, Fiji and Samoa; (2) Aleutian and Midway Areas; (3) Areas of the Andaman Islands [Bay of Bengal]; (4) Important points in the Australian Area'.

There was, manifestly, a yawning gulf in strategic appreciation between fighting the US Pacific Fleet should it interfere with these deployments and

Operation MI, which proposed taking the entire Combined Fleet to mid-ocean to seek it out. In a series of meetings between 2 and 5 April 1942, Kuroshima and Combined Fleet Operations Officer Captain Yasuji Watanabe presented the outline of Operation MI to the NGS and, once again, employed the threat of Yamamoto's resignation to overcome opposition. It came down to a trial of wills between Yamamoto and NGS Chief Admiral Osami Nagano, who backed down and approved the operation with the addition of a secondary operation against the Aleutians. Initially little more than a face-saving frill that might even have provided a useful diversion, following the Doolittle raid on Tokyo the idea of a wide oceanic perimeter to protect the sacred Emperor from another such affront turned it into a significant operation in its own right.

This was no way to formulate an operation on which hung the fate of both the IJN and the Japanese Empire, but strong personalities will expand to fill a vacuum of authority. At precisely the same time, Admiral King was trying to take over the bureaus of the (civilian) Department of the Navy, a process not halted until President Roosevelt issued an Executive Order revoking King's initiatives. There was, however, never the slightest doubt about what would happen to any officer who dared encroach on King's prerogatives. In Japan the NGS usurped the functions of the Navy Ministry in the formulation of national policy, but was in turn imposed upon by Yamamoto. Thus with reference to Operation MI, Yamamoto's role was roughly equivalent to those of the US Secretary of the Navy, Commander US Fleet and Commander Pacific Fleet put together, too much for one man.

King and Yamamoto had parallel careers. Yamamoto qualified as a pilot in 1925 at the age of forty, King in 1927 at forty-eight. Yamamoto was second in command of the Kasumigaura Aviation Corps between 1924 and 1925, King of the Norfolk Naval Air Station between 1929 and 1930. Yamamoto was captain of the new aircraft carrier *Akagi* between 1928 and 1929, King of the *Lexington* between 1930 and 1933. Yamamoto was head of the Technical Division of the Navy Ministry's Aeronautics Department between

1931 and 1933 and the first chief of the newly independent Aeronautics Bureau from 1935 to 1936, while King was chief of the Bureau of Aeronautics (BuAer) from 1933 to 1936. Yamamoto had command of the First Carrier Division from 1933 to 1934, King rising to similar responsibilities between 1936 and 1939. Each had his own particular cross to bear. Yamamoto's was that Japan's labour surplus precluded the development of the construction machinery that was to play such a vital role in the hands of the US 'Seabees' (Construction Battalions); King's was that the lines of demarcation between army and navy prevented him from developing long-range, land-based naval aviation. Thus while he was at BuAer, King issued the specifications for the Catalina, basically an airship with wings, while in a similar situation Yamamoto challenged Japanese industry to produce the revolutionary Nell long-range attack bomber, thereby setting a trend whose fruits we have seen.

Although not in the same league as the Japanese, relations between the US Army and Navy were tense, with the added complication that the Army Air Corps had its own agenda. During the months before Midway, in addition to his bold assault on the principle of military subordination to civilian authority, King was involved in a ruthless power play over the allocation of shipyard resources and the control of land-based aerial anti-submarine operations over the Atlantic. In sum, while most admirals aspired to be a Nelson, leading their fleet to victory, King's model was Jervis, the fierce old man who made Nelson's exploits possible. King handled the politics and made sure that the USN had a full say in the formulation of Allied strategy, leaving Nimitz free to concentrate on operations. Yamamoto was a key player at the political and strategic levels but his instincts inclined him to be a Nelson, not a Jervis, and in February 1941 he speculated:

> If there's a war, it won't be the kind where battleships sally forth in leisurely fashion as in the past, and the proper thing for the commander-in-chief of the Combined Fleet would be, I think, to sit tight in the Inland Sea, keeping

an eye on the situation as a whole [as Nimitz chose to do]. But I can't see myself doing anything so boring ...   ✓

At the same time, Yamamoto may have believed that he was marked by destiny to lead Japan in peace as well as war. His devoted acolytes certainly entertained Napoleonic ambitions for him, and when he was asked what he thought would happen to him if Japan lost the war he replied, 'either the guillotine or St Helena'. Roosevelt had not yet locked the Allies into the 'unconditional surrender' formula and it is possible Yamamoto calculated that victory at Midway would make him the unquestioned master of the IJN, thus able to challenge the army for political supremacy and, national 'face' having been saved, to demand the substantial concessions necessary to end the war.

This is a charitable interpretation, the alternative being that Yamamoto should not have had command of a rowing boat. There does not seem to be any middle ground, the latter verdict being inescapable if he was closely involved in the formulation of Operation MI, whereas if his eyes were fixed at the top of a staircase of vaulting ambition, it would explain why he failed to notice that the first step was rotten. Something very odd had to be at work for a man regarded as one of the most intelligent naval officers of his generation to find himself sitting helplessly 300 miles away in the battleship *Yamato*, the building of which he had eloquently opposed, while the naval air element he had done so much to develop suffered an avoidable defeat. Simple incompetence cannot explain it – like many of the great blunders of history, it bears the hallmark of a failure to keep the eye on the ball that dooms military operations just as certainly as it does golf shots.

The linch-pin of Operation MI was to seize the Midway islands and convert them into a forward air base. The islet of Kure would be turned into a base for floatplanes brought in with the Occupation Force, Sand Island would become the base for Emily flying boats from Jaluit while the airfield on Eastern Island, rehabilitated and expanded by two labour battalions, would be used by Bettys

Officers of the Naval General Staff, Combined Fleet and First Air Fleet aboard *Akagi*.

Front row from left: 6–Ugaki, 7–Nagumo, 9–Nagano, 10–Yamamoto, 11–Kuroshima. Genda is 3rd from right, second row.

flown in from Wake and by Zeros transported by the carriers of the Mobile Force. NGS officers had argued that the IJN lacked the logistical train to support the base and that Hawaii-based Flying Fortresses would render the labourers' efforts in vain, only to see their entirely valid objections brushed aside. But even before that the islands had to be secured, and as far as anything is certain in war that was not going to be achieved by about three thousand assault troops preceded by a mere two to three days of preliminary bombardment.

The IJN's experience at Wake in December 1941 was an unheeded warning. The failed first assault had cost the IJN two destroyers sunk and several other ships damaged, despite the destruction of eight of twelve marine fighters (the only aircraft on the atoll) in a raid by twin-engined bombers from Kwajalein, and severe damage to the land defences by further bombing raids on successive days. The second attempt involved the fleet carriers *Hiryu* and *Soryu* in addition to the land-based bombers, and although the five hundred marines had lost all of their aircraft, most of their heavy guns and had suffered a hundred casualties, the thousand-man Special Naval Landing Force still had to be put ashore by the desperate expedient of beaching two old destroyers converted into troop transports.

Midway was a far more formidable proposition, and the Japanese were fully aware of it. They should therefore have known that the islands could not be taken by the modest invasion force assigned to it unless first literally ploughed up by preliminary bombardment. Yet this was ruled out by the requirement for the airfield to become operational as soon as possible after its capture, and the plan specified *less* bombardment than had proved necessary at Wake. There was no hope of achieving the absolute surprise of Pearl Harbor, long-range patrolling by Midway-based Catalinas made operational surprise very unlikely and the radar on Sand Island (which Wake had lacked) precluded tactical surprise. In addition, the reefs fringing the islands would rip the bottom out of the converted destroyers well short of the beaches and it would take at least six round trips by all five of the Daihatsu landing craft they carried to ferry the troops ashore. Even if every man of the landing force had been a champion swimmer as well as a war god, the assault would still have failed.

Yet this was the keystone for the whole enterprise and the reason why the carriers were sent blitzing ahead of the rest of the fleet to their doom. Mahan's stricture against ships engaging shore batteries was an article of faith in the IJN, such that when Watanabe proposed sending the battleships to bombard Midway after the loss of the carriers, Yamamoto rebuked him: 'You ought to know' he said, 'that of all naval tactics, firing one's guns at an island is considered the most stupid'. In fact Operation MI provided for night bombardment by the heavy cruisers of Vice Admiral Takeo Kurita's close support force, but what their guns could do, battleship guns could clearly have done better. It is incomprehensible that a principle derived from the vulnerability of wooden warships should have been applied to steel monsters that hugely outgunned the coastal artillery on Midway. Nonetheless, it was the reason why the Mobile Force was burdened with the schizophrenic mission of reducing the atoll's defences while remaining on guard to engage enemy carriers.

In addition, if the scheme was to work the enemy had to do exactly what was expected of him. This was most clearly shown in the posting of the IJN submarines to intercept the US fleet when it sortied from Pearl Harbor, which only took up their stations on 3 June, two days later than Operation MI intended. But since the I-boats could stay at sea for weeks, why cut it so fine in the first place? No possible harm to the Japanese interest could come from infesting the waters around Pearl with submarines for a week or two in advance, and as things turned out it might have saved them from defeat.

There is a further oddity in the composition of the Mobile Force itself. Since they were not going to be used for shore bombardment, added little AA armament and carried fewer floatplanes than the heavy cruisers, why did the battlecruisers *Haruna* and *Kirishima* form part of Nagumo's force while their sister ships *Kongo* and *Hiei* were hundreds of miles behind them with the Second Fleet? It is almost as though the Combined Fleet planners allotted every vice admiral and rear admiral a command appropriate to his rank and then tried to put it all together, deepening the impression that Operation MI was more concerned with institutional politics than with defeating the US Pacific Fleet.

This would be a good moment to re-examine the IJN order of battle given in **Appendix A** in conjunction with **Map 10** (in the chapter 'Point Luck'), both to appreciate the size and complexity of the operation and to speculate what it was supposed to achieve. The Aleutians diversion was the product of internal politics and a hysterical reaction to the Doolitle raid, but at least it had a rationale, however flawed, and the rest of the Combined Fleet was more

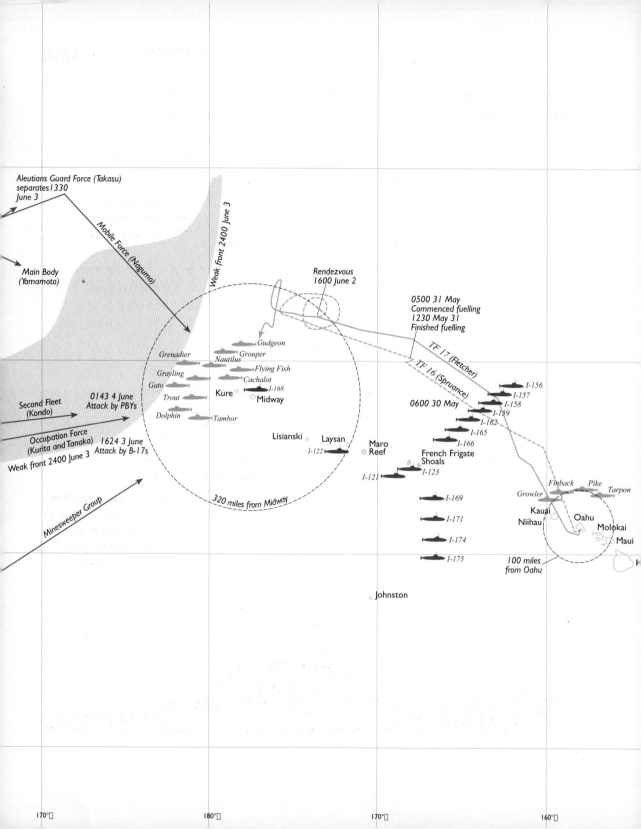

Aleutians Guard Force (Takasu)
separates 1330
June 3

Mobile Force (Nagumo)

Weak front 2400 June 3

Main Body
(Yamamoto)

Rendezvous
1600 June 2

0500 31 May
Commenced fuelling
1230 May 31
Finished fuelling

TF 17 (Fletcher)

TF 16 (Spruance)

Grenadier
Grouper
Gudgeon
Nautilus
Grayling
Flying Fish
Gato
Cachalot
Trout
Kure
I-168
Midway
Dolphin
Tambor

Second Fleet
(Kondo)

0143 4 June
Attack by PBYs

*Occupation Force
(Kurita and Tanaka)*

1624 3 June
Attack by B-17s

Weak front 2400 June 3

0600 30 May

I-156
I-157
I-158
I-159
I-162
I-165
I-166

Lisianski
Laysan
I-122

Maro
Reef

French Frigate
Shoals
I-123
I-121

Minesweeper Group

320 miles from Midway

I-169

I-171

I-174

I-175

Growler
Finback
Pike
Tarpon

Kauai
Niihau
Oahu
Molokai
Maui

100 miles
from Oahu

Johnston

170°   180°   170°   160°

than powerful enough for the central thrust. It is the inconsistencies within the latter that are so baffling. What purpose could there have been for dividing the First Fleet and sending four battleships, as well as the two special torpedo cruisers, north, without air cover, to a position where they could not immediately support either the Midway or the Aleutians operations? The light carriers *Hosho* and *Zuiho* can only have been assigned to the heavy divisions of the First and Second Fleets to provide CAP – so why were they equipped with obsolete Claude fighters, and with Kate attack bombers when the latter could have been put to better use by the Mobile Force? The last point underlines the biggest question of all – in a maximum effort involving virtually the entire Combined Fleet, one which seriously depleted the crucial strategic oil reserve, why were the cutting-edge Air Units all significantly under strength?

It is when we come to examine vital steps that were supposed to have been taken before the plan went into effect that puzzlement turns to incredulity. The entire philosophy of the IJN was that it would always be more highly motivated and better prepared than its more numerous enemies, but after six months spent chasing the Allied navies out of Far Eastern waters and the Indian Ocean, the men of the First Air Fleet/Mobile Force were tired and badly in need of rest. Morale was still high, but the combat readiness of the Air Units had been sharply eroded. They were not granted the necessary time to recover and Nagumo's after-battle report, despite a sense of personal failure so

**Map 6
Disposition of
submarine forces at
0900 on 3 June 1942**

Japanese submarines

U. S. submarines

Haruna in 1939:
much bombed at
Midway she was
finally sunk in
July 1945

great that he was only with difficulty persuaded not to commit suicide, put the blame squarely where it belonged.

> ...since there had been a considerable turnover in personnel, practically no one got beyond the point of basic training. Inexperienced fliers barely got to the point where they could make daytime landings on carriers. It was found that even some of the more seasoned fliers had lost some of their skill. No opportunity was available to carry out joint training, which of course made impossible any co-ordinated action between contact units, illumination units, and attack units. The likelihood of obtaining any results from night attacks, therefore, was practically nil.

Night attack with torpedoes was the tactical touchstone for the IJN and was to inflict savage reverses on the USN in the battles off Guadalcanal. As the report went on to make clear, Nagumo – who was a torpedo, not an aviation specialist – was referring not only to his mixture of weary and inexperienced fliers, but also to the surface-warfare component of the Mobile Force, which had not been able to practise essential battle drills during the six months it had been acting as an escort to the carriers.

The same could not be said of the fresh and well-oiled 'Hashira Jima fleet', as the men of the First Air Fleet mockingly dubbed the battlefleet that had so far ventured out of its anchorage in Hiroshima Bay only to train, clustered around the beautiful *Yamato*, the bearer of the name of the Japanese race and a ship so massive that she made the older battleships look like cruisers. The sole purpose of this force was to do or die in the climactic encounter, and now that at last it was sailing to give battle, it was doing so hundreds of miles behind the weary Mobile Force.

As the British journalist Basil Liddell Hart wrote, battleships were to admirals what cathedrals were to bishops, and *Yamato* was the depository of far too much faith and treasure to be risked in the forefront of an adventure thousands of miles from the sacred shores of Nippon. Since she was the flagship, Yamamoto had to sail in her, but as an icon she, along with the previous flagship *Nagato* and her sister ship *Mutsu*, had to be held back until lesser warships had cleared the way. The fact that their screen was made up of old destroyers and that they were accompanied by one of Ugaki's trademark Special Duty Forces, which could only become operational once Midway was completely secure, argues that Operation MI did not contemplate using *Yamato* as the unstoppable battering ram she was designed to be.

Perhaps, crowned with victory, Yamamoto might have sailed her into Tokyo Bay to compel the surrender of the Tojo government, as happened to its successor on the deck of the battleship *Missouri* three years later. Whatever the unwritten hopes behind it, the more one examines Operation MI the more it seems to make sense as politics or even as a mystical celebration of power, in a way it utterly fails to do as a military operation.

It may seem far-fetched to suggest that the operation was rushed in order to set it in motion by Navy Day, but the explanation given by Ugaki – that it was necessary in order to have sufficient moonlight for night action – is flatly contradicted by Nagumo's estimate of capability. Given the personalities involved it is reasonable to conclude that the date was chosen because Yamamoto was the only serving officer who had fought at Tsushima and the historical continuity was an omen too powerful to be ignored. There is a somnambulist quality to the ambivalently worded letter Yamamoto wrote to his long-time mistress that day: 'On the morning of the twenty-ninth we leave for battle, and I'll be at sea in command of the whole force for about three weeks. Not that I'm expecting very much of it. Now comes the crucial time.' The self-deprecation was, of course, designed to ward off the evil eye, but most people in his position would also have done some contingency planning. Instead, Operation MI consisted of a series of linked leaps of faith, as summarised by the unhappy Nagumo:

a) Although the enemy lacks the will to fight, it is likely that he will counter attack if our occupation operations progress satisfactorily.

b) The enemy conducts air reconnaissance mainly to the West and to the South but does not maintain a strict vigil to the Northwest or to the North.

c) The enemy's patrol radius is about 500 miles.

d) The enemy is not aware of our plans.

e) It is not believed that the enemy has any powerful unit, with carriers as its nucleus, in the vicinity.

f) After attacking Midway by air and destroying the enemy's shore based air strength to facilitate our landing operations, we would still be able to destroy any enemy task force that may choose to counter attack.

g) The enemy's attempt to counter attack with use of shore based aircraft could be neutralised by our fighter cover and AA fire.

With the exception of the last premise every one of these assumptions not only proved false but in some cases flew in the face of facts known to the Combined Fleet staff, if not Nagumo, before battle was joined. Of them all, the belief that the enemy must be provoked into doing battle was the most important, so let us now see just how wrong it was.

5

INTELLIGENCE

Despite the widely held belief that it is an oxymoron, the field of information-gathering and assessment is rightly called military intelligence. Musashi wrote, 'to know myriad things by means of one thing is a principle of military science' and according to the Duke of Wellington, 'all the business of war, and indeed all the business of life, is to endeavour to find out what you don't know by what you do, that is what I called guessing what was at the other side of the hill'. But because the information available is seldom precise enough to preclude alternative interpretations, there will always remain the intuitive element that we saw Ugaki speculating about in the previous chapter. This is why Nimitz is rightly honoured for the decisive action he took on the basis of the assessment of Japanese intentions provided by his COMINT specialists.[1]

Paradoxically, the crucial intelligence contribution may have been what decryption, traffic analysis and radio direction-finding could not tell him, because Yamamoto's Main Force maintained hermetic radio silence. It is extremely unlikely that Nimitz would have risked his carrier task forces as he did had he known that the Midway operation involved two more carriers and seven more battleships. He only knew that four or five carriers and four battleships were with the Mobile Force and Second Fleet, and that two carriers were with the Fifth Fleet in the Aleutians operation.

Six months earlier the US Pacific Fleet had benefited from a similar blessing, albeit very well disguised, when Kimmel was left out of the loop of top secret COMINT reports that would probably have caused him to take his battleships to sea. Had he done so, Nimitz believed that Nagumo's six carriers would, in all likelihood, have sunk them in deep water, beyond hope of salvage and with far greater loss of life. This underlines the fact that even if COMINT had provided Nimitz with a far more complete picture before Midway than it actually did, there were still fundamental command issues at stake that no amount of operational intelligence could resolve. Not the least of these was how his carriers would fare if they failed to land a knock out-surprise punch and the battle became a slugging match between evenly matched forces.

Regrettably, US documentation of the COMINT story is incomplete, while the Japanese destroyed their records and were extremely cagey in postwar interviews, so one or two important points will probably remain unresolved. What should be stressed is that in the absence of any other sources, the USN was totally dependant on COMINT, even for the sort of information that was freely available to their enemies from the American press. A particularly egregious illustration was the story headlined by several US newspapers on 7 June 1942, which revealed that the Americans had foreknowledge of Japanese intentions which could only have come from reading enciphered radio traffic. Within a few weeks the IJN initiated significant changes in its communications security procedures, including a long overdue revision of the location designators (such as 'AF' for Midway) and unit call signs that had provided vital keys to the serial cracking of their ciphers.

Although one can sympathise with King's contention that the press should be told nothing until the end of the war, and then only who had won, the more interesting aspect of this episode is that with the dissemination of information tightly circumscribed and considerations of 'face' paramount, the IJN did not collectively learn from its mistakes. It continued to use lower-grade ciphers for 'mere' administrative traffic, apparently unaware that logistical preparations are as valuable as operational orders for the purpose of predicting intentions. For example, what seems to have convinced Nimitz that Operation MI could not be a deception was a routine administrative message. Fletcher recalled expressing surprise when, on 27 May, Nimitz told him to prepare for battle at Midway.

> Yes, Midway [Nimitz emphasized]. You have to go there because the Japanese are going to try to take it. In fact, they are so positive they have already ordered a Captain of the Yard to report there on August 12.[2]

One notable casualty of this bureaucratic blind spot was Yamamoto himself, killed over Bougainville on 18 April 1943 in an aerial ambush ordered by Nimitz following the interception of a routine signal giving details of a travel schedule that brought Yamamoto's Betty within the extreme range of Guadalcanal-based US fighters.

The first indication that the Japanese had turned their attention once more to the central Pacific area came during the night of 4/5 March, when two of Japan's new Emily flying boats flew over Oahu and dropped some bombs, doing no damage but sparking fears that the Japanese carriers were back. Lieutenant Commander Joseph Rochefort, head of the Combat Intelligence Office at Pearl (Op-20-02, known as station 'Hypo') and nearly as unorthodox in dress as Yamamoto's Kuroshima (although we can acquit him of any thought that this might have been professionally advantageous in King's navy), revealed that the Emilys had been refuelled by a submarine in the protected waters within French Frigate Shoal, about 500 miles west-north-west of Oahu. This helped to balance an earlier gaffe by Commander Edwin

Layton, Nimitz's Intelligence Officer, who worded a warning of possible further Japanese attacks on Pearl incautiously, prompting King to order Nimitz to declare a state of 'fleet opposed invasion' whereby he assumed command over the Army and its Air Corps in Hawaii.

The Japanese raid was in retaliation for the US carrier raids, but it was a foolishly premature revelation of the Emily's amazing range. As a direct result Nimitz was to post minor naval units to French Frigate Shoal and all of the other unpopulated islets and shallows stretching from Hawaii towards Midway, thereby denying them to the Japanese when they needed them to perform reconnaissance of Pearl in advance of Operation MI. It also enabled Rochefort to clarify that the 'Operation K' in future Japanese communications referred to this scouting mission and not, as some insisted, to an invasion of Hawaii.

Rochefort also warned Midway to expect a visitor from Jaluit and on 10 March the Marines' Buffalo fighters were just able to catch up with an Emily flying a weaving pattern about 50 miles out, which suggests that it was testing the radar on Sand Island. The Emily was both fast and heavily armed and would have been expected to outrun or outfight any reaction it provoked, and in any case it had time to report the range at which it was detected. This may have been added to the IJN estimate of Midway's air defences provided by submarines, an exception to their generally misleading combat intelligence and too accurate to be the product of periscope observation. Presumably scouts, who either swam or were put ashore by night, obtained it.

Starting in February 1942, Hypo and its sister station 'Cast' on Corregidor, in the Philippines (later evacuated to Melbourne, Australia, where it became active on 20 March), tracked the forward deployment of Japanese air units

---

Map 7
Operation 'K' thwarted

The aircraft tenders *U.S.S. Thornton* and *Ballard* and the destroyer *U.S.S. Clark* were posted at French Frigate Shoals, preventing *I-121* and *I-123* from refuelling Emily flying boats from Jaluit. The oiler *U.S.S. Kaloli* and the converted yacht *Crystal* were posted at Pearl and Hermes Reef along with the tug *Vireo*. *Vireo* detached to assist *U.S.S. Yorktown* on 5 June.

29 May Yacht *Crystal* posted to Pearl and Hermes Reef, joined by *Vireo* on 1 June and *Kaloli* on 3 June.

29 May *Thornton* and *Clark* seen at French Frigate Shoals by *I-123*, causes Operation 'K' (reconnaissance of Pearl Harbor by Emilys) to be aborted.

4 June *Ballard* relieved them after delivering stores and John Ford to Midway.

 Japanese submarines

 Converted Tuna boats posted on 30 May

Converted yacht

 Tug

U.S. Naval vessels

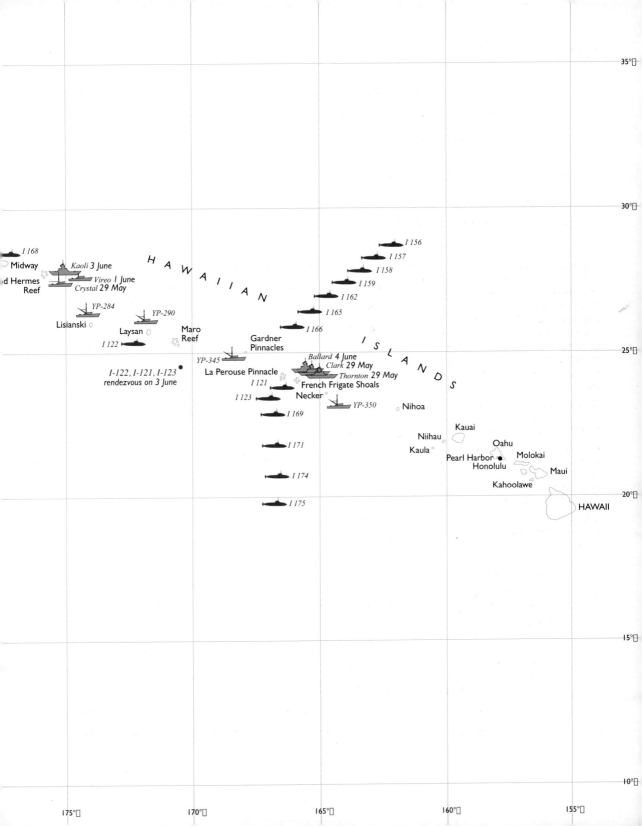

35°

30°

I 168

Midway

Hermes
Reef

Kaoli 3 June

Vireo 1 June

Crystal 29 May

I 156

I 157

I 158

I 159

I 162

I 165

I 166

YP-284

Lisianski

YP-290

Laysan

I 122

Maro
Reef

Gardner
Pinnacles

YP-345

La Perouse Pinnacle

I-122, I-121, I-123
rendezvous on 3 June

I 121

I 123

Ballard 4 June

Clark 29 May

Thornton 29 May

French Frigate Shoals

Necker

YP-350

Nihoa

Kauai

Niihau

Kaula

Oahu

Pearl Harbor

Honolulu

Molokai

Maui

Kahoolawe

I 169

I 171

I 174

I 175

HAWAII

H   A   W   A   I   I   A   N

I   S   L   A   N   D   S

25°

20°

15°

10°

175°

170°

165°

160°

155°

and equipment to the Marshall Islands. The COMINT stations warned that it presaged an attack on Midway before, in fact, the Japanese had formulated any such intention, but this was not crying 'wolf' in the context of the time, rather the reverse. Exaggerated overestimates of Japanese capabilities were entertained in Washington DC at this time, including fears of an attack on the West Coast, nurtured by some desultory shelling by submarines, hilariously satirised in Stephen Spielberg's film *1941*.

The field of conjecture narrowed from 13 March, when the cryptanalysts began to read the naval cipher designated JN-25 fairly consistently and continued to do so until 27 May, when a new and temporarily unreadable cipher was introduced. There was no 'open sesame' moment, and as late as 26 May Nimitz reported to King, 'generally speaking our present intelligence is mainly the decoding (*sic*) of 40 percent of the messages copied, and only 60 percent of possible messages are copied'. Furthermore, there was often disagreement among Hypo, Cast and Op-20-G (the Communications Security Office in Washington) over the substance, as well as the interpretation, of the deciphered messages.

Although Captain John Redman, head of Op-20-G, was not an intelligence specialist, he was seconded by Commander Joseph Wenger, who was. He also enjoyed the inestimable advantage of working directly under his brother, Rear Admiral Joseph Redman, at a time when the high command was taking new shape following President Roosevelt's Executive Order 9096 of 12 March 1942, which combined the offices of Commander-in-Chief US Fleet and Chief of Naval Operations in the person of Admiral King. One interpretation that can be given to the various disputes within the naval intelligence community in Washington at this time is that the Redmans were seeking to increase the influence of the Office of Communications at the expense of the Office of Naval Intelligence and of Rear Admiral Richmond Turner at War Plans. The latter became so exasperated that one of his last exercises of fast-eroding authority was to issue a directive on 20 May 1942, stating that unless they could produce hard evidence to the contrary, Op-20-G, Hypo and Cast should 'not comment in such a way as to indicate that C-in-C 5th Fleet is to command any force now concentrating in Northern Empire Waters, but are to assume that Admiral Turner's views are correct'. At issue was Turner's belief that Fifth Fleet was the sea-frontier command for northern Japan and not the nucleus of an Aleutians task force – which, unfortunately for him, it was.

There was also disagreement between the Pacific stations and Op-20-G over the Japanese 'AF' and 'AK' designations. Cast had identified 'AF' as Midway on 7 March 1942, with Hypo concurring, and neither Nimitz nor King appears to have seriously doubted it. Thus the most famous COMINT anecdote of the Midway campaign was simply a plan cooked up by the Pacific stations to end the bickering with Op-20-G and was not the breakthrough of myth and movie. Sometime in May, Layton prevailed upon Nimitz to send Midway an order (by the submarine cable that concealed the enormous increase in traffic between Pearl and Midway from the Japanese in the weeks before the battle) to transmit a plain language radio message back to Pearl saying that their water condenser had broken down. On 22 May, Cast reported the following intercept from Naval Intelligence in Tokyo: 'The AF air unit sent following radio message to Commandant 14th District AK on 20th – quote Refer this unit's report dated 19th, at the present time we have only enough water for two weeks. Please supply us immediately unquote.' Although this put an end to the 'AF'/ 'AK' dispute, it was only a storm in the teacup of the naval intelligence community and seems not to have impinged on high-level decision-making in the slightest.

On 14 May 1942, King again directed Nimitz to declare a state of fleet-opposed invasion, citing a possible Main Force attack on Midway and Oahu during the first week of June, with a simultaneous attack on the Aleutians, but not yet discarding the possibility that other operations would be mounted against Ocean and Nauru Islands, or that the offensive out of New Britain and New Guinea, which had just culminated in the battle of the Coral Sea, might be renewed. By this time Nimitz was convinced that the Layton–Rochefort interpretation of the available COMINT was correct and that Midway, not

Joseph Rochefort after a very belated promotion to Captain

Oahu, was the target, but after General Delos Emmons, the Army Commander in Hawaii, protested against sending his bombers to the atoll, Nimitz assigned Captain James Steele to play the role of devil's advocate at Hypo. Despite this, and even after having been included in the highly restricted COMINT distribution, Emmons was not reassured. On 25 May his staff prepared a tail-covering critique of placing too much reliance on reports of Japanese intentions, instead of basing planning on estimates of their capabilities, which the army felt included a direct assault on Oahu. While his staff bristled, Nimitz was merely amused and gracefully accepted an apology, along with a jeroboam of champagne, from Emmons after the battle.

While Op-20-G and Turner were wrangling, Nimitz and King reached almost total agreement concerning Japanese intentions, as shown by their Situation Summaries of 16 and 17 May respectively. Nimitz included the minor caveat 'unless the enemy is using radio deception on a grand scale, we have a fairly good idea of his intentions', but continued, 'there may well be three separate and possibly simultaneous enemy offensives. One involving cruisers and carriers against the Aleutians, probably Dutch Harbor. Second against Port Moresby involving present forces that area. Probably [a] reinforced third against Midway for which it is believed the enemy's main striking force will be employed.'

King's assessment was more detailed and stunningly accurate, not merely correctly identifying the objectives for all of the Japanese naval divisions identified by COMINT, but also containing a unique insight into Operation MI, which did not, despite an obeisance to it in his after-battle report, much influence Nimitz's deployment for the coming battle. King stated that important elements of the Combined Fleet were unaccounted for and that there were 'some indications that [the] remainder of 1st Fleet may take up supporting position west of Midway', its purpose being to ambush the US Pacific Fleet when it came out to defend Midway. The assessment seems to have been the work of King's intelligence officer, Captain George Dyer, whose contribution remains oddly unremarked.[3]

The approach course of the Mobile Force was revealed in a routine request for weather information from Nagumo, intercepted on 18 May, which included the gratuitous information that he planned to make air attacks from 50 miles north-west of 'AF' from 'N minus 2 days until N day'. That was precisely the range of the (old) radar on Sand Island, tending to support the above hypothesis concerning the mission of the Emily shot down on 10 March. But this was of minor significance in comparison with knowing from what direction the attack would come and although the intercept left the date of 'N day' unresolved, it was sufficient for Nimitz order Task Force 16 (Halsey) and Task Force 17 (Fletcher) to return to Pearl with 'all deliberate speed'.

Nimitz also recalled all submarines from their patrols and the first thirteen to return were stationed on 200 and 150-mile radii to the north and west of Midway. Later arrivals were posted 800 miles north-west of Oahu, and the last to return formed an inner screen for Pearl, a mere 100 miles out. Nimitz proudly wore a submariner's dolphins and symbolically assumed command of the Pacific Fleet on the deck of the submarine *Grayling*, so we may be sure that Rear Admiral Robert English's disposition of the submarines corresponded very closely to Nimitz's views. Given the poor performance of the Mark 14 torpedo at this time his commander-in-chief's faith may have been misplaced, but he was not hedging his bets and committed his forces very much according to what Layton and Rochefort were telling him.[4]

By contrast Rear Admiral Robert Theobald, whom Nimitz now designated as the commander of cruiser-based Task Force 8 with responsibility for countering the Japanese thrust at the Aleutians, never overcame his suspicion that the information he was being given about Japanese intentions was too detailed and therefore likely to be a deception operation. The action he took was based on the assumption that Attu and Kiska were too insignificant to merit a major Japanese effort, and that their real intention was to get behind his task force. It was a fair assessment and history would have been even unkinder to him than it has been had he risked his command for such worthless pieces of real estate. After Operation MI was cancelled, Yamamoto sought compensation further north and if Theobald had sought to engage the Aleutians force upon news of the Japanese defeat at Midway, he might indeed have found himself cut off by a reinforced fleet, eventually including the big carrier *Zuikaku*.

Other intercepts advised Nimitz that the Japanese were obtaining good results from traffic analysis and radio direction-finding, prompting warning messages to be sent not only to Halsey and Fletcher to enforce strict radio silence on their chattering Air Groups, but also to General Douglas MacArthur in Australia. MacArthur took prompt and drastic action to correct the weakness, with sad consequences for many inexperienced aircrew who were lost over the ocean during the following months. Never one to miss a trick, he also suggested turning the insight to US advantage by creating a 'spoof' task force in the Coral Sea, an idea which Nimitz seized upon. The seaplane tender *Tangier*, cruiser *Salt Lake City* and the Melbourne COMINT station, directed by the brilliant Lieutenant Commander Rudolph Fabian, forthwith began to generate spurious radio traffic. Tokyo duly detected this, and reassuring reports that a US carrier task force was active far away in the Coral Sea were sent to Yamamoto on his way to Midway.

Less reassuring was that on Japanese 1 June and US 30 May (the same day, the international date line intervening) the COMINT group on board the *Yamato* detected a long report designated 'urgent' from a US submarine on the route of Rear Admiral Raizo Tanaka's Occupation Force. On 2/1 June, the traffic analysts in Tokyo reported an unprecedented increase in high-priority radio transmissions from Pearl Harbor and indications of enemy task forces at sea around Hawaii and the Aleutians. On the same day, both the Japanese base on Wake and the submarine *I-168* reported longer-range and greatly increased air patrols out of Midway, while on 3/2 June Tokyo reported radio direction-finding triangulations of a task force near Midway.

Some have seen this as the moment when Yamamoto was trapped by the need to maintain radio silence and therefore did not warn his subordinates that the all-important element of surprise was lost. But the information available did not lend itself to any such firm conclusion, while it was reasonable to assume that Nagumo had also received the warnings. It was certainly cold-blooded to permit the crowded transports to continue on course as bait, but to a degree that was implicit in Operation MI from the beginning. Ugaki smugly wrote in his diary that 'if the dispatched message were a report of discovering our forces it would surely serve to alert the enemy, thus contributing to making our [bag of] game in battle heavier'. In other words, the Combined Fleet staff were not concerned about the premature discovery of the Occupation Force and calculated that it increased the probability of wrong-footing the US fleet by drawing it to the south of Midway.

They could not have known that there was no chance of this, and that Nimitz's COMINT cup had overflowed when Hypo unlocked the Japanese date cipher on 25 May. Retroanalysis of earlier intercepts permitted Rochefort to identify 'N day' as 6 June, central Pacific time, and that the Aleutians would therefore be attacked on 3 June and Midway on 4 June. Despite strong last-minute reservations even among his own staff, Nimitz ordered them to plan accordingly.

On 27 May the changes in the JN-25 cipher that were supposed to have taken place nearly a month earlier finally went into effect, holding up against sustained attack through most of 1942. For all the virtuosity of the USN cryptanalysts, it took a combination of the haste to launch Operation MI and the consequent over-use of radio communications by the Combined Fleet, with lack of liaison between the Intelligence and Communications Bureaus of the NGS and, finally, administrative problems in the distribution of the new cipher, to grant Nimitz just sufficient information to form a firm judgement of his opponent's intentions.

Even so, the decisive factor was the outstanding moral courage of this officer – and of the self-styled son-of-a-bitch in Washington who backed his judgement, although it ran counter to his own belief that the carriers should be held back. Nimitz knew that time was on his side and that the prudent course was to let the Japanese wave break on Midway while his submarines attritted the Mobile Force, before sending in his carriers to finish it off. Had he done so, the Japanese trap might have worked. Yet both at Midway and in the immediately preceding Coral Sea engagement Nimitz chose to confront, on more or less level terms, an enemy who had previously defeated his own and Allied armed forces with embarrassing ease. This showed a faith in his men, their training and their equipment that elevates men to the ranks of great commanders when they win, but also assures them of dismissal and, in the case of US officers, the prolonged nausea of a Congressional investigation when they do not.

Unfortunately there was a sad, spiteful coda to this remarkable story. Rochefort may have given his commander the means with which to win at Midway, but in the process he had stepped on the toes of ambitious officers who knew how the game was played. He was recalled from Hawaii, relieved of radio intelligence duties and posted to the Floating Dry-Dock Training Center in California. Pausing only to ensure that as much credit as possible accrued to Op-20-G, which remained in the hands of the astute Wenger, John Redman then became Communications Officer on Nimitz's staff, in due course becoming an admiral like his brother. Later in the war Rochefort returned to COMINT duties on King's staff, an intriguing assignment in view of the fact that the reason given for his disgrace was his alleged failure to keep the notoriously unforgiving King properly informed. Nimitz twice recommended him for the Distinguished Service Medal, but it was not awarded until 1986, forty-four years after he had earned it and nine years after Rochefort's death.

On 2 May Nimitz arrived at Midway in a Catalina to present medals to the pilots who downed the Emily on 10 March and to promote Naval Air Station Commander Cyril Simard to captain and the Marines' Harold Shannon to colonel. He also made an 'informal' inspection of the defences of the atoll so rigorous that Simard and Shannon knew something serious was afoot even before the admiral asked them what they required to hold Midway against a major amphibious assault. Shannon asked for reinforcements for the Marine Aircraft Group and his Sixth Marine Defense Battalion, plus more AA guns to add to the twelve 3-inch, dual-purpose guns that he already had, along with the older 7, 5 and 3-inch naval guns of the Sea Coast Artillery Group. A veteran of the Great War, he also asked for as much barbed wire as possible. Although the main function of the Naval Air Station and the long-range PBY-5 flying boats of patrol squadron VP

Shoho wrecked, battle of the Coral Sea

23 was to act as a sentry for Hawaii, Simard joined Shannon in pleading for a greater offensive capability, arguing that the best way to defend the islands was to keep the enemy at arm's length.

Nimitz agreed, but upon his return to Pearl found himself fully taken up with events far to the south, where the Coral Sea engagement was developing into the first set-back imposed on Japanese expansion. Briefly, between 1 and 8 May the *Yorktown* and *Lexington* task forces under Fletcher, with an Australian/US cruiser support group under Rear Admiral John Crace RN, prevented an invasion of Port Moresby in southern New Guinea, sank the light carrier *Shoho* and put three bombs into the fleet carrier *Shokaku*, which nearly caused her loss to fire. In exchange, the Allied forces lost the destroyer *Sims*, the fleet oiler *Neosho* and 'Lady Lex', the latter also to secondary fires. *Yorktown* was damaged by near misses and was hit by one semi-armour-

piercing bomb that detonated deep within but did not disable her. The Japanese also suffered crippling losses to the Air Units on *Shokaku* and her sister ship, *Zuikaku*, but believed they had sunk two carriers (the *Neosho* receiving a posthumous promotion) and one battleship each of the *California* and *Warspite* classes (the heavy cruisers USS *Chicago* and HMAS *Australia*, actually untouched). This battle is generally reckoned a draw, but if thwarting the intentions of a more powerful enemy and severely blunting his cutting edge is not considered a victory, then the bar is set too high.

Lexington wrecked, battle of the Coral Sea

The Japanese attempted to do two things at the same time and succeeded neither in landing a joint Navy/Army invasion force at Port Moresby nor in trapping the Allied fleet. The land-based aircraft of both sides failed to obtain any hits by level-bombing from altitude – doubly fortunate for the Allied cruisers when they were attacked by their own Flying Fortresses – while the

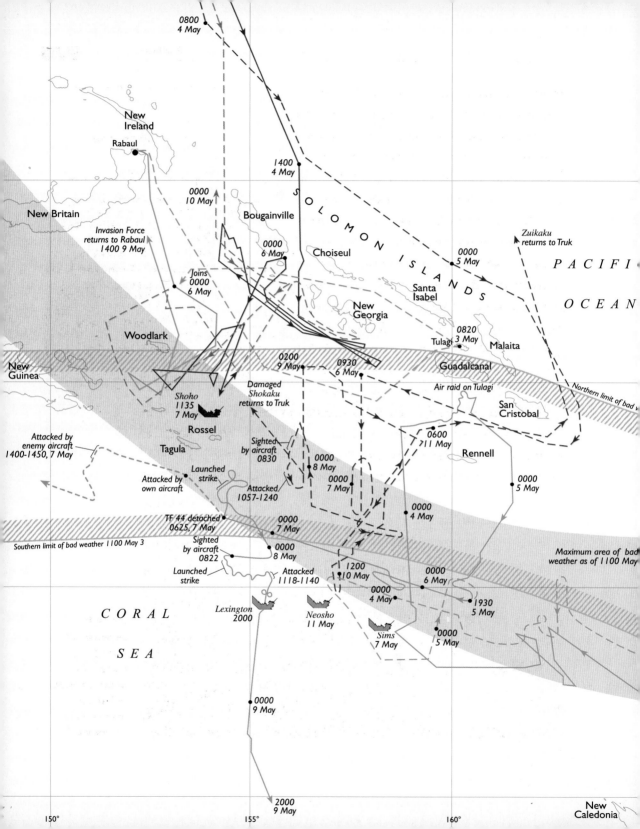

New Ireland

Rabaul

New Britain

New Guinea

0800
4 May

1400
4 May

0000
10 May

Bougainville

0000
6 May

Choiseul

S O L O M O N   I S L A N D S

Santa
Isabel

New
Georgia

0000
5 May

Zuikaku
returns to Truk

P A C I F I

O C E A N

Invasion Force
returns to Rabaul
1400 9 May

Joins
0000
6 May

Woodlark

0200
9 May

0930
6 May

Tulagi

0820
3 May

Malaita

Guadalcanal

Air raid on Tulagi

Northern limit of bad w

Shoho
1135
7 May

Damaged
Shokaku
returns to Truk

Rossel

San
Cristobal

Attacked by
enemy aircraft
1400-1450, 7 May

Tagula

Launched
strike

Sighted
by aircraft
0830

0000
8 May

0000
7 May

Rennell

0600
11 May

0000
5 May

Attacked by
own aircraft

Attacked
1057-1240

0000
4 May

TF 44 detached
0625, 7 May

0000
7 May

Southern limit of bad weather 1100 May 3

Sighted
by aircraft
0822

0000
8 May

Maximum area of bad
weather as of 1100 May

Launched
strike

Attacked
1118-1140

1200
10 May

0000
6 May

0000
4 May

1930
5 May

0000
5 May

C O R A L

Lexington
2000

Neosho
11 May

Sims
7 May

0000
5 May

S E A

0000
9 May

New
Caledonia

2000
9 May

150°

155°

160°

meagre results obtained by the US torpedo bombers led to the unfair suspicion that they had not pressed home their attacks. In the first battle ever fought without visual contact among the surface elements, radar tipped the balance in favour of the US carriers by enabling them to scramble and direct their CAP more effectively, despite the embarrassingly evident superiority of the Zero. But the tactical lessons of the battle received limited diffusion within both navies over the following month, and it was no accident that the key player at Midway was *Yorktown*, whose air battle control had been tested in combat and whose damage-limitation procedures reflected the lessons learned from the loss of *Lexington*.

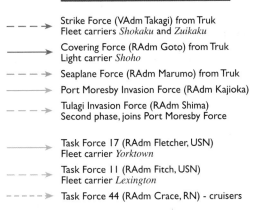

Map 8
Battle of the Coral Sea

- - - → Strike Force (VAdm Takagi) from Truk
Fleet carriers *Shokaku* and *Zuikaku*

———→ Covering Force (RAdm Goto) from Truk
Light carrier *Shoho*

- - - → Seaplane Force (RAdm Marumo) from Truk

———→ Port Moresby Invasion Force (RAdm Kajioka)

- - - → Tulagi Invasion Force (RAdm Shima)
Second phase, joins Port Moresby Force

———→ Task Force 17 (RAdm Fletcher, USN)
Fleet carrier *Yorktown*

- - - → Task Force 11 (RAdm Fitch, USN)
Fleet carrier *Lexington*

- - - -→ Task Force 44 (RAdm Crace, RN) - cruisers

Once Nimitz was able to return his attention to the central Pacific, even after declaring a state of fleet-opposed invasion on 14 May there were still constraints on his freedom of action. High command is seldom a matter of saying go and he then goeth, and a great deal of negotiation was required

The last moments of *Lexington*: a sight the Japanese were to become familiar with at Midway

before Nimitz could begin to reinforce Midway as he wished. But after the exchange of intelligence assessments with King commented in the previous chapter, he began to pour in as many resources as the atoll could hold. An early step was to upgrade the radar installation on Sand Island, increasing both its range and its ability to detect the height, as well as the bearing, of incoming aircraft – and to differentiate them from the omnipresent albatrosses, or 'gooney birds', that nest on Midway.

The first new aircraft to arrive were the radar-equipped, amphibian PBY-5As of patrol squadron VP 44, each carrying one torpedo, which began to fly in on 22 May. On the same day, the atoll's preparedness for battle suffered a severe set-back when an accident destroyed sixteen of thirty-one storage tanks and half of the aviation-fuel stocks. Replacement fuel was promptly shipped in drums, which proved invaluable after the Japanese bombers had destroyed the rest of the tanks. Before that, however, once the army's thirsty Flying Fortresses and Marauders arrived to monopolise the installed fuel lines, all of the other aircraft had to be refuelled laboriously from drums with manual pumps, an exhausting task that drew down on the stamina of the Marine infantry and distracted them from their primary mission.

Before the build-up began, the Marine Aircraft Group on Midway was composed of VMF 221, equipped with Buffalo fighters, and VMSB 241, with Vindicator dive bombers. The Marine pilots had achieved a high degree of proficiency with these types, but on the 26 May the aircraft ferry *Kitty Hawk* brought seven F4F-3 Wildcat fighters and nineteen SBD-2 Dauntless dive bombers, along with twenty-two more pilots, of whom seventeen were newly qualified. These aircraft were in no way inferior and were in some respects superior to the types with which the carrier Air Groups were being re-equipped, but their arrival had the perverse effect of reducing overall combat effectiveness. The Marine Air Group commander, Lieutenant Colonel Ira Kimes, logically allotted them to his more experienced pilots, which meant that when they went into battle, many aircraft were flown by men who were unfamiliar with them, with each other, or both. Lastly, on 31 May, a detachment of *Hornet*'s VT-8 squadron that had missed the carrier at Pearl flew in with six of the new Avenger torpedo bombers. Most of this inchoate force got into the air on 4 June, but it was a triumph of quantity over quality and the gallant aircrews paid a terrible price (see **Appendix B**).

Kitty Hawk and the cruiser *St Louis*, which made a lightning call on Midway on 25 May, also delivered part of the Third Defense Battalion from Hawaii, along with twelve more 3-inch DP guns, eight 37mm and twelve twin 20mm AA cannon. Also on board were five light tanks and two companies of the Second Marine Raider Battalion, under Captain Donald Hastie, to provide the mobile infantry reserve that the Marines had lacked on Wake. Named 'Carlson's Raiders' after their commanding officer, Lieutenant Colonel Evans Carlson (whose executive officer was Major James Roosevelt, the President's eldest son, official recognition of the Marines' contribution to the battle not suffering thereby), they had just completed basic training, but were reputedly as desperate a collection of eager cut-throats as even the US Marine Corps has ever attracted. While Shannon festooned the islands with barbed wire, the Raiders put fangs into the shoreline with a variety of obstacles and home-made mines of every description, then burrowed out firing positions linked by trenches and tunnels.

An intriguing reinforcement arrived on board the seaplane tender *Ballard*, which had acted as mother ship to a late-arriving flotilla of eleven torpedo (PT) boats. This was John Ford, director of some of the greatest Westerns ever filmed and a commander in the US Navy Reserve, who had been urgently summoned from the mainland by Nimitz himself. It seems fair to interpret Nimitz's action as an indication that he fully appreciated Midway's iconic significance for domestic propaganda as the besieged fort, with his carriers playing the role of the US Cavalry. But when the time came, Simard ordered Ford to act as a spotter for him on the Sand Island power house, certain to be a prime target for the Japanese bombers. The equivalent installation on Eastern Island was levelled and Ford was wounded by a near miss after the unique experience of filming the 'one big chunk' of shrapnel that hit him. The Marines on the roof with him advised him to stay away from the Navy doctor and bandaged him themselves. Perhaps Simard was not altogether content with the part assigned to him in Nimitz's movie ...

It was certainly a mistake to burden Midway with Army Air Corps bombers following the fuel-dump explosion. On 29 May, belatedly realizing that Simard and his tiny staff were being swamped by the logistical demands of the rapidly growing Navy, Marine and Army Air Groups, Nimitz sent Commander Logan Ramsey, the operations officer at Pearl Harbor's Naval Air Station, and his staff. Ramsey barely had time to make his presence felt before the battle began, but his opposite number, Captain Chisao Morita of the Midway Expeditionary Force, was at that time buttoned up under strict radio silence on *Akagi*. So although the word 'scramble' applied with literal accuracy to the air operations conducted by Ramsey, Morita was unable to alter a plan that refrained from scouting Midway in order not to alert the Americans, even after it became apparent that the element of surprise had been lost. Incredibly, the Bettys and flying boats based at Wake and the Marshall Islands were to play no role in the battle, even though Midway was within their range.

Map 9
Midway Atoll

From 30 May, Ramsey co-ordinated the PBYs and B-17s in a huge search operation covering an arc of 180° from north-north-east to south-south-west with an outer radius of 700 miles. The slower flying boats commonly spent eighteen hours in the air, setting out well before the bombers and returning after dark, which led to a number of collisions with the marker buoys in the lagoon. Additionally, on the first day, two of the Catalinas were badly shot up by a Betty out of Wake and a Mavis out of Wotje at about the 500 mile mark, demonstrating that, as Ramsey commented, '*any* type of Japanese plane could, and did, assume the offensive against the PBY'. Although better able to defend themselves, the B-17s were not designed nor their crews trained for reconnaissance, so the main burden of patrolling was borne by the PBYs, while Oahu drew down on its own patrolling capability to send replacement aircraft.

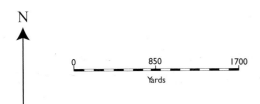

N

0 — 850 — 1700
Yards

Reefs around
Midway atoll

Shallows

Seward Roads

Welles Harbor

Shallows

Brooks Channel

LAGOON

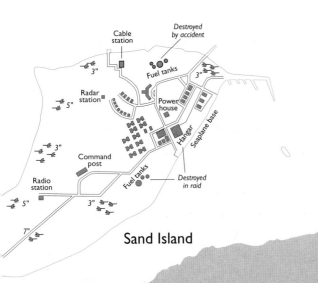

Cable
station

*Destroyed
by accident*

Fuel tanks

3"

Radar
station

3"

Power
house

5"

3"

Hangar

Seaplane base

Command
post

Fuel tanks

*Destroyed
in raid*

Radio
station

5"

3"

7"

Sand Island

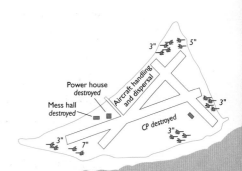

Power house
destroyed

Mess hall
destroyed

Aircraft handling
and dispersal

3"

5"

3"

CP destroyed

3"

3"

7"

Eastern Island

OCEAN

Stress levels were raised by the presence of Major General Willis Hale of VII Army Air Corps, who protested that too much was being demanded of his detachment on Midway and then flew back to Pearl on 2 June, wafted on his way by a sigh of relief, even from his own officers, 'to make strong representations to that effect'. This had the salutary effect of prompting Nimitz to send Kimes a much-needed executive officer (XO). In a classic case of the left hand not knowing what the right hand was doing, Kimes's previous XO had departed on the *Kitty Hawk* on a routine tour rotation, and on his arrival on 3 May, the officer sent belatedly to replace him was handed 'enough work for six men'. That Kimes was deprived of an XO just when his command had doubled in size, and new aircraft and crews needed to be integrated with the old, must have contributed to a lower level of preparedness in the Marine Aircraft Group than would otherwise have been the case.

Thus, despite the advance warning provided by COMINT, the reinforcement of Midway was very much a last-minute affair that put appalling strain on the local command structure, as well as on the limited resources available. A big part of the reason why Nimitz's sense of urgency did not filter down the chain of command was because he had to protect at all costs the source of the intelligence upon which he was acting. The result was that Midway was far from being the fourth, unsinkable US aircraft carrier in the battle, as it is sometimes portrayed. Nimitz's hopes were more realistic, and although his general instructions (Op Plan 29-42) of 27 May stressed the need to 'hold Midway and inflict maximum damage on the enemy by strong attrition tactics', he clearly expected that damage to be inflicted by the carriers. Midway's role was to send scouting aircraft out as far and as wide as possible and then to be ready to resist several days of bombardment, followed by a night assault.

The nervous tension on Midway as the day predicted for the Japanese assault drew closer can readily be imagined, but in accordance with Murphy's Law, the first Japanese vessels to be sighted in the morning of 3 June were the most insignificant contingent in Operation MI. These were part of the

Minesweeping Force proceeding independently from Wake, which were sighted 470 miles south-west of Midway by Ensign James Lyle in a PBY-5 and accurately reported at 0904 hours. Further west, Ensign Jewell Reid in his PBY-5A was not so precise, and at 0925 he excitedly reported sighting the 'Main Body' 700 miles out and at 262°, before moving into a shadowing position and revising his report to 'six large ships in column formation' at 1040. Twenty minutes later, he revised it again to eleven ships steering east at 19 knots.

Another PBY was ordered to fly towards the reported position, and at 1130 it reported two cargo ships and two escorts 270 miles west-south-west. Faced with three widely separate sightings, at 1200 Simard dispatched a B-17 with long-range tanks and a naval observer on board to seek out the 'Main Body'. This B-17 was intended to guide six more, under the command of Lieutenant Colonel Walter Sweeney, each equipped with an auxiliary bomb bay fuel tank and six 500-pound 'demolition' bombs, which took off half an hour later. The scout found a further two transports and two destroyers some 700 miles out at 1640, but by that time Sweeney's force had already attacked Reid's 'Main Body', actually the Midway Occupation Force, and had succeeded in straddling one transport.

Even as the Army bombers were groping their way back to Eastern Island, where the runway lights were left on to guide them, the Navy was preparing to launch a daring second strike. The last B-17 was recovered at 2145, but half an hour earlier four PBY-5As, which had only arrived that afternoon from Oahu, took off from the runway under the command of Lieutenant William Richards, each with a torpedo under one wing. Although they became separated, all four found the Occupation Force employing radar, and at about 0130 on 4 June, Richard's aircraft had the unique satisfaction in this battle of achieving a torpedo hit and detonation on the tanker *Akebono Maru*, killing eleven men and wounding thirteen. In a parallel attack, Lieutenant Douglas Davis also released at point-blank range, but the only damage sustained by *Kiyozumi Maru* was to the eight men who were wounded when Davis's gunners strafed the decks. These accurate attacks out of the night must have seemed exceptionally ill-omened to the Japanese troops cowering helplessly on board the transports.

They lived to die another day, on Guadalcanal, because the bait was not taken. Simard and Ramsey did not waver from their primary responsibility and on 4 June a fighter CAP was flown off to cover the departure of eleven flying boats from the lagoon and eleven amphibians, followed by sixteen B-17s, from Eastern Island. All were airborne well before dawn at 0437, and the Catalinas flew out to cover the entire 180° search arc, not merely the area within which previous sightings had been made. VP 23 had the north-western sector, and at 0532 Lieutenant Howard Ady radioed the electrifying report that he had sighted 'many carriers'. This was followed at 0544 by a report of 'many planes heading Midway from 320 [degrees] distant 150 miles' from Lieutenant William Chase in another PBY. At 0552, having meanwhile flown to cloud cover behind them, Ady confirmed two carriers and two battleships, albeit giving a position placing them further from Midway and nearer the US carriers by some 25 to 30 miles.

An order to turn north was radioed to Sweeney's B-17s on their way to attack the Occupation Force again and, once the Sand Island radar confirmed the incoming strike at over 90 miles range, every aircraft ready to fly was ordered into the air. First to go were VMF 221's twenty Buffalos and four Wildcats (two more Wildcats, late returners from the morning CAP, followed fifteen minutes later), under Major Floyd Parks, then six Avenger torpedo bombers under Lieutenant Langdon Fieberling. Immediately after them the four sleek, twin-engined Marauders, under Captain William Collins, roared down the runway for their first practical experience of launching torpedoes, followed by sixteen Dauntlesses, under Major Lofton Henderson, and twelve Vindicators, under Major Benjamin Norris. One Buffalo and one Vindicator turned back with engine trouble and barely made it to their revetments before the Japanese arrived.

One of the most criticized US decisions of the battle was that half of the fighters were sent to intercept the incoming raid, while the rest were retained

at the 10-mile mark as a CAP, rather than sending some to escort the bombers. But the priority for the commanders at Midway was to defend the islands, and while the B-17s had the range to return to Oahu and the PBYs could, and did, refuel from tenders at Lisianski and Laysan, all of the rest would certainly have been lost if the airfield were rendered inoperable. Faced with a similar dilemma, the carriers were to make much the same choice.

Bel Geddes' depiction of the leading VMF-221 Wildcats intercepting the Japanese strike

The Japanese strike consisted of thirty-five Kates from *Hiryu* and *Soryu*, thirty-six Vals from *Akagi* and *Kaga* and nine Zeros from each of the four carriers. Fuchida, the leader of the first strike at Pearl Harbor, was recovering from an emergency appendectomy on *Akagi* and in his absence the Midway strike was led by *Hiryu's* Air Unit Commander, Lieutenant Joichi Tomonaga. The Kates flew at 14,000 feet in three-plane 'Vs', forming one large arrowhead to facilitate communication by hand signals, the Vals in similar formation above and behind them and the Zeros a further step above the two bomber formations.

So it was that when the eight Buffalos and three Wildcats of Parks's group dived on the bombers for the single, slashing attack that they were able to make before being mobbed by Zeros, their fire was concentrated on the Kates. They downed three and damaged a dozen others, the leading *Hiryu* group suffering the most. This was the torpedo-attack élite of the First Air Fleet and would, if level-bombing specialist Fuchida had not been incapacitated, have been retained to lead the second strike, at this time sitting on the carrier decks ready to launch if enemy surface ships were sighted.

Leading the Wildcat division, Captain John Carey sighted the intruders first and radioed 'Tally ho! Large formation of bombers ... accompanied by fighters'. But it was the Japanese who became the hunters and, once the advantage of height and radar-granted surprise was gone, the Marines were massacred. Carey got a bullet through the windshield and another through both legs from the Val rear gunners even before the Zeros arrived, after which only one Wildcat survived intact, by diving away vertically at full throttle. Carey and another Wildcat pilot were to crash-land back at Eastern Island but only one Buffalo returned, too shot up for further service, its pilot full of admiration for the Japanese, who maintained 'superb air discipline, staying in tight vee formations and keeping on their compass course'. This despite the fact that the strike leader and two others had to dive to put out fires from their wing tanks, only to reform and fly on, trailing smoke.

The inner CAP of twelve Buffalos and three Wildcats was too spread out, and was itself intercepted by Zeros before it could get in among the bombers. In return for two Zeros, a single Buffalo made it back in flightworthy condition and eight went down, along with the Wildcat piloted by Captain Francis McCarthy, promoted and decorated a month and two days earlier for his part in shooting down the probing Emily. In a head-on confrontation, Second Lieutenant Charles Kunz suffered the shattering experience of having bullets crease his scalp above both ears, and Kimes had to authorize several doses of 'medicinal' whisky to calm him enough to sleep that night.

Three Buffalos and the two remaining Wildcats suffered battle damage, leaving VMF 221 with two combat-worthy aircraft and mourning fourteen dead and four wounded pilots. Captain Phillip White, pilot of the sole inner CAP Buffalo to survive intact, wrote a bitter after-battle report.

> The F2A-3 is <u>not</u> a combat aeroplane. the Japanese Zero Fighter can run rings around [it]… It is my belief that any commander that orders pilots out for combat in [it] should consider [them] lost before leaving the ground.

A number of ground observers witnessed the death of Second Lieutenant Martin Mahannah, fresh from flight school, who baled out of his flaming Buffalo but was machine-gunned in the air and in the water by the two Zeros that had shot him down, along with a comrade who went to his rescue, whose body was never found. To Mahannah's anguished classmate, Charles Hughes, spared by the malfunction that had forced his early return, it seemed that the Buffalos 'were tied to a string while the Zeros made passes at them'.

Although the casualties inflicted on *Hiryu*'s Kates spared Midway three of the 1,780-pound 'land bombs' they carried and were to have important repercussions later in the day, VMF 221 had failed to keep the raiders away and it was now down to the AA gunners on the islands and on the PT boats. Ford was astonished at how calm the men around him were, 'lackadaisical, as though they had been living through this sort of thing all their lives.' The 3-inch guns claimed a further two Kates, one of them from *Hiryu*, and damaged four more, while the light flak downed an insolently stunt-flying Zero and one Val as it pulled out over the seaplane ramp on Sand Island. But the main purpose of AA is to prevent accurate bombing and this it did, for the damage was surprisingly light and not one of the grounded aircraft was hit.

The remaining fuel tanks were hit and some were set on fire, but the most grievous loss was caused by a direct hit on the Eastern Island command post that killed Major William Benson and two other Marines. Four more Marines died in a spectacular explosion of munitions stored in a VMF rearming pit, and an Army Air Corps lieutenant and an enlisted man died in an otherwise empty aircraft revetment. Twenty men suffered minor injuries, including Ford, who was knocked unconscious and wounded in the arm. The ammunition explosion and smoke from the fuel tanks gave the impression of greater damage than had actually been inflicted but the veteran Tomonaga was not impressed. His radio knocked out when Parks's group nearly destroyed his Kate, he now wrote a message on a blackboard for his wingman to radio back the fateful message, 'There is need for a second attack wave'.

It never came, however, and what the garrison might have done had things developed otherwise remains in the realm of speculation. Although VMF 221 was virtually eliminated, Midway's ability to defend itself and to hit back was otherwise still intact. At an exorbitant price, the marines had downed a few Japanese aircraft that might have made a difference later, but their greater success was to keep Nagumo's attention focused on them.

After the battle, Rear Admiral Raymond Spruance observed that the Americans had been 'shot with luck' and, although he did not say so, one of the larger pellets was that Bull Halsey had to be hospitalized with acute dermatitis upon his return to Pearl Harbor on 26 May 1942. Halsey recommended his cruiser commander, Spruance, to replace him in charge of Task Force 16 (*Enterprise* and *Hornet* groups), overall carrier command devolving on Frank Fletcher, who arrived two days later in the damaged *Yorktown* with Task Force 17. Uneasy about his performance in the Coral Sea, King came close to demanding that Fletcher be replaced as well, although by whom, if not Nimitz himself, is not clear. After a searching interview, Nimitz expressed his confidence in Fletcher and so what was to prove precisely the right command structure for the forthcoming battle came into being. Fletcher's Coral Sea experience led him to fight a cagier battle than

Halsey would have done, while Spruance moderated the hyperaggressiveness of Halsey's staff on board *Enterprise*.

Foremost among the latter was acting Chief of Staff Commander Miles Browning, who combined the functions of Nagumo's Chief of Staff Rear Admiral Ryunosuke Kusaka and Air Operations Officer 'Armoured Sleeve' Genda. In a reversal of the usual US/Japanese roles, the latter fatally persuaded Nagumo to adopt a measured response at the crucial moment, while Browning urged Spruance to launch a pell-mell attack, in accordance with the views he had expressed in an eerily prescient 1936 memorandum.

Every carrier captain has known the bitter experience of rushing his aircraft up and down the deck to meet changing probabilities in the situation and to care for the return of a scouting flight, just as the situation was becoming critical. Every carrier we have has known what it means to be 'bopped' with all planes on deck, because her hands were tied by uncertainty as to her next move ... [1]

The outcome at Midway is generally believed to have depended very heavily on the quality invoked by Nimitz's planners when they bestowed the name 'Point Luck' on latitude 32° north, longitude 173° west, some 325 miles north-east of Midway, where the task forces were to rendezvous at 1600 on 2 June. But of the factors that we have reviewed so far only the random health problems affecting the two front-line teams can be attributed to blind chance. One other element beyond human control was the weather, which provided

Raymond Spruance replaced 'Bull' Halsey (right) on the eve of the battle

cloud cover for the Japanese approach to Midway. But it did the same for the US task forces on 4 June, causing one of the search aircraft launched by the Japanese Mobile Force to pass overhead without seeing them. Nagumo may have imposed what proved to be fatal delays on his air operations by launching against Midway from further away than he had intended in order to exploit this front, but this in turn kept him clear of most of the US submarines. The wind direction enabled the Japanese to steer directly for Midway while launching and recovering, but prevented the US carriers from closing the distance while performing the same evolutions, contributing to the loss of many undamaged aircraft. A fair verdict is therefore that the weather favoured the IJN.

Although hindsight permits us to see that Fuchida's appendicitis, Halsey's dermatitis and Genda's pneumonia were among the drops that caused the bucket to overflow, it was already filled to the brim by a cascade of poor Japanese decisions made with a carelessness bordering on frivolity. Yamamoto judged the largest contributory factor in his defeat to have been the failure of his submarine force to perform its allotted tasks, which in addition to the aborted Operation K included greeting the US Pacific Fleet with salvos of Type 95 torpedoes after it sortied from Pearl. As events developed the US task forces were past the I-boat patrol line before the due date anyway, but the submarines took up station two days late because Vice Admiral Teruhisa Komatsu, commander of the Sixth Fleet at Kwajalein, was not informed how crucial the timing was. When Arima asked Kuroshima if he should send Komatsu instructions additional to the general order, he was told it was unnecessary. It was also Kuroshima who persuaded Yamamoto not to relay the COMINT warnings and he seems to have believed that the subordinate commanders involved in this enormously complex operation all knew what was expected of them, without making sure they did.

By contrast and although there was far less time to do so, Op Plan 29-42 was gone over thoroughly in a meeting on 27 May presided over by Nimitz's Chief of Staff, Rear Admiral Milo Draemel. The two task-force commanders and their operations officers thoroughly grilled Layton and Nimitz's War Plans Officer, Captain Charles 'Socrates' McMorris, whose assistants Captain Lynde McCormick USN and Colonel Omar Pfeiffer USMC had drafted the plan. This was in accordance with King's long-held view (see **Appendix C**) that 'there will be neither time nor opportunity to do more than prescribe the several tasks of the several subordinates (to say "what," perhaps "when" and "where," and usually for their intelligent co-operation, "why"); leaving to them – expecting and requiring of them – the capacity to perform the assigned tasks (to do the "how")'. Nonetheless, Nimitz came close to defining the 'how' in his cover letter to Fletcher and Spruance.

> In carrying out the tasks assigned in Op Plan 29-42, you will be governed by the principle of calculated risk, which you will interpret to mean the avoidance of exposure of your force to attack by superior enemy forces without prospect of inflicting, as a result of such exposure, greater damage to the enemy.

Information was disseminated further according to what the division and squadron commanders needed to know before the ships sailed, the notoriously indiscreet pilots being briefed only after they had flown out to rejoin the carriers from the airfields where they were based when in port. Those given the big picture were stunned at the scale of the Japanese operation and full of admiration for the detailed information they were given. When Midway's copy of the plan arrived by secure cable, Kimes commented that the only thing lacking was Hirohito's bathtub with an outboard motor, while *Enterprise* navigator Commander Richard Ruble was heard to speculate 'that man of ours in Tokyo is worth every cent we pay him'. The rumour mill ('scuttlebutt') had plenty to work with in the highly charged atmosphere on

Yorktown dry-docked in Pearl Harbor to repair Coral Sea damage

Oahu, particularly after *Yorktown* returned to Pearl late on 27 May and Nimitz declared that she must be able to resume operations within three days. Promptly dry-docked, her bomb damage was made good in less than two, as much a comment on the low destructive power of the bomb that hit her as on the efficiency of the dockyard.

The general mood of the fleet was one of eager anticipation, such reservations as existed being among the pilots, who had reason to feel uneasy about their equipment in the days before the battle. The fighter squadrons on the other carriers were already equipped with F4F-4s and were by now resigned to them, but *Yorktown*'s pilots were shocked to find them more sluggish than their F4F-3s (they were 800 pounds heavier). Although their folding wings permitted more of them to be packed into the hangars, this also reduced the amount of ammunition they could carry. No less disappointed were the torpedo-bomber crews who had been looking forward to receiving the new TBF – as we have seen, the first Avenger group arrived at Pearl too late and flew to Midway instead. The most acute concern of the dive-bomber crews was that their three-power telescopic sights and windshields fogged up when diving from cruising altitude into the warm and humid air over the ocean.

There were also personnel and organizational problems. *Hornet*'s combat experience was limited to hosting the Doolittle raid on Tokyo, while relations within her Air Group were bad, bordering on poisonous – Lieutenant Commander Stanhope Ring's official designation was CHAG (Commander *Hornet* Air Group), and his pilots called him 'sea-hag'. But responsibility for the abysmal showing by the Air Group at Midway can only be laid at the feet of *Hornet*'s captain, the soon-to-be Rear Admiral Marc Mitscher and a future star of the Pacific War, whose driving ambition made him intolerant of dissent. Some historians have held Ring primarily to blame, contrasting his acquiescence with the successful defiance by *Enterprise* Air Group's Lieutenant Commander Clarence McClusky of an order by Browning to launch his aircraft at excessive range on 5 June. Yet by that time McClusky was a wounded hero and, even so, it is doubtful whether he would have dared to act in this manner if Browning's patron Halsey had still been in command. Ring may have lacked personal authority, both in his dealings with his pilots and with Mitscher, but he had no combat experience to draw on and no reason to challenge the decisions of his commanding officer.

The McClusky/Browning confrontation suggests there may also have been a history of bad blood among the officers on *Enterprise* – flat-out insubordination never has a short fuse. Like Browning, Mitscher was a pioneer naval aviator, and both had a lethal combination of strong opinions and a lack of up-to-date familiarity with the aircraft under their command. Neither, it seems, fully appreciated what a mismatch there was among the performance characteristics of the three types of aircraft that they had on board, in particular the short range of the F4F-4 and how different payloads affected the range of the Dauntless. What they did know was that the length of take-off required went from the half-deck of the Wildcat to the as-long-as-possible of the Devastator with a torpedo slung underneath. In conjunction with the light breeze prevailing from the south-east that prevented the US carriers from closing the range during launch and recovery, bad things followed from those narrow certainties.

The tactical equation for the Japanese commanders was greatly simplified by the superior lift of all of their aircraft and, especially, the extended 'loiter' capability of the drop-tank-equipped Zeros. Although they also needed to sail into the wind in order to launch fully laden bombers, in light air they could launch Zeros and recover all types across a broad aspect. Until the introduction of the steam catapult and the angled deck, launch and recovery could not take place simultaneously because aircraft awaiting launch had to be concentrated ('spotted') aft. After landing they had to be run forward, over a net that would be raised to protect them from following aircraft whose tail hooks might fail to engage one of the arrester wires that were stretched a few inches above the after-deck. All of the carriers at Midway had three elevators connecting the flight deck with the hangar, variously disposed but all

Ordnance men
loading 500lb
demolition bomb
on a Dauntless
aboard *Enterprise*

requiring intricate choreography on both decks to strike recovered aircraft below, perform maintenance and refuel and rearm them, ready to emerge once more for launching in the sequence required by the operations officers. Both sides might order a badly damaged aircraft to ditch or push it over the side if it was found to be unserviceable. The nightmare of the ground crews was not so much a crash as last-minute changes that required a major reshuffle of their charges.

Criticism of Mitscher's and Spruance/Browning's decisions must therefore be tempered by the consideration that for three hours in the morning of 4 June their opposite numbers inflicted repeated changes in operational requirements on their crews. The strike force caught on the decks of *Kaga*, *Akagi* and *Soryu* at 1022 was exactly the same as the one that had been ready to launch at 0715 – but had in the meantime been struck below and partially rearmed twice. In many ways this was another manifestation of 'armoured sleeve' arrogance – the ground crews of the Japanese carriers were so well drilled that Genda and Kusaka counted on them being able to do what turned out to be the impossible. Although both sides committed the sin of 'order, counter-order, disorder', the Americans did so in forgivable haste to strike first, with the result that a poorly organized strike carried out promptly beat a more orderly and technically better one that took too long to prepare.

Obedience to first principles is particularly important for the inexperienced and, not counting the massacre of the aircraft-less HMS *Hermes* in the Indian Ocean, six of the seven carriers at Midway had no previous experience of a carrier-to-carrier engagement. Only the Coral Sea veteran *Yorktown* had and, with another aeronaval battle imminent, this should have made a totem of her Air Group, directed by the well-respected Lieutenant Commander Oscar Pederson. It was therefore with a sense of disbelief we may share, and barely concealed indignation, that on 27 May Fletcher heard Nimitz refuse his request to retain and reinforce his existing squadrons and learned that his Air Group was to be dismembered. Not knowing that he would soon be engaged in another battle, Pederson had requested some shore time for his fliers, but in a particularly egregious example of bureaucratic indifference to unit pride, *Yorktown* (CV-5) now sailed with new fighter, bomber and torpedo squadrons bearing the designation VF-3, VB-3 and VT-3, pertaining to *Saratoga* (CV-3). The further redesignation of *Yorktown*'s retained Bombing Five as Scouting Five (VS-5) can only have been made to satisfy the tidy mind of some pencil-pusher.[2]

Most of VT-3 had never operated from a carrier and its experienced CO, Lieutenant Commander Lance Massey, had only assumed command on 24 May. VB-3 under Lieutenant Commander Maxwell Leslie had served on *Enterprise* in April, but had not seen combat. For the fighter squadron the saving grace was that although its CO and XO were rotated ashore and it was redesignated VF-3, sixteen of the pilots remained and their new commander was Jimmy Thach, one of the greats of aerial warfare. Despite having received orders to take command of his own squadron, his friend Lieutenant Commander Don Lovelace volunteered to serve as Thach's XO and together they flawlessly handled the prickly command transition, familiarization with the new aircraft and the integration of seven newly hatched pilots. But there was no time for them to test the tactics Thach believed would enable them to counter the Zeros and, tragically, one of the fledglings botched his first landing on *Yorktown* on 30 May, jumping the net into Lovelace's aircraft and killing him.[3]

Had the Americans been defeated at Midway all of the above would have been exhaustively weighed as contributing factors – but they were not, so its significance has been understated. The key point, which bears emphasizing, is that the USN regarded men and machines as interchangeable parts and battle as a managerial exercise, to be embarked upon with a strict eye on profit and loss, while the Japanese saw it as an art form in which will and élan were the decisive elements. Nagumo's after-battle report thus drew only three (blindingly obvious) conclusions and praised those who had allegedly practised 'body-crash' tactics as 'exceptional even in the traditionally glorious history of the Japanese Navy'. Nimitz's report was devoid of bombast and concluded with thirty-five 'Lessons and Conclusions from the Action' that ranged from equipment minutiae to strategic analysis. It was this profound difference in attitude that defined the battle and, to a large extent, the war.

The other Air Groups also had ill-omened accidents to lament. On 28 May, Lieutenant Commander Eugene Lindsey, CO of VT-6, stalled his Devastator on final approach to *Enterprise* (CV-6) and crashed astern. Badly bruised, he and his gunner were rescued by the plane guard *Monaghan* and were returned by breeches buoy on 31 May. On 29 May, a Dauntless flown off *Hornet* (CV-8) on anti-submarine patrol went down and although it was seen on radar and a destroyer was immediately dispatched to the site, no trace of it was found. In addition to maintaining a constant schedule of medium and long-range patrols, the air staffs on board *Enterprise* and *Yorktown* had to work out procedures for the forthcoming battle by blinker, it having been discovered that the supposedly very short-range talk between ships (TBS) radio could sometimes be detected hundreds of miles away.

Although Fletcher, on *Yorktown*, was acting Commander Carriers, Halsey's staff was with Spruance on *Enterprise*. Bearing in mind that Fletcher's self-confidence cannot have been improved by learning of King's displeasure during his interview with Nimitz, it is not surprising that Spruance exercised considerable overall command functions even before Fletcher formally passed them to him after *Yorktown* was disabled. For example, it was agreed that fighter CAP direction for all three carriers was to be handled by Lieutenant Commander Leonard Dow, Spruance's Communications Officer. A further departure from the normal hierarchy was occasioned by the fact that Ring, the least experienced, was the senior of the three Air Group commanders and would have led any combined strike force. There were too many anomalies for any satisfactory solution to be worked out in the time available, and each carrier was to fight the battle largely as if unique and alone.

Doctrine stated that the strike elements should attack together, therefore the slow torpedo bombers should launch first, followed by the dive bombers, with the fighters flying off last. This had been the procedure in the Coral Sea,

where the fighters had also been divided evenly between strike escort and CAP duties. But Op Plan 29-42 gave unequivocal and overriding priority to the protection of the carriers and this worked to the particular detriment of the torpedo bombers. There would not be enough fighters to escort both them and the dive bombers, and with the majority of the fighters held back for CAP duty there was an either-or decision to be made. In two of the three Air Groups it went in favour of sending the fighters in high, not only to protect the dive bombers, but also to gain the diving speed without which they were believed to be little more than Zero-bait.

On 31 May Mitscher presided over a formal meeting with Ring, his four squadron commanders and their deputies. Also present were *Hornet*'s Air

Eugene Lindsey returning to *Enterprise* by breeches buoy

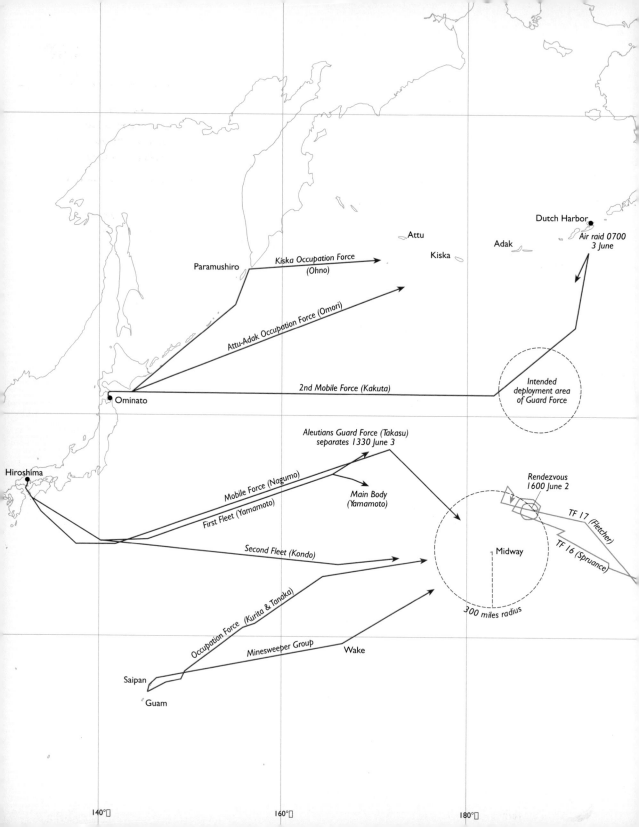

Dutch Harbor
Air raid 0700
3 June

Attu

Kiska

Adak

Paramushiro

Kiska Occupation Force
(Ohno)

Attu-Adak Occupation Force (Omori)

2nd Mobile Force (Kakuta)

Ominato

*Intended
deployment area
of Guard Force*

Aleutians Guard Force (Takasu)
separates 1330 June 3

Hiroshima

Mobile Force (Nagumo)

First Fleet (Yamamoto)

Main Body
(Yamamoto)

Rendezvous
1600 June 2

TF 17 *(Fletcher)*

Second Fleet (Kondo)

TF 16 *(Spruance)*

Midway

Occupation Force (Kurita & Tanaka)

Minesweeper Group

Wake

300 miles radius

Saipan

Guam

140°   160°   180°

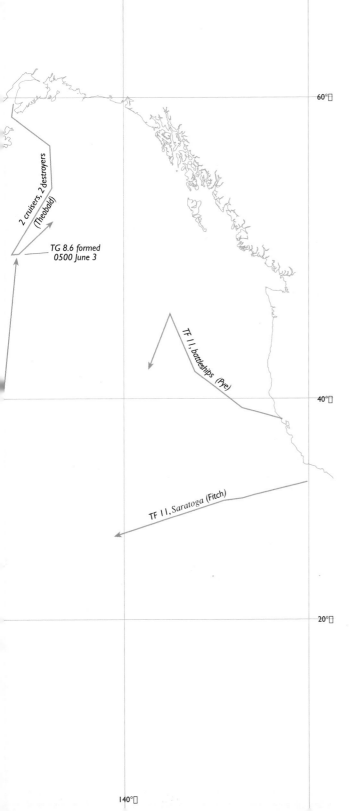

Map 10
Approach to battle:
opposing fleets at
0000 hrs, 4 June

Japanese Fleet
U.S. Fleet

2 cruisers, 2 destroyers
(Theobald)

TG 8.6 formed
0500 June 3

TF 11, battleships (Pye)

TF 11, Saratoga (Fitch)

60°

40°

20°

140°

Officer and Captain Charles Mason, who, but for the imminent battle, would have taken command of the carrier upon Mitscher's promotion to rear admiral, effective from the next day. Only one voice was heard, however: arguing that the results in the Coral Sea demonstrated that the torpedo bombers were less vulnerable, Mitscher overruled the COs of both VT-8 and VF-8, Lieutenant Commanders John Waldron and Samuel Mitchell, and decreed that the ten fighters he was allotting to the strike force would stay with the dive bombers all the way.

Mitscher also decided to launch twenty CAP and strike-escort fighters first, followed by the fifteen dive bombers of Lieutenant Commander Walter Rodee's VS-8 with 500-pound bombs and the nineteen aircraft of Lieutenant Commander Robert Johnson's VB-8 with 1,000-pound bombs, Ring opting to fly with the latter. The torpedo bombers would then be brought up and launched while the first wave was climbing to 20,000 feet. In Mitscher's scheme the dive bombers would attack first, permitting the torpedo bombers to approach undetected. Waldron did not believe a word of it and warned his crews to be prepared for all the enemy fighters to attack them unabated.

With the greater mutual confidence that came from having operated together the longest, there was no such formality on *Enterprise*. McClusky would lead the combined dive-bomber group that would launch first, adding his own aircraft to the seventeen of Lieutenant Wilmer Gallaher's VS-6 with 500-pound bombs (eleven also with 100-pound bombs under their wings), followed by the fifteen dive bombers of Lieutenant Richard Best's VB-6 with 1,000-pound bombs. Only the CAP fighters were to be flown off first, the ten strike escorts launching after the fourteen torpedo bombers of VT-6 in the second deck-load.

McClusky delegated the escorting details to Lieutenant James Gray of VF-6 who, with Lindsey in the sick bay, agreed a plan with the XO of VT-6, Lieutenant Arthur Ely, that the fighters would go with the dive bombers, reasoning that they could use their height advantage to come to the assistance of the trailing torpedo bombers when the time came. Ely was to break radio silence if attacked, but it was clearly necessary for visual contact to be maintained. Unfortunately, when Lindsey resumed command on the morning of 4 June, Gray and Ely each thought the other had explained this arrangement to him and as a result Lindsey briefed his crews to expect close fighter support, which gave rise to savage rancour later.

From the start, Fletcher intended to use battle-tested Task Force 17 as the flank guard in case the Japanese hooked towards Midway from further north. *Yorktown's* Air Group was to be employed in a manner that coincided with the preference of Pederson, who had long ago realized that he could best direct operations from on board. Thach was instructed to maintain a CAP of six aircraft at all times from before dawn to dusk, while at any time half of Lieutenant Wallace Short's VS-5 (formerly VB-5 and still disgruntled about it) would be scouting on a radius of 200 miles to the east and north, carrying 100-pound bombs in case they should find an I-boat on the surface, while the other half was on stand-by with 500-pound bombs. Once all of the threats and targets had been properly evaluated, a strike force made up of Massey's VT-3, Leslie's VB-3 with 1,000-pound bombs, and Thach with an eight-fighter escort would launch, in that order. At an informal meeting on 3 June, Massey and Leslie both generously urged Thach to escort the other. Thach, who had yet to encounter Zeros but whose Coral Sea veterans judged the torpedo bombers to be more vulnerable, decided to go in low.

Each Air Group thus produced a different solution. *Yorktown's* was manifestly superior and a larger number of aircraft would have survived the battle had it not been for the several factors that inhibited Fletcher from ensuring Mitscher and Spruance conformed. But Fletcher cannot be faulted for his handling of his primary responsibility. He placed himself and his most experienced battle group in the place of greatest exposure and, had Yamamoto's Main Force suddenly appeared, was ready for it. The fog of war was pierced but not dispersed by COMINT and Fletcher, no less than Nagumo, had to deal with uncertainty about where and when enemy forces might appear. But Nagumo had over a month to plan how his homogenous and veteran force would cope with the twin responsibilities of taking Midway and guarding against a US counterattack, whereas Fletcher had less than a week, most of it at sea without the means to confer with his unfamiliar and inexperienced subordinates, to decide how to cope with the possibility that he was sailing into the gigantic trap that Operation MI was intended to set. He deserves more credit than he has received.

When Musashi wrote, 'hit first, in order to make a powerful stroke after hitting', he meant that the opponent must be taken out of his own battle plan and put off balance before the killing stroke could be delivered. Between 0710 and 0830, Midway-based US aircraft kept Nagumo's carriers almost continuously under attack, at the cost of five US Navy Avengers lost and the survivor crippled, two US Army Marauders lost and the other two crippled, six of sixteen US Marine Corps Dauntlesses shot down, two ditched and two returned too shot up for further service. Four of eleven Vindicators also failed to return, two more returning damaged. In addition, fourteen US Army B-17s bombed from 20,000 feet without loss but, like the rest, without actually achieving any of the hits they jubilantly reported.

I have not been able to establish why the fast Avengers and Marauders were launched first and the Vindicators last, or why each element attacked

Two USMC Vindicators take off: the one in the foreground flown by James Marmande disappeared on 4 June

separately. An assumption – and no more – is that Simard and Ramsey were focused on their long-range patrolling responsibilities, and Kimes on his mixed and mismatched squadrons, so the co-ordinating function fell through the cracks. Entirely by chance, the faster Marauders caught up with the Avengers within sight of the Mobile Force and to Fuchida 'it looked as if [they] had planned a converging attack from both flanks, but fortunately for us the timing was off'.

Unfortunately for Fieberling's Avengers, they were intercepted by a swarm of Zeros while still at cruising altitude, and although they dived through cloud to reach attack height, five of them were shot down with their torpedoes on board. *Hiryu*, their prospective target, saw three fall and a fourth jettison its torpedo and abandon the attack. This was Ensign Albert Earnest's aircraft with the turret-gunner dead, 17-year old radioman-belly-gunner Harry Ferrier rendered unconscious with a head wound, and the pilot also wounded and compelled to drop his torpedo to recover control after his

elevator wires were cut. Only desultorily pursued once he no longer posed a threat, bearing the marks of more than seventy bullets and cannon shells and with only his trim tabs to work with, Earnest made it back to Midway. He was to be awarded two Navy Crosses, one for the action and the other for bringing the aircraft back for priceless combat evaluation.[1]

Fuchida was more impressed by the attack of the Marauders, and would have been amazed to learn that they came not merely from two different squadrons, but from separate bombardment groups and had never even practised flying in formation together. Collins flew the lead aircraft from the 69th Bombardment Squadron, while Lieutenant James Muri had the lead for the two from the 18th Reconnaissance Squadron, and at least three of the four dropped their torpedoes accurately, forcing *Akagi* to turn into them with two passing to port and one to starboard. The fourth bomber was observed from the battlecruiser *Haruna* to 'disappear spectacularly beneath the water', and after the attack was over observers on *Akagi* noted what they thought was a

Earnest's *Avenger* back on its wheels again after crash-landing back at Midway

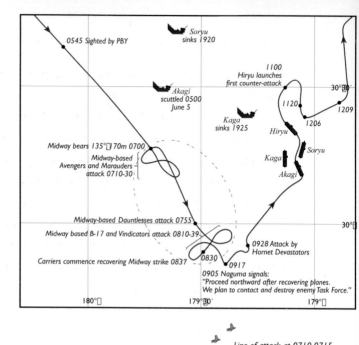
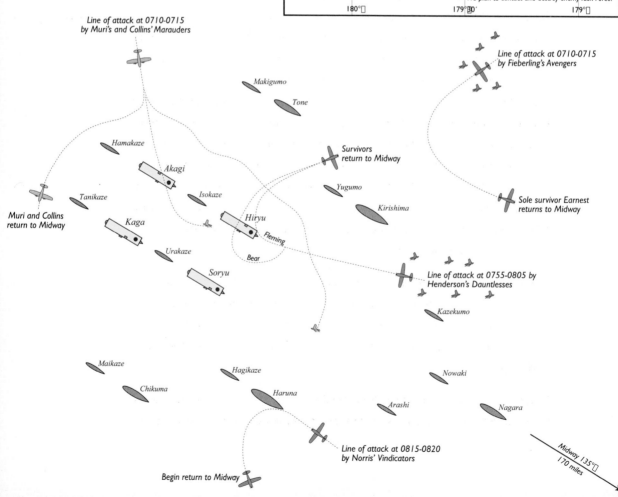

bomb explosion in their wake, which was probably the torpedo dropped by this aircraft.

Fuchida counted six Marauders and believed he saw three downed by fighters and a fourth, 'which skimmed straight over *Akagi*, from starboard to port, nearly grazing the bridge'. This one was probably the victim of AA fire because he saw it burst into flames immediately afterwards and plunge into the sea, while on *Hiryu*, less than a mile beyond *Akagi*, they believed it had attempted to make a 'body-crash' on them. Both the surviving Marauders were badly shot up, Muri's aircraft having more than five hundred holes in it and all three gunners wounded, but again the CAP fighters did not pursue them and the damaged aircraft made it back to Midway. Collins's after-battle report was acid: 'No bomber is a match for a bunch of fighters and particularly so when the few guns it has won't shoot and the gunners have not had sufficient training to shoot them.'

Map 11
Probable deployment of Mobile Force at 0700, 4 June

The Avengers and Marauders had drawn the CAP down and several Zeros had exhausted their ammunition, but unfortunately the Midway dive-bombers were too far behind to exploit the opportunity. Furthermore, although the 'many planes' bearing given by Chase proved sufficient for the Midway aircraft to find the Mobile Force, no report emerged from these two attacks to either correct the number or the location of the carriers given by Ady an hour earlier, despite the stern reminder issued by Nimitz after the reporting shambles on 3 June.

> Successful and timely employment of striking forces is almost wholly dependent on reliable combat intelligence with emphasis on enemy composition, position and condition. Damage to enemy must be carefully evaluated and reasonably certain results reported. Reports must get through promptly.

Nimitz had good reason to be dissatisfied with the relatively poor return on the comprehensive search operations he had ordered and blamed it on the

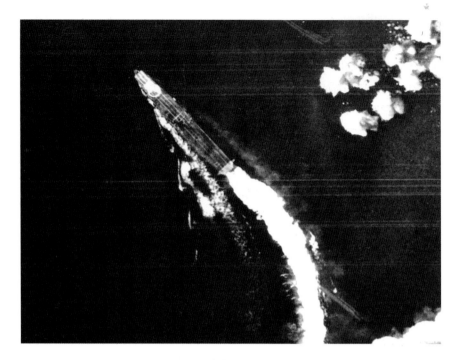

Hiryu **making
a battle turn to
evade bombs
from Midway
flying fortresses**

vulnerability of the PBY, which prevented close observation of enemy formations. But although one PBY was indeed shot down on 4 June by fighter
floatplanes when scouting the Occupation Force, US sources do not confirm
the several attacks made on patrol aircraft that were logged by the Mobile
Force.

This reporting failure remains something of a mystery, because all Midway
aircraft and the submarine cordon were on a common radio frequency
monitored continuously by all surface craft, yet after the early sightings
Fletcher and Spruance received no further useful combat intelligence from
any of them. It may have been no more than the result of poor navigational
skills and reporting procedures, but the former, at least, seems highly unlikely.
Navigators who were capable of finding Midway in the dark should have been
able to pinpoint the location of the Mobile Force to within yards in broad
daylight.

To rub salt into the wound, the execrable navigation of the last of a mere seven Japanese search planes (the famously late-launching #4 floatplane from *Tone*) took it well north of its intended pattern, and at 0728 it reported sighting 'what appears to be ten enemy surface ships' at a time when the US carriers were only halfway through launching their first strike. Who was then the lucky one?

Definitely not Lofton Henderson, leading his sixteen US Marine Corps Dauntlesses, who approached the Mobile Force forty minutes after the Marauders had left and ran into a CAP of fresh pilots flying fully fuelled and armed Zeros. Intercepted just after he had initiated the long, shallow dive of a glide-bombing attack, his aircraft was the first to fall, followed swiftly by five others. Now in the lead, Captain Richard Fleming was mobbed, his gunner wounded and his instrument panel smashed, but he nevertheless pressed on into a storm of flak and released at *Hiryu* from 400 feet. He and two of three others, who bombed 'by the book' along the length of the carrier, obtained near misses, but Second Lieutenant Robert Bear dived to sea level and made a broadside attack with his forward-firing guns blazing.

In what may have been the first attempt to employ what later became an established technique, Bear 'tossed' his bomb at *Hiryu*, both he and the bomb flying over her separately, and very low indeed, the latter to explode in the water 300 feet beyond while the intrepid Bear returned to Midway unharmed. *Hiryu* recorded simultaneous attacks by four dive bombers and four strafing fighters in addition to Fleming's attack, so Bear's solo effort evidently made a great impression. This time the CAP fighters chivvied the departing dive bombers further than they had the first wave and two went down from battle damage on the way back. Lieutenant Daniel Iverson, having dived into 'almost an entire ring of fire from the flight deck' , near-missed astern and then zoomed up into a swarm of Zeros, laconically recording that he was hit 'several times', including one bullet that cut his throat microphone cable. No less than 210 holes were counted in his aircraft back at Midway.

Even as Henderson's dive bombers began their attack, Sweeney's B-17s, down to fourteen after two early returns, droned up from the south at 20,000 feet and sighted the Mobile Force. They drew most of the heavy AA fire while some Zeros made ineffectual passes from below, and this distraction no doubt saved the lives of some of the low-flying Marines. Photos from their bomb bays show *Akagi*, *Hiryu* and *Soryu* manoeuvring violently, but in fact the flagship was not targeted. *Soryu* recorded 'about eleven' bombs near her from three B-17s, *Hiryu* two near her out of nine bombs dropped by nine level bombers and *Kaga* three astern, incorrectly attributed to dive bombers.

That only twenty-three of eighty-four bombs dropped were recorded is not significant – they burst on impact and when the sea erupted there was no way of knowing how many bombs were involved. Fuchida thought that only *Soryu* had been attacked by level bombers and that *Hiryu* was the target of a simultaneous attack by glide bombers, but saw 'dark geysers of water' obscuring both. In conjunction with the smoke pouring from the funnels of the carriers travelling under full power, the huge splashes made by their bombs misled the army pilots, who reported five definite hits on three of them.

The result of the foregoing events was that the second element of VMSB 241, Norris's group of eleven 'Wind Indicators' – as the SB2U-3s were unaffectionately known – had an almost clear run in. The least experienced group of pilots in the most inadequate aircraft to take part in this battle, they were dead men flying without the distraction provided by their squadron-mates in the dive bombers and by Sweeney's B-17s. Norris evidently judged that their good fortune should only be pushed so far and led them all against *Haruna*, the nearest substantial target. As they dived, Zeros slashed at the rear of the formation, killing 18-year-old Private Henry Starks, of whom his pilot, Second Lieutenant Daniel Cummings, sadly commented, '[he] had never before fired a machine gun in the air and could not be expected to be an effective shot much less protect himself'. Second Lieutenant George Koutelas reported the target 'ringed with near misses, also one direct hit on the bow', and although *Haruna* took the glide-bombing approach to be the signature of torpedo bombers, her report specified two 'very near' and three near misses with bombs, while the battle diagram shows three on either side.

One aircraft was unable to release its bomb and Cummings, finding his angle of approach wrong for the battlecruiser, chose not to waste his bomb and flew off alone to look for another target. Nevertheless six out of nine bombs within 100 feet of a fast-manoeuvring target made this one of the most accurate attacks by any group of US bombers in the whole battle. Unfortunately, during the return flight one over-eager pilot turned back to pursue a Japanese scouting floatplane and the Zeros got him, while another aircraft simply disappeared, the delayed victim of battle damage. Cummings ditched 5 miles from Midway, while another Vindicator ran out of fuel and made a water landing in the lagoon, the crew plucked from the water by a PT boat while their plane was still afloat.

More than one of the returning pilots owed his dry landing to the biblical pillar of smoke by day and fire by night lit by the Japanese among the oil tanks and fuel lines on Sand Island, completing the job begun by the accident on 22 May. Thereafter all refuelling was done by hand, a task greatly simplified by the large number of aircraft that would no longer require it. Among these were the surviving Avenger and Marauders, considerately crash-landed to the side of the runways. Two Dauntlesses and two Vindicators were also unfit for further service while four of Sweeney's B-17s blew out tyres upon touching down amid bomb fragments and wreckage from US and Japanese planes. Simard, Ramsey and Kimes did not join their pilots' celebration of their survival and of what they believed was crippling damage done to the enemy. 'We estimated they would be back in three or four hours', Kimes commented. 'Fighting airplanes to repel air attack were practically nil, so there was a pretty anxious time as we waited for the Japs to show up.'

After the attack by the Marauders, and in response to Tomonaga's signal that a second attack was necessary, Nagumo ordered the torpedo bombers spotted on *Kaga* and *Akagi* to be rearmed with land bombs, which also cleared the decks for the rotation of the CAP fighters. The rearming continued while he waited for clarification of the first, exasperatingly imprecise, report from *Tone* #4, but at 0745 he signalled the fleet, 'prepare to carry out attacks on enemy fleet units. Leave torpedoes on the planes which have not yet been changed to bombs', and radioed *Tone* #4 to 'ascertain types and maintain contact'.

Shortly thereafter, anti-submarine patrols reported strafing two periscopes (*Grouper* and *Nautilus*, closing in response to the PBY sighting reports), and the cruiser *Nagara* and several destroyers were dispatched to attack them. At around 0800, *Chikuma* reported 'carrier-based planes' incoming (probably Norris's Vindicators), but then *Tone* #4 radioed the reassuring report that the US force was 'composed of five cruisers and five destroyers'.

For the next half-hour the carriers circled and drew apart under bombardment by the dive bombers and B-17s, but the biggest bombshell of them all was the next report from *Tone* #4: 'The enemy is accompanied by what appears to be a carrier'. Nagumo and his staff barely had time to consider this information before their own aircraft, returning from Midway, were briefly fired upon by the cruiser and destroyer screen and then circled overhead, some of them damaged and all of them low on fuel and urgently requesting permission to land.

This was a lot to cope with, and the officers on *Akagi* did not take it well when Rear Admiral Tamon Yamaguchi, commander of the Second Carrier Division, signalled 'Consider it advisable to launch attack force immediately'. His flagship *Hiryu* and her sister ship *Soryu* each had eighteen Vals spotted, while at least half of the fighters on CAP had been in the air for a relatively short period and could have been ordered to accompany the strike. Far away in *Yamato*, the Combined Fleet staff officers assured Yamamoto, who wanted to send a similar message, that there was no need to break radio silence because 'of course' Nagumo would launch immediately. He intended to do so, but Kusaka and Genda counselled him to land the Midway strike force first, and he accepted their advice.

Both Kusaka and Genda survived the war, and their version of this fateful decision was that some of the Midway strike force would have had to ditch if not landed immediately. But it certainly took longer to move the spotted aircraft forward or to strike them below than it would have done to launch them, so this is not an adequate explanation. Kusaka was known to favour a single, combined strike, the Kates on *Akagi* and *Kaga* were not yet ready to launch and the Mobile Force was undoubtedly in disarray, but even the sum of all these factors did not constitute a valid reason to ignore the 'strike-first' principle.

Something else was at work, and it was probably resentment of Yamaguchi, who had made no secret of his belief that Nagumo and Kusaka were incompetent and that he should be in command. Genda may have been as

A pillar of smoke by day: burning oil tanks on Sand Island with nonplussed 'gooney' chicks in the foreground

influenced by his concern for his fellow aviators as he later stated, but Kusaka protested too much, and one is left with the lingering suspicion that considerations of 'face' influenced him to recommend the rejection of Yamaguchi's disrespectfully given advice. Instead he concurred with Nagumo's decision to order the Mobile Force to turn north after recovering the Midway strike, closing the distance in accordance with surface torpedo-attack doctrine, when they should have stood off to take advantage of the greater range of their aircraft.

Nagumo at least was receiving up-to-date, if inaccurate, combat intelligence, whereas his opposite number Fletcher had nothing to go on beyond the early morning reports. Both admirals suffered from unconscionable delays in receiving the text of radio reports, but one of the worst was that Ady's 0532 report only reached Fletcher after 0600, when he immediately signalled Spruance to 'proceed south-westerly and attack enemy carriers as soon as definitely located. I will follow as soon as planes recovered'.

In the Coral Sea, an inaccurate early report of two enemy carriers had led to the launching of both US carriers' Air Groups against what proved to be cruisers, although timely information from a patrolling B-17 permitted them to find and destroy the *Shoho*. With only two of the four or five carriers predicted by COMINT located and with most of VS-5 patrolling a full 180° sweep to the north, unrecallable without identifying himself to Japanese radio direction-finding, Fletcher's tactical options were limited, but coincided with how he wanted to fight the battle. *Enterprise* and *Hornet* were sent to throw a heavy first strike, while *Yorktown*'s Air Group remained in reserve and under his direct control.

Task Force 16 sailed south-west to close the distance, the air staff furiously computing the optimum point of which they should turn south-east, into the wind but parallel to the reported course of the Japanese task force. On *Enterprise*, Browning was frantic to catch the Japanese carriers with their Midway strike returning and persuaded Spruance to launch at 0700, when he calculated the Japanese would be 155 miles away, near the limit the F4F-4s could fly and also engage in combat for any useful length of time.

The radius of *Hornet*'s fighters, condemned to loiter overhead while the other squadrons launched and assembled in 'deferred departure', was perforce from the start less than the minimum required, and even the more sensible *Enterprise* launching configuration left little room for error. And error there was, because Ady's report had placed the Japanese carriers nearer Task Force 16 than they actually were and, as we have seen, they turned north upon completing recovery of the Midway strike, which together put the predicted point of interception about 55 miles east of the true location.

At 0638 Spruance informed Mitscher by blinker of his intention to turn into the wind and launch at 0700, and notified him that Task Force 16 would resume course 240° once launching was complete and deferred departure had taken place, closing the distance and giving the Air Groups a fixed line, or 'Point Option', for their return course. The message included the predicted point of interception but, mindful of Fletcher's 'definitely located' proviso and that all of the Japanese carriers had not been accounted for, specified that the air groups should fly out in 'search-attack' formation. This was poor staff work: the purpose of 'deferred departure' was concentration, which was absolutely necessary if radio silence was to be maintained, whereas 'search-attack' involved the scouting squadrons going ahead in an extended line abreast to cover a broader swathe of the ocean, in touch with each other and with the following heavy-attack squadrons and fighter escort by radio. One or the other, not both.

Although Mitscher went through a form of consultation with Ring and the squadron commanders, it can only have been he who decided to ignore Spruance's guidance and instead to adopt a compact 'group-parade' formation and to explore the gap between *Yorktown*'s hemispheric search arc and the line *Enterprise* air group intended to take (231°). After each of the airmen had produced a different navigational solution, Ring decided that *Hornet* air group would fly out on 265°.

This seems to have been the last straw for the smouldering Waldron, whose opinion was once again ignored, and about thirty minutes into the flight he broke radio silence to tell Ring that he was going the wrong way and that VT-8 was turning south-west. This was flagrant, indeed ostentatious and compound mutiny. Although the term 'dead right' applies with ghastly literalness to Waldron's judgement about where the Japanese carriers were to be found, he could have simply slipped away and there was something undeniably vengeful about broadcasting his act of rebellion for all to hear.

Map 12
***Hornet* Air Group attack**

——— Japanese Mobile Force
——— Task force 16
- - - - - VT 8
— — — VF 8
— ·· — ·· VS 8
— ·— ·— · VB 8

The dive-bombers flew on in a large arrowhead, with Ring's three-plane section in the lead, to his right Lieutenant Commander Walter Rodee's VS-8 with fifteen aircraft, and to his left Lieutenant Commander Robert Johnson's VB-8 with sixteen, the fighters overhead. As the formation reached the two-hour mark, the fuel gauges in the F4F-4s indicated they had reached their point of no return. The first to turn back was a member of VF-8 commander Mitchell's own division, who flew alongside him twice, pointing to his fuel gauge, and on the second occasion broke away, followed by his section leader who believed he had obtained permission to do so. An hour later, fuel exhausted, they ditched together and spent five days adrift until rescued by a PBY.

Not long after this further act of indiscipline, Mitchell led the rest of VF-8 back on a course that might have found Task Force 16 had it maintained the Point Option course, but although some were able to detect *Hornet*'s homing beacon, they were unfamiliar with the equipment and were unable to close on it with sufficient precision. They sighted the wakes of the task-force ships but kept going, believing them to be Japanese, and eventually all ran out of fuel. Three were rescued by PBYs on 8 June and three more on 9 June, but two were never found.[2]

The rot continued as the dive bombers flew on to the estimated point of interception, some of them picking up the horrifying last transmissions of VT-8. Ring continued for a while on 265°, then led the formation in a wide sweep to the south before setting a return course. In the process he lost both

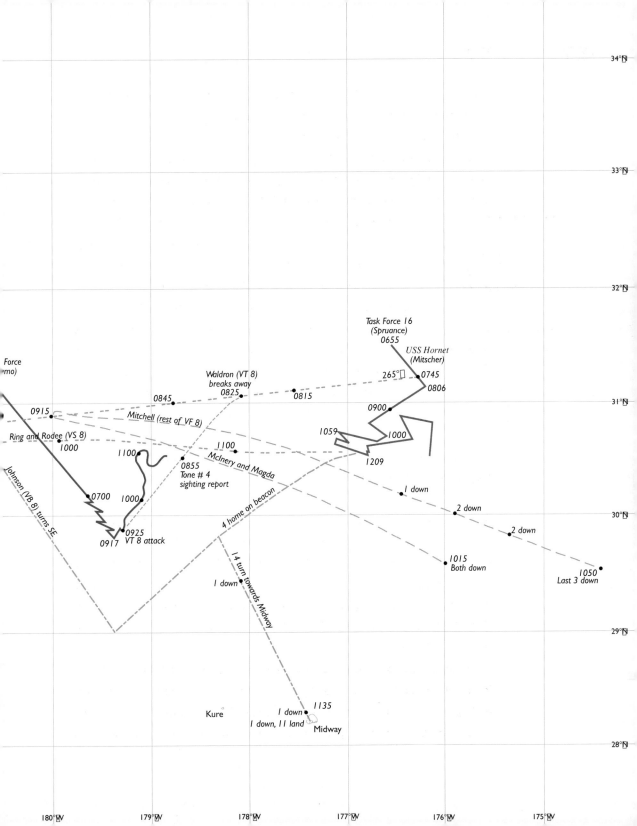

34°N

33°N

32°N

Task Force 16
(Spruance)
0655

USS Hornet
(Mitscher)

265° 0745
0806

0900

0915   1059   1000

Ring and Rodee (VS 8)   1209
1000

Force
mo)

Waldron (VT 8)
breaks away
0825   0815
0845

31°N

Mitchell (rest of VF 8)

1100

1100   McInery and Magda
0855
Tone # 4
sighting report

1 down

2 down

2 down

Johnson (VB 8) turns SE

0700   1000

0917   0925
VT 8 attack

4 home on beacon

1015
Both down

1050
Last 3 down

30°N

14 turn towards Midway

1 down

29°N

Kure

1 down   1135
1 down, 11 land   Midway

28°N

180°W   179°W   178°W   177°W   176°W   175°W

squadrons and even the two other aircraft of his own section, which rejoined VB-8. Ring was an excellent navigator but confidence in him was by now so badly shaken that although Rodee took VS-6 back on the same course, he did so after calculating it himself, losing touch with the Air Group commander. One can readily imagine Ring's state of mind as he flew back alone.

Meanwhile, Johnson led his squadron south-east on 320°, the course of the Japanese Midway strike as reported by Chase four hours earlier, then turned north-east for Point Option. With some of his men shorter on fuel than others, he then tried to lead them all south-east again towards Midway, the bird in the hand of the quandary he had put them in. Four dive bombers could detect the homing beacon and continued to land safely on *Hornet*, the rest followed Johnson and one soon ditched followed by another about 10 miles out.

Midway radar detected the approach of the remaining twelve aircraft, and Simard scrambled his sole functional F4F-3 and four operational B-17s. Johnson's bombers dropped their bombs on the outer reef to show that they were friendly, but the AA gunners took this amiss and opened fire on them. One more bomber ditched in the lagoon and three others were damaged before they were able to land. Until Simard advised him of their arrival, Mitscher believed he had lost 14 dive bombers, in addition to 10 fighters and all of VT-8, over half of *Hornet*'s Air Group in return for no damage to the enemy whatever. To compound this lamentable result, *Hornet*'s action report contains the following remarkable insight into Mitscher's mental rigidity: 'About one hour after the planes had departed the enemy reversed course... We did not break radio silence to report this to the planes'.

KILLING STROKE

How Mitscher's career not only survived the débâcle, but also prospered, is beyond the remit of this book. It seems to have taught him some much-needed humility, and in the overall scheme of things the men of *Hornet* air group who died on the morning of 4 June 1942 helped to make him a better, perhaps even a great admiral. To a degree he was also saved by the fact that the US Navy could not afford to draw attention to the gross breakdown in discipline that had taken place and this, along with Mitscher's understandable desire to find a redeeming feature, led to the canonization of Waldron and his men. If, as General George Patton succinctly put it, the purpose of war is not to die for one's country but to make someone else die for his, then respect for VT-8's heroic death-charge must be tempered by the acknowledgement that it served very little purpose, not even causing its target *Soryu* to take violent evasive action.

The Japanese had not picked up Waldron's breach of radio silence, but *Tone* #4 saw VT-8 after it turned south and at 0855 radioed *Akagi*, 'ten enemy torpedo planes are heading toward you'. Whoever else may or may not have been lucky this day, there can be no argument about the crew of this reconnaissance flight, who kept stumbling over vital combat intelligence and somehow, despite being monitored by radar and even visually from Task Force 16, were never found by the fighters directed against them.

Waldron's squadron had no such luck and was spotted at a range of 20 miles by *Chikuma*, which at 0920 directed *Akagi*'s CAP Zeros to an early interception by firing her main armament at the torpedo bombers. It was all over very swiftly, with the Devastators either going down in flames or exploding in mid air as cannon shells detonated their torpedoes. *Soryu* recorded two torpedo tracks at 0930, one of which must have come from the aircraft of Ensign George Gay, who swore that he could 'see the little Jap captain up there jumping up and down and raising hell' when he flew past *Soryu*'s bridge. Wounded and with his gunner dead, Gay was finally brought down in the middle of the Mobile Force, where he prudently hid under his life raft and had a ring-side seat for what followed. Haunted by survivor guilt, the rest of his life was a long, sad coda to this moment and a reminder that some of the worst wounds leave no visible scars.

Hornet's launch order was ill-conceived but it was accomplished quickly, whereas on *Enterprise* it took so long to respot the deck after launching VS-6 and VB-6 that at 0745 Spruance, urged on by Browning, ordered McClusky to proceed alone. Gray's fighters were now launched out of sequence, without informing him that the dive-bombers had flown on ahead. After reaching his assigned altitude, the only planes he could see to escort were a squadron of torpedo bombers at 1,500 feet. Gray took these to be Lindsey's VT-6, his own charges, but they were in fact Waldron's VT-8. The last of Lindsey's squadron launched at 0800 and he led it south-west on 240°, believing that Gray was overhead as agreed. Order and counter-order had produced the proverbial result and the *Enterprise* squadrons now made their way towards the enemy following three separate courses.

Much of what went wrong can be attributed to the fact that the Air Groups were unaccustomed to forming up in strict radio silence, but to compound this difficulty each Group employed a different radio frequency, there were chronic equipment failures and radio reception was poor. A combination of these problems meant that Gray, waiting for the agreed summons, did not dive in support of VT-8, which entered low cloud at the crucial moment, or hear Lindsey when VT-6 made its own gallant attack half an hour later. Instead he circled over the mobile force at 22,000 feet, where he could pick up his carrier's homing signal, waiting for the dive bombers to appear. At 0956, his fuel situation critical, he radioed the first contact report since Ady's sighting four hours earlier, four minutes later sending a further message that must have had Nimitz, Fletcher and Spruance, along with their respective staff officers, tearing their hair out in frustration.

> This is Gray. We are returning to the ship due to lack of gas. We have been flying over the enemy fleet. They have no combat patrol. There are six destroyers, two battleships and two carriers. Course about north.

Far below, unseen and unheard, VT-6 had just made its attack. After turning north-west at 0935, Lindsey sighted the Japanese fleet at about 0945 and separated from Ely and the second division to try to make a hammer-and-anvil attack on the fleeing *Kaga*. Directed by fire from *Tone*'s main armament the *Akagi* fighters that had just destroyed Waldron's squadron were now joined by part of the *Soryu* contingent and tore into VT-6, Lindsey and Ely being among the first to go down, rapidly followed by seven others.

Kaga did not record any tracks, but reported that the torpedo attack was 'followed up with dive bombing', presumably some of the Devastators flying over her after dropping their torpedoes. Once again the Zeros broke off when they were sure the threat was spent and five VT-6 aircraft got away, one so severely damaged that it was pushed over the side after returning to *Enterprise*,

VB-6 Dauntless piloted by Goldsmith on return to *Enterprise*

another being forced to ditch on the way back, its crew adrift until picked up by a PBY on 21 June, making them the last of the downed aviators to be rescued. The survivors felt betrayed by their fighters, but responsibility rests with Browning and Spruance and with the lack of training in navigation that made the line-of-sight homing beacon on *Enterprise* the only hope Gray had of getting his thirsty aircraft home. He was shattered when he learned of the fate of the torpedo bombers.

> ... the shock was as total as that which one could expect from a death in his immediate family. These were shipmates and dear friends of many years.

The killing stroke was about to be delivered (see **Appendix D**), so Gray's comment that 'they have no combat air patrol' is of extremely great interest. Where was Genda's 'armoured sleeve'? During the Midway strike three Zeros had been lost and thirteen damaged, *Akagi* losing another to the gunners of VT-6, but each ship carried three spares, with the result that there were still seventy operational fighters available. No less than thirty-seven of these were on CAP when Gray made his report, three of them specifically launched from *Soryu* to engage a formation of 'high level bombers' that can only have been his fighters. At 1015, *Hiryu* and *Soryu* launched a further three Zeros each, bringing the CAP total to forty-three, the contingents being (number of undamaged aircraft, including spares, in parentheses): *Kaga* fifteen (eighteen); *Akagi* nine (sixteen); *Hiryu* ten (twelve); and *Soryu* nine (twenty-one).[1] Genda's boast implied that half of the fighter force would be more than enough to defend the mobile force from a carrier attack, so what went wrong?

The standard explanation is that the torpedo bombers caused a breakdown in CAP discipline and drew all of the fighters down to sea level, but VT-8 and VT-6 were dealt with by the low CAP provided by the *Akagi* and *Soryu* fighters, who also engaged the last low-level attack by VT-3/VF-3, joined by at most one or two from the other air units. The Japanese knew the role that dive bombers had played in loss of the *Shoho* and the near-loss of the *Shokaku* in the Coral Sea, and the fact that they called them 'Helldivers' (actually the name of once and future Curtiss dive bombers) indicates that they respected them. Yet over twenty fighters belonging to the most experienced naval Air Units in the world somehow not only failed to intercept, but did not even see three squadrons of dark-blue Dauntlesses approaching. If Gray saw no high CAP at 1000, and there was still none twenty to twenty-five minutes later, there must have been a fundamental flaw in IJN air-defence procedures.

McClusky and thirty-two *Enterprise* dive bombers (one VS-6 aircraft had turned back with engine trouble) reached the estimated interception point at 0920 to find open ocean. In fairness to Browning, and in mitigation of his abandonment of deferred-departure procedure, if Ady's report had been accurate the timing would have been perfect and they would have arrived over the Mobile Force when the Midway strike was still being cleared away. As it was, McClusky continued to fly south-west for fifteen minutes and then

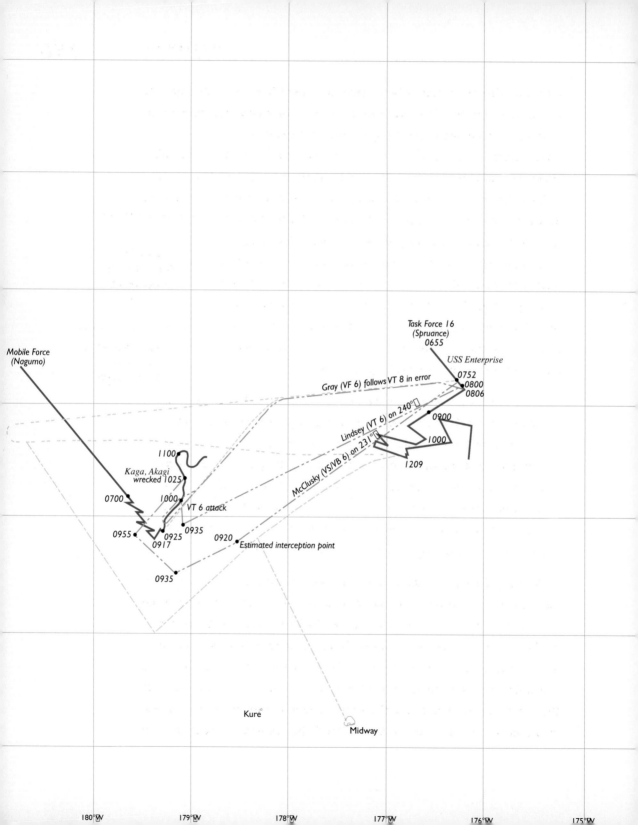

Task Force 16
(Spruance)
0655

Mobile Force
(Nagumo)

USS *Enterprise*
0752
0800
0806

Gray (VF 6) follows VT 8 in error

Lindsey (VT 6) on 240°

Lindsey (VT 6) on 231°

0900

1000

1209

McClusky (VS/VB 6) on 231°

1100

Kaga, Akagi
wrecked 1025

0700

1000

VT 6 attack

0955

0925

0935

0917

0920

Estimated interception point

0935

Kure

Midway

180°W
179°W
178°W
177°W
176°W
175°W

turned north-west to begin a box search that might have found the Japanese fleet anyway, but at 0955 he saw the destroyer *Arashi* racing back from depth-charging *Nautilus* and turned to fly parallel to her course.

Five minutes later, the Mobile Force appeared in McClusky's binoculars about 35 miles away and he unhelpfully radioed 'This is McClusky. Have sighted the enemy'. Instead of asking for a much-needed location report, Browning grabbed the microphone to order him to attack, as though he might have been there for some other purpose. Several pilots thought they were approaching their own task force after nearly three hours in the air, including one VB-6 pilot, sputtering in to ditch because of fuel exhaustion, who turned and glided as far away as possible once he realised his mistake. For the rest, the biographer of their carrier waxed lyrical about their unimprovably good fortune.

Map 13
Enterprise **Air Group attack**

——— Japanese Mobile Force
——— Task force 16
— - - — *Enterprise* attacks

> In a dive bomber's dream of perfection, the clean blue Dauntlesses – with their perforated dive flaps open at the trailing edges of their wings and their big bombs tucked close and pointing home, the pilots straining forward, rudder-feet and stick-hands light and delicate, getting it just right as the yellow decks came up, left hand that would reach down and forward to release now resting on the cockpit edge, gunners lying on their backs behind the cocked twin barrels searching for the fighters that did not come – carved a moment out of eternity for a man to remember forever.[2]

McClusky decided to attack *Kaga* and *Akagi*, the two closest carriers, and assigned the first to his own section, followed by Gallaher's VS-6, and the second to Best's VB-6. Apparently transmitting simultaneously such that neither heard the other, Best radioed 'Group Commander from six baker one. Am attacking according to doctrine'. Previously a fighter pilot, this was McClusky's first mission as leader of dive bombers and he was unaware that the nearer aircraft should take the further target to bring both under attack at the same time. Thus it was that at 1022, just as Best began to dive on

Kaga, McClusky's section, followed by VS-6, abruptly pushed over in front of him. Best pulled out, but only Lieutenant Edwin Kroeger and Ensign Frederick Weber followed him towards *Akagi*, the rest hurtling down on the doomed *Kaga*.

The 500-pound bombs of VB-6 probably did little structural damage, but the first one to hit *Kaga* landed among the twenty-five Kates that were waiting to take off, turning the stern of the ship into a huge fireball punctuated by exploding torpedoes. Among those killed in their cockpits was the leader of the attack bombers at Pearl Harbor, Lieutenant Commander Tadashi Kusumi. Not all of the Kate aircrew shared his fate – both of the Japanese veterans on board Robert Ballard's 1998 Midway expedition had been on reconnaissance and anti-submarine patrolling duties and were in *Kaga*'s ready room rather than sitting in their aircraft when the bombs hit. The second bomb hit a refuelling cart opposite the island and enveloped it in flames, this or another hit killing everyone on the bridge, including Captain Jisaku Okada. Then the 1,000-pound bombs of VB-6 penetrated amidships and started an uncontrollable fire in the engine room, where most of *Kaga*'s estimated eight-hundred fatalities were concentrated. Those on board stopped counting after four hits and five near misses, and *Kaga* was wrecked beyond hope of salvage.

Although the damage done to *Akagi* by the 1,000-pound bombs of the three VB-6 bombers that attacked her was not so comprehensive, it was no less deadly. Best's bomb penetrated near her midships elevator, Kroeger's punched through her deck and exploded close enough alongside to hole her hull, while Weber's, which the Japanese recorded as the 'fatal hit', detonated in the hangar deck aft, the explosion blasting up through the flight deck amid the spotted Kates. Fuchida, who had earlier commented to Genda what fun it all was, recalled his reaction.

I was horrified at the destruction that had been wrought in a matter of seconds. There was a huge hole in the flight deck just behind the amidship elevator. The elevator itself, twisted like molten glass, was drooping into the hangar. Deck plates reeled upward in grotesque configurations. Planes stood tail up, belching livid flames and jet-black smoke. Reluctant tears streamed down my cheeks as I watched ... fire spread among the planes lined up wing to wing on the after flight deck, their torpedoes began to explode, making it impossible to bring the fires under control. The entire hangar area was a blazing inferno, and the flames moved swiftly toward the bridge.

The attacks were nearly simultaneous – Lieutenant Norman Kleiss of VS-6, racing away at sea level after registering the second hit on *Kaga*, saw *Akagi* erupt 'like a haystack in flames', but as they flew away the *Enterprise* dive-bomber crews were puzzled to see a third carrier on fire from stem to stern. Crawling up to the bridge, Fuchida also saw it and believed the Mobile Force had been the victim of synchronized attacks.

The third carrier was *Soryu*, the victim of an entirely separate attack by half of *Yorktown* Air Group. After recovering the morning scouting sweep that had encountered only Japanese floatplanes, Fletcher concluded that there were no carriers on his flank and turned Task Force 17 south to close on the only confirmed sighting. Still awaiting word that the missing Japanese carriers had been located, he conferred with his Flag Captain Elliott Buckmaster, Air Officer Commander Murr Arnold, and the Air Group's Pederson. They decided to launch the twelve torpedo bombers of VT-3 and seventeen dive bombers of VB-3 as soon as they were in fighter range, although reducing the fighter escort to six. VS-5's seventeen dive bombers, with a six-fighter escort, would be spotted for a second strike, and the thirteen remaining fighters of VF-3 would be dedicated to CAP. Although Thach protested that his tactics required four-plane sections, the senior officers on *Yorktown* took the time to explain the overall situation to the strike leaders, putting their mission in perspective.

The torpedo bombers began to launch at 0830 and the last of Thach's escort was in the air by 0905. By about 0945, the three components were in visual contact, Leslie's dive bombers at 15,000 feet, Massey's torpedo bombers at 1,500, two fighters at 2,500 feet and four at 5,500 feet. Leslie signalled his force to arm their bombs but to his horror the newly installed electrical switch released his instead, which along with three others whistled down through Thach's fighters before Leslie could warn the rest of his force to use the manual switch. Like the *Enterprise* torpedo bombers, the strike was to fly out on 240° for 150 miles and then turn north-west, but since Task Force 17 was further to the west, the formation flew nearly directly to the Mobile Force.

Map 14
***Yorktown* Air**
Group attack

———— Japanese Mobile Force
———— Task Force 17
———— Task force 16
- - - - - - *Yorktown* attacks

They had not even reached their estimated interception point when first Massey, then Thach and Leslie saw smoke on their right shortly after 1000 and turned towards it. Once the carriers were sighted, VT-3 climbed to 2,500 feet to gain speed by diving to drop height, the VF-3 escort conforming, and at 1010 *Chikuma* fired her main armament at them to direct the CAP towards this new menace. The *Yorktown* attackers were approaching along VT-6's escape route and were promptly hit by a swarm of Zeros, some attacking Thach's fighters while the rest went for the torpedo bombers.

The veteran Ensign Edgar Bassett of the higher fighter group was killed almost immediately, but thereafter the VF-3 commander led his untried wingmen, one of whom also had radio failure, in the first test of his soon-to-be famous 'Thach weave', whereby one fighter led a pursuer under the guns of another. In an epic aerial duel he downed three, his wingmen probably getting one more, but the Zeros had done their job and kept them away from the torpedo bombers – although that calculation worked both ways. Aviation Radioman Lloyd Childers, the only VT-3 gunner to survive, recalled:

> I observed the F4Fs above us mixing it up with the Zeroes. At one point, when I was not shooting at a Zero, I saw [one] coming almost straight down, not smoking, smacking the water within a hundred yards of us. So, I knew the F4Fs were not losing every encounter, even tho' badly outnumbered.[3]

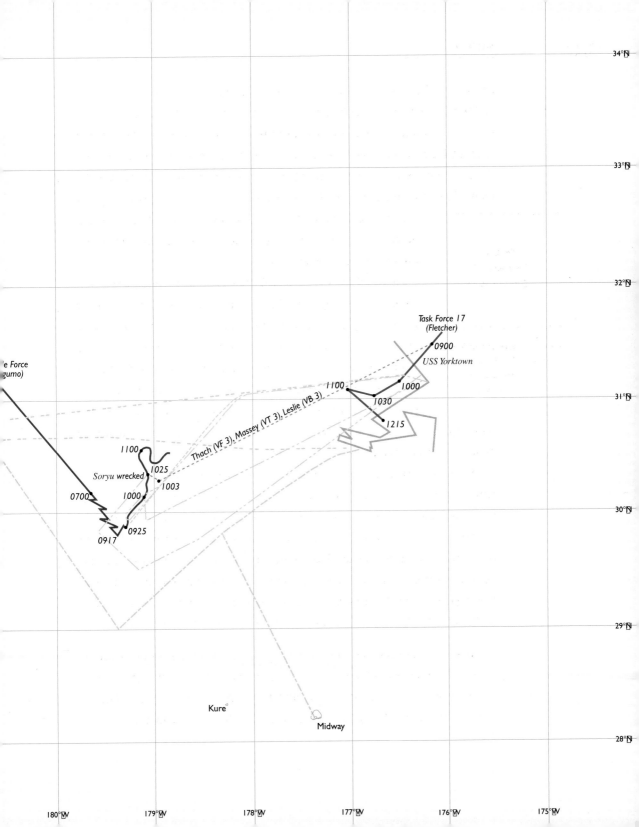

34°N

33°N

32°N

e Force
gumo)

Task Force 17
(Fletcher)

●0900

USS Yorktown

1100 ●1000
● ●
1030

1215
●

31°N

Thach (VF 3), Massey (VT 3), Leslie (VB 3)

1100

1025

Soryu wrecked ● 1003

0700 1000 ●

0925

0917

30°N

29°N

Kure °

Midway

28°N

180°W   179°W   178°W   177°W   176°W   175°W

The Devastators flew on escorted only by the experienced Machinist Tom Cheek and the rookie Ensign Daniel Sheedy. Also separated from their charges, they were compelled to defend themselves, Cheek killing two Zeros and Sheedy, despite being wounded in the legs, winning a head-on confrontation with another at wave-top level. Six or seven for one was an unprecedented outcome for a battle between Wildcats and Zeros, and although Thach judged the skill level of his opponents to be low, the much-cursed F4F-4 unarguably kept his young pilots alive, while similarly inexperienced Japanese pilots died.

VT-3 adopted a tight, layered formation that permitted the gunners to concentrate their fire on attackers from astern, shooting down at least one Zero and keeping the rest at bay for the loss of one torpedo bomber set on fire after the gunner was killed, from which Ensign Wesley Osmus baled out. The early interception forced Massey to dive earlier than he had intended in order to get the defenceless bellies of his aircraft as close to the water as possible, but *Soryu* successfully evaded the charge and VT-3 flew on towards *Hiryu*, much the furthest away of the carriers.

Massey was among the first to go down in flames after the squadron divided to make converging attacks. Childers reported 'a melee with about 30 Zeros going crazy in the most undisciplined, uncoordinated attack that could be imagined'. *Hiryu* recorded separate attacks by sixteen torpedo bombers at 1013, during which she evaded seven torpedoes, and by five torpedo bombers at 1030, with three tracks passing ahead and two astern. US accounts, however, speak only of five torpedoes released at a range of 600-800 yards, at about the same time as the other carriers were being wrecked.

VT-3's attack was a stern chase closing at no better than 75 knots, and involved overtaking the carrier before turning to drop (*Hiryu* could do 34 knots, the torpedoes only 33). The attack was clearly carried out with sublime steadiness in the midst of a Zero feeding frenzy, as well as intense AA fire, and speaks volumes for the leadership of Massey. Even if Childers reported three times the number of Zeros actually involved, in addition to those tied up by

VF-3, one-third of the entire mobile force CAP was committed to stopping this attack. This time the fighters did not break off but pursued the survivors, tending to confirm that their discipline had at last broken down. Not so that of the torpedo bomber crews, who evoked admiration even from their enemies. During the withdrawal Aviation Radioman Robert Brazier, mortally wounded and unable to man his guns, continued to give his pilot, Captain Wilhelm Esders, a running commentary on the persistent attacks made by several Zeros. Thanks to Brazier, Esders evaded them by flying at near stalling speed about 20 feet above the water, waiting until they were committed before turning into their line of attack, until the last of them flew alongside and waved before climbing away.

Leslie tried to co-ordinate his attack with Massey's but lost radio contact with him after 1020 and a few minutes later pushed over on *Soryu*, which had turned into the wind to launch as soon as the threat from VT-3 had passed. Bombless, the squadron commander strafed until his machine-guns jammed and then pulled out, but immediately behind him Lieutenant Paul Holmberg saw his own bomb burst erupt beneath the Vals on *Soryu*'s deck. Lieutenant DeWitt Shumway, leading the third division and the last man to attack *Soryu*, reported five direct hits and three near misses from the nine aircraft preceding his own.

The Japanese recorded two more hits after Holmberg's, evenly spaced along her length, any more going unremarked as the ship was disembowelled by the horrendous secondary explosions that killed two-thirds of her complement. The much-loved Captain Ryusaku Yanagimoto gave the order to abandon ship at 1045 and chose to perish in the flames that enveloped the bridge. Five VB-3 pilots made the disciplined decision not to attack a clearly doomed ship and three of them attacked the destroyer *Isokaze* while two dived on *Haruna*, the alternative target of choice during this battle.

All three sections of the *Yorktown* air group attack were notably more effective than those from *Hornet* and *Enterprise*, the former being an unmitigated disaster and the latter being redeemed by McClusky's initiative and the coolness and skill shown by Best and his two wingmen in not joining the *Kaga* overkill. The full effects of the bungled *Enterprise* launch were still to be felt, however. AA fire downed one VS-6 bomber during the attack and damaged Ensign Frank O'Flaherty's aircraft, forcing him to ditch nearby, but a further six from VS-6 and seven from VB-6 went down during the return flight. Five VS-6 aircraft were lost after fighting off a second attack by Zeros (see next chapter), but only two of the VB-6 bombers had battle damage when they ditched from fuel exhaustion, which, as we saw, claimed one of them even before the attack. They were victims of the additional weight and drag of the 1,000-pound bomb during the deferred departure and the long outer dog-leg.

Nonetheless the effectiveness of the 500-pound bombs had been circumstantial, something emphasized later when the Japanese hit *Yorktown* with three of similar weight and only temporarily disabled her. Although the range/payload equation was to give rise to a near-mutiny on *Enterprise* the next day, *Yorktown* Air Group had shown how it should be done by planning the operation in a mutually respectful and professional manner. Arnold and Pederson could not have known that Thach and his little group would do so well, but even if they had given him two more F4F-4s, as originally intended, the VF-3 contingent would still have been outnumbered and taken out of the escort role. Events were soon to prove that their decision to hold back the bulk of the squadron for CAP was correct.

Against the isolated example of chivalry reported by Esders must be set the fate of three American airmen who were plucked from the sea by the Japanese. Wesley Osmus, whom we last saw parachuting from his aircraft at the beginning of VT-3's charge, was picked up by *Arashi*, and received medical attention, food and water, as did VB-6's Frank O'Flaherty and Aviation Machinist Bruno Gaido after they were retrieved by *Makigumo*. They were not mistreated until the ships' captains had consulted their superiors, but who exactly gave the order that doomed them is not clear. *Arashi* and *Makigumo* were from different destroyer divisions, so presumably the order came from the cruiser *Nagara*, the flagship of the Mobile Force screen, to which Nagumo transferred his flag at 1130. The first combat-intelligence report arising from the interrogation of the prisoners was from *Arashi* at 1300, and in Nagumo's log it is recorded with a note that Osmus 'died on 6 [5] June and was buried at sea', which omitted to mention that the cause of death was beheading. A few days later, O'Flaherty and Gaido were tied to five-gallon kerosene cans filled with water and pushed overboard while they were still alive.[1]

Self-defeating brutality was a common Japanese reaction when events did not develop to their satisfaction and although second to none in reptilian cruelty, these crimes pale in significance next to the decision that was now taken to give battle with the sole remaining carrier. It would have been more sensible to fall back on Vice Admiral Nobutake Kondo's Second Fleet and its carrier *Zuiho*, but it is clear from Ugaki's diary that if Nagumo had thought to do this he would have been superseded, as he was later in the day for ordering a withdrawal following the further loss of *Hiryu*. From several orders issued by Yamamoto, it is apparent that he and his staff clung to hope of capturing Midway, even after the three carriers had been wrecked.

Map 15

Hiryu* vs *Yorktown

In his rambling analysis of the defeat, Ugaki could not bring himself to admit that this had been the fatal flaw from the start, and concluded, 'Thus the distressing day ... came to an end. Don't let another day like this come to us during the course of this war! Let this day be the only one of the greatest failure of my life!' It was not, and on 15 August 1945 Ugaki died as futilely as he had lived, taking a number of impressionable young men with him on a Kamikaze mission that did not even find the enemy, in defiance of his Emperor's broadcast calling for resistance to cease.

With *Akagi*'s communications knocked out, command of the Mobile Force briefly devolved onto Rear Admiral Hiroaki Abe on board *Nagara*, who let Yamaguchi off the leash at 1050 and received the immediate acknowledgement, 'All our planes are taking off now for the purpose of destroying the enemy carriers'. Not quite. The flight deck was immediately cleared by dispatching eighteen Vals, led by Lieutenant Michio Kobayashi, and six Zeros, led by Lieutenant Yasuhiro Shigematsu. But there were thirty CAP Zeros still in the air, as well as an *Akagi* Kate returning from anti-

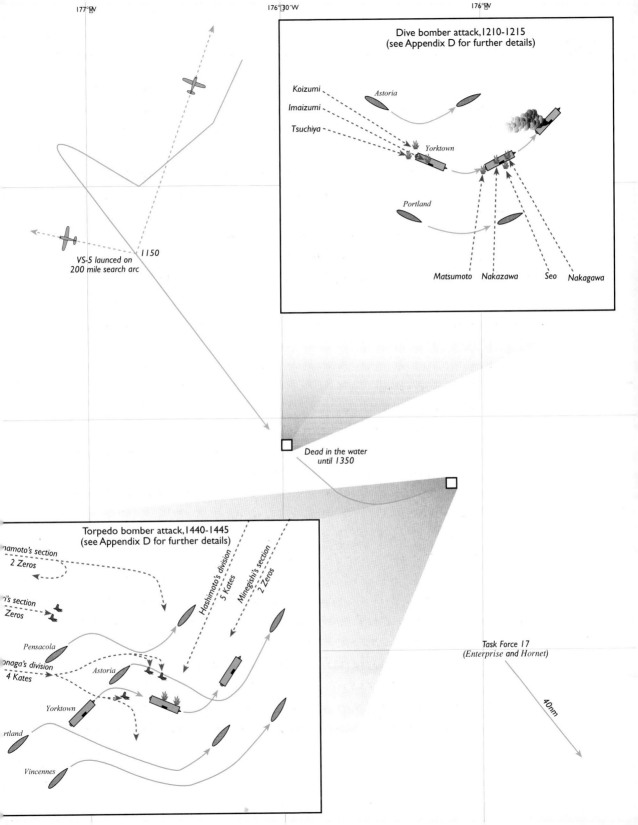

177°W   176°30'W   176°W

1150

VS-5 launced on
200 mile search arc

Dive bomber attack,1210-1215
(see Appendix D for further details)

Koizumi

Imaizumi

Tsuchiya

Astoria

Yorktown

Portland

Matsumoto   Nakazawa   Seo   Nakagawa

Dead in the water
until 1350

Torpedo bomber attack,1440-1445
(see Appendix D for further details)

amoto's section
2 Zeros

Hashimoto's division
5 Kates

Minegishi's section
2 Zeros

i's section
Zeros

Pensacola

onaga's division
4 Kates

Astoria

Yorktown

rtland

Vincennes

Task Force 17
(Enterprise and Hornet)

40nm

submarine patrol, and one of the circling Zeros had to ditch from fuel exhaustion while the first strike was being launched. Yamaguchi really had no choice but to recover the remainder before bringing up *Hiryu*'s remaining Kates for a second strike, the result being that the first was only half what might have been launched two hours earlier, when both carriers of the Second Carrier Division had their Vals spotted. The legacy of operational ambivalence also meant that some of the Vals now launched were still carrying thin-shelled 'land' rather than semi-armour-piercing bombs.

It was certainly correct to counter-attack immediately, and no time would be wasted searching for the enemy because *Chikuma*'s #5 floatplane, which had taken over shadowing duty from *Tone* #4, left its radio on 'send' to guide the strike. Also in attendance was a *Soryu* survivor, a prototype Yokosuka scout bomber later nicknamed 'Judy', but this was plagued with radio problems and had to fly back to report. Although the Japanese did not follow the US dive bombers back to their carriers, they did overtake some of them and a desire for vengeance caused Shigematsu to forget his primary obligation. All six Zeros peeled off to attack a formation of five VS-6 bombers led by Lieutenant Charles Ware, which defended itself to such good effect that two of the fighters were damaged and had to turn back, without having downed a single dive bomber. Ware's aircraft and three others of this group later disappeared without a trace, damage sustained or simply the additional fuel expended in this engagement probably being the cause. But the combination of their fierce resistance and Shigematsu's indiscipline meant that the Vals began their attack unescorted.

Yamaguchi's quick response caught the US carriers in the process of landing their strike aircraft, and although Dow on *Enterprise* had eight of *Hornet*'s VF-8 at 20,000 feet and eight of his own VF-6 at 10,000 feet, twenty-five more Wildcats were stuck at the front of the flight decks while recovery took place. Dow was therefore not in a position to lend immediate assistance to *Yorktown*, which was out of visual range 30 miles to the north-west, and it was her own fighters that did most of the damage to the attackers. Radar was very far from

Yorktown **after
bomb from Iwao
Nakazawa's Val
penetrated the
boiler room**

being a precision instrument at this time and at 1152, when the 'bogeys' were first picked up at a range of 32 miles, Pederson told his pilots that there were fifty of them.

Twelve VF-3 fighters had just been launched in a CAP rotation that left *Yorktown* without any high cover at precisely the wrong moment. They were theoretically in two six-plane divisions led by Lieutenants Richard Crommelin and Arthur Brassfield, but in fact radio communications were so sporadic that Pederson found himself directing individual pilots if, and when, their radios worked properly. Thus Lieutenant Scott McCuskey, of Crommelin's division, was unaware that he was being trailed by Brassfield's wingman Ensign Harry Gibbs when he ploughed through the First Division of Vals. Gibbs was so pleased at making his first kill that he followed it down, but McCuskey flew on alone to scatter the Second Division as well. Brassfield then made a solo attack that destroyed three Vals in less than a minute, and the majority of the First Division Vals jettisoned their bombs at this point, some because of damage but some, Kobayashi among them, in order to counterattack. They were rapidly disabused of the idea that Vals could fight Wildcats on level terms but, if only by forcing the F4F-4s to use up their scarce ammunition,

Scott McCuskey was out of ammunition when he met Michio Kobayashi

bought time for some of their remaining comrades to get within range of *Yorktown*.

Much too late, Shigematsu and three other 'Zeros' now caught up after their encounter with the *Enterprise* dive bombers. Another of them immediately paid the price for indiscipline by breaking away to make a solo attack on Lieutenant Duran Mattson's Wildcat, thereby flying into the gunsight of his wingman, Ensign Horace Bass. Mattson then had a head-on confrontation with a Val whose markings identified it as the leader of the Second Division, in which the superiority of six .50 machine-guns over two .303s was convincingly demonstrated. Pederson had earlier directed Crommelin and his wingman Ensign John Bain to fly to 18,000 feet and they now made two dive-

and-zoom attacks on the bombers before running into the remaining Zeros, Crommelin claiming one and Bain another.

The battle now moved into range of the ships' 5-inch guns and was joined by four planes each from VF-8 and VF-6 sent by Dow. One VF-8 section got among the bombers amid a dense flak barrage, from which two Vals and Ensign Stephen Groves's aircraft were seen to go down in flames. The VF-6 fighters intercepted four of the remaining Vals but suffered weapon and radio malfunctions and broke off the engagement when the formation flew into the even thicker curtain of fire that was now being put up by the task force's massed light AA.

Michio Kobayashi, leader of the Val strike, whose good luck did not last

Three First Division Vals attacked *Yorktown* from astern at about 1210, two being hit even as they released their bombs. One land bomb burst close astern and another hit the flight deck aft of the island, tearing a 12-foot hole in the deck and killing or wounding the gun crews of the quadruple 1.1-inch guns that had just cut the parent aircraft into three pieces. The third bomb also burst astern, but now the four Vals of the Second Division that had been reprieved by VF-6's electromechanical problems made their attack from the starboard side. One missed close alongside, but two hit *Yorktown* with semi-armour-piercing bombs. causing a cloud of black smoke to almost obscure the ship.

The bombless Kobayashi had remained within sight and as the five surviving Vals made off at low level he radioed, 'Fires break out on carrier'. Intent on the target he did not see McCuskey close to point-blank range, only to have his guns go click, but two VF-6 Wildcats with plenty of ammunition then found him and we can only speculate what this conscientious officer would have said to his impetuous colleague Shigematsu had he returned. Pederson picked up another Val on radar about 10 miles out and directed

Brassfield towards it. Brassfield found it circling Esders, who had been forced to ditch, and at 1239 recorded his fourth confirmed kill as the thirteenth Val lost on this mission splashed into the ocean.

Without detracting from the cool competence of Oscar Pederson or from the skill and determination of the US pilots, there is no diluting the Japanese escort leader's responsibility for the crippling losses suffered by the Vals. *Yorktown* was caught in the midst of CAP rotation and the initial interception had the advantage of neither surprise nor height. Had they remained in close support, Shigematsu's six Zeros might well have fended off the attacks by the two dispersed VF-3 divisions, in particular the charges by McCuskey and Brassfield that caused so many Vals to jettison their bombs. Yet the good fortune of finding the high CAP down was also wasted by Kobayashi's decision to approach at 10,000 feet, especially hard to understand after he had witnessed the devastating success of attacks from higher altitude by the US dive bombers on the Mobile Force. The dog-fighting episode also suggests he did not appreciate that his aircraft no longer enjoyed the technological edge that had permitted them to operate unescorted during the air war over China.

If the attack was less damaging than it might have been, it still left *Yorktown* dead in the water and seldom has Churchill's aphorism that in war everything goes on all the time been more apt. Fletcher had cancelled the second strike by VS-5 and at 1133 launched ten of them

Carpenter repairing the hole Nakagawa put in *Yorktown*'s wooden deck while smoke belches from her damaged boiler room: note massive battle ensign

**Kate of
Tomonaga's
section banks
past *Pensacola*
to attack
*Yorktown***

Kate of Tomonaga's section banks past *Pensacola* to attack *Yorktown*

to search north and north-west, the VF-3 division on CAP was called down and the two that were soon to engage Kobayashi's Vals were launched by 1150. Two minutes later, as Pederson was directing the newly launched fighters to intercept the fifty 'bogeys' on his radar screen, two returning *Enterprise* dive bombers were forced to make emergency landings, followed by the recalled CAP division and by Thach and three other VF-3 fighters, the first to return from *Yorktown*'s strike. Cheek, the last to land, found his aircraft bounding unchecked along the deck and quick-wittedly nosed it in to prevent a repetition of the accident that had killed Lovelace on 30 May. The Wildcat, still upside down, was struck below, but the arresting gear had been damaged and Leslie's VB-3, arriving together at this time, was ordered to orbit out of

gunnery range while repairs took place and the ship freed herself to take evasive action.

   After the attack, *Yorktown* could neither fly off the aircraft she had on board (those in the hangar having been liberally doused by the sprinkler system) nor land the ones in the air. VB-3 had meanwhile lost Leslie and Holmberg, who ran out of fuel and ditched near the cruiser *Astoria*, the rest landing on *Hornet* after being 'bounced' by fortunately inaccurate VF-6 fighters, which were not having a good battle. The painfully wounded Sheedy, flying the last of the VF-3 strike fighters, was following VB-3 in to land when tragedy struck – his damaged right landing gear collapsed and as the plane slewed around his guns fired into *Hornet*'s island, wounding twenty and killing five men,

Torpedo from Hashimoto's section hits *Yorktown*

including the son of Vice Admiral Royal Ingersoll, Commander-in-Chief of
the Atlantic Fleet. After Sheedy's plane had been cleared away, the fighters
that had used up their ammunition and fuel began to land, six of the
Yorktowners going to *Enterprise* and six to *Hornet* amid their own CAP
rotations, choreographed by Dow who now came into his own as overall
director of fighter activity.

After transferring his flag to *Astoria* at 1324 Fletcher recovered radio contact
with Spruance. Their satisfaction at the confirmed destruction of three enemy
carriers was tempered by the damage done to *Yorktown* by a fourth and
possibly a fifth from positions unknown, and by the staggering losses among
their own Air Groups. Fifteen of seventy-nine fighters, thirty-eight of forty-
one torpedo bombers and twenty-six of a hundred dive bombers were lost or
unserviceable, while of the undamaged aircraft nine fighters and seven damp
dive bombers were stranded on *Yorktown*, ten dive bombers were on patrol

and eleven were on their way back from refuelling at Midway. Although there is no record of any negative comments, the two other admirals cannot have been impressed by the performance of Mitscher's Air Group. This may have influenced Spruance and Browning to plan the second strike around the twenty-five operational dive bombers of VS/VB-6 and VB-3 on board *Enterprise*, almost disregarding the fifteen of Rodee's VS-8 and the four of VB-8 that had made it back to *Hornet*. The plus side was that with fifty-six Wildcats available, there was reason to be optimistic about parrying any further Japanese thrusts.[2]

Yamaguchi would have wished for such an embarrassment of riches. Even

**Elliott
Buckmaster**

as the US admirals conferred, he launched his second strike at 1330. This consisted of ten torpedo-carrying Kates led by Tomonaga flying the shot-up aircraft in which he had returned from Midway, now only able to carry half its normal fuel load. Of her original complement of attack bombers *Hiryu* had lost four, with five damaged in the Midway strike, and had gained only the solitary *Akagi* survivor. The six Zeros of the escort were led by the commander of *Hiryu's* fighter unit, Lieutenant Shigeru Mori, and the second section by Warrant Officer Yoshijiro Minegishi, who had much to prove after returning early from the first strike. The third, two *Kaga* survivors, was led by the future 'ace', Petty Officer Akira Yamamoto.

By this time the Japanese admirals were fully apprised of the situation and knew from the prisoner interrogations and the report of the returning Judy that they were dealing with three carriers, as well as the aircraft from Midway. *Hiryu* had become a sitting duck, yet it does not seem to have occurred to anyone that she should hit and run. The feeling on *Yamato* was that the Mobile Force must redeem itself and this view seems to have been shared by Nagumo and Kusaka on *Nagara*, while Yamaguchi appears to have shared the Thanatotic philosophy of his Naval Academy classmate, 'Life-exists-in-death' Ugaki.

Yet even now the response was very far from the spirit of the 'Banzai' charge. Thirty young men were dispatched carrying ten aerial torpedoes, while two heavy cruisers and eleven of the most modern destroyers in the IJN, with a total of 104 torpedo tubes loaded with the superb Long Lance and twice as many reloads, milled around waiting for Kondo's Second Fleet to come up instead of closing with the enemy. If tactical retreat was out of the question for reasons of 'face', then the correct solution was for the whole of the Mobile Force to charge immediately, seeking an early night engagement, which would at the very least have tied up US aircraft resources and spared *Hiryu*. Bearing in mind that the B-17s and Dauntlesses were singularly unsuccessful against the smaller warships, and that the larger US cruiser force was balanced by the Japanese battlecruisers and the effectiveness of the Long Lance, it was surely a gamble worth taking, one that torpedo specialist Nagumo should have found irresistible. But he did not, nor did Yamamoto urge him to it and this, I believe, is the true turning point, and the moment when the factors discussed earlier came together to make the Japanese defeat irrevocable.

Tomonaga's attack belongs in any anthology of men at war, but so does the effort of *Yorktown*'s engine-room personnel who restored power and had her under way by 1350, five minutes before radar detected the second Japanese strike 35 miles out, Mori's Zeros above and behind the Kates flying at 4,000 feet. Already in the air over *Yorktown* were three fighters each from VF-3 and VF-6 launched from *Enterprise*, now 40 miles away, led by the indefatigable Scott McCuskey. Pederson directed four of them to intercept, retaining two to cover the launch of eight F4F-4s led by Thach, frantic to avoid being caught on deck again while his ship was under attack. The huge battle ensign at her mast began to snap as *Yorktown* slowly accelerated to 19 knots before turning to gain just enough wind over her hastily repaired deck to get Thach and his men into the air at 1440, amid the thunder of 5-inch guns as the enemy came within range.

The first to make contact were Gibbs and his section leader, Lieutenant William Woollen. Both had scored against the Vals, but now ran into a properly conducted escort and although Woollen flamed one Kate, Minegishi and his wingman sent both him and Gibbs to watery landings. McCuskey and Ensign Melvin Roach caught Mori and his wingman trying to kill the very experienced and unco-operative Machinist Doyle Barnes, who had only just taken off from *Yorktown*, and swiftly shot them both down. McCuskey went on to the rescue of two other fighters being given a combat tutorial by the *Kaga* pilots and damaged Akira Yamamoto's wingman. Undeterred, Yamamoto doggedly resumed close escort duty alone.

The honours were therefore about even as the aerial brawl now moved to low level over Task Force 17. The Zeros had, however, got nine of the ten steadily diving Kates within attacking range of *Yorktown*, which they assumed must be another carrier and not the one reported in flames following the first strike. Tomonaga's First Division came in first from astern and was met by Thach and his XO, Lieutenant William Leonard. Although Thach set the strike leader's aircraft on fire, he was chagrined to see Tomonaga hold it level long enough to make a good drop before his wing came off. Leonard forced another to jettison before shooting it down, but his wingman was unable to prevent a third from launching its torpedo before the Kate blew up in his face. The sole remaining First Division Kate dropped at an acute angle and got away, only to be shot down by late-arriving reinforcements from Task Force 16.

But now, thanks to the sacrifice of Mori and his wingman and of Tomonaga's group, the Second Division was able to make a less harried attack. It enjoyed the continuing protection of Minegishi's section, which shot down and killed Ensign George Hopper, the last to launch from *Yorktown*, and of the redoubtable Akira Yamamoto, who put some more holes into Barnes's aircraft and later drove off Thach himself. The Kates were further assisted by AA fire that shot Ensign Milton Tootle off their backs in the closing seconds and although the torpedo on the *Akagi* aircraft hung up, the other four launched successfully. *Yorktown* lacked the speed to evade them all and two torpedoes slammed into her port side in quick succession, causing her lose all power and rapidly to take on an alarming list. Buckmaster, unable to counterflood and fearing that she must soon capsize and trap the crew below, gave the order to abandon ship within fifteen minutes of being hit.

At 1445 the commander of the Second Division radioed *Hiryu*, 'I carried out a torpedo attack against an enemy carrier and saw two certain hits', while at precisely the same moment Fletcher's dogged insistence on reconnaissance finally produced the dividend it deserved. Lieutenant Sam Adams of VS-5, launched from *Yorktown* at 1150 and at the limit of his fuel, reported sighting one carrier, two battleships and assorted cruisers and destroyers. Here the USN had a stroke of luck on a par with the earlier meandering of *Tone* #4, because Adams was 38 miles south-west of where he should have been and, indeed, thought he was. Spruance now authorized the attack that Browning had been agitating to launch for the past hour, but to crown a day of indifferent staff work, *Hornet* was only advised at 1517 that the strike was to be launched at 1530. By that time Mitscher had ordered a CAP rotation and had moved his dive bombers forward to land two *Yorktown* fighters, along with his own and the VB-8 bombers only now returning from Midway. The strike was further weakened by Spruance's decision to retain all the fighters to protect Task Force 16, which could easily have resulted in the massacre of the unescorted dive bombers.

It is likely that Browning's treatment of *Hornet* air group was again influenced by the fact that Ring would have had command of a combined strike force. With McClusky wounded and Leslie marooned on *Astoria*, leadership of the second *Enterprise* strike devolved on Gallaher of VS-6. His own squadron was now reduced to seven, including Ensign Richard Jaccard who had flown in McClusky's section on the first strike, while Best's VB-6 was down to three, so the bulk of the strike was provided by the fifteen dive bombers of *Yorktown*'s VB-3, now led by Shumway. *Enterprise* recorded launching only twenty-four dive bombers, thirteen with 500-pound and eleven with 1,000-pound bombs, the discrepancy presumably arising from an early return by a VS-6 aircraft. *Hornet* began to launch as the last of the mixed *Enterprise* group took off, and at 1600 Mitscher ordered the first sixteen, armed with 500-pound bombs, not to wait for the rest but to proceed under the command of Lieutenant Edgar Stebbins, leaving all the senior officers behind.

Happily for most of the aviators who were now flying towards the Mobile Force, its destroyer screen was either standing by the burning carriers or providing close escort, and none were on picket duty to spot incoming aircraft. Of the floatplanes that might have observed the departure of the strike, contact was lost with *Chikuma* #5 at 1619 and *Tone* #3 at 1630, both shot down earlier by VF-6 fighters directed by Dow. Although *Tone* #4's guardian angel once again saved it from a similar fate, it developed engine trouble and had to fly back. Half of the remaining thirteen floatplanes were searching the north-to-north-east quadrant at a range of 150 to 180 miles (241 to 290 kilometres), range but no thought seems to have been given to defensive patrolling. Meanwhile, on *Hiryu* they were readying *Soryu*'s Judy and their remaining bombers for the fourth strike of the day and the aircrew, particularly the fighter pilots who had been in action or on stand-by since before dawn, were drawing on their last reserves of stamina.

11

FINISH

A s the bombers disappeared Spruance radioed Fletcher, 'Task Force 16 Air Groups are now striking the carrier which your search plane reported. Have you any instructions for me?' 'None', Fletcher replied. 'Will conform to your movements.' Two admirals had been obliged to transfer their flags from shattered carriers to escorting cruisers that day, but while one of them clung to his authority, the other sensibly renounced his in favour of the man who was best able to exercise it. It was Fletcher's misfortune that, twenty-eight years earlier, his had been one of a scandalously large number of Medals of Honor awarded for a minor action at Vera Cruz under the command of his similarly decorated uncle, and King felt the episode had brought the US Navy into disrepute. Following the Eastern Solomons battle in late August 1942 Fletcher was shelved, a poor reward for having won the first three aeronaval battles of the war, but also a demonstration of the depth of talent among the senior ranks of the USN.[1]

As though to illustrate that the IJN was not similarly blessed, Nagumo's record shows three messages logged between 1655 and 1656. One was a demand from Ugaki to 'report progress of attacks on Midway, particularly whether or not friendly units will be able to use shore bases on Midway tomorrow'. Another, from Nagumo, ordered the Mobile Force to advance at 24 knots on 120°, more towards Midway than the American carriers. It should not have required the further loss of *Hiryu* to concentrate minds on the fact that the US Pacific Fleet was present in force, something that had been known since 0820 and was brutally confirmed two hours later, but even now the original sin of Operation MI still exerted its malign influence.

The third message was from Yamaguchi, reporting that the Kates had left a carrier of the *Enterprise* class burning, but that two additional carriers had been sighted 10 miles away, against which he was preparing to send six Vals and six Kates.[2] The ground crew had done an amazing job, and even some of the newly returned Kates were ready to go, but the aircrew were bone weary and nobody had eaten since breakfast. So he decided to postpone the strike until 1800, when it could attack out of the setting sun, and ordered a special meal of sweet rice balls to be prepared for the entire crew. Yamaguchi, like the late captain of *Soryu*, was unusual among the senior officers of the IJN in not being afraid to show a human touch, but there is a hint of resignation about this decision. US patrol aircraft had been sighted and he had to assume that his location was known. There were fourteen Zeros overhead, but there had been many more flying over *Kaga*, *Akagi* and *Soryu* when they were wrecked, and although he believed his planes had crippled two US carriers, he now knew that there were two more, in addition to whatever Midway could send against him.

Gallaher sighted the Mobile Force at about 1650, some 30 miles north-west of the estimated interception point, and led the formation around it to attack out of the sun and from the 'unexpected' side, climbing steadily in order to gain velocity during the final approach. These were excellent tactics, and he was also cool enough to order the heavier punch of Shumway's VB-3 to be directed at a nearby battleship (our old friend *Haruna*), calculating that the more vulnerable *Hiryu* could be dispatched by his own Group. But the Yorktowners had a score to settle, and although Shumway later swore that he diverted to the carrier only after seeing Gallaher's bombs miss, the timing indicates that this should be taken with a pinch of salt.

The first logged sighting of the bombers was made by *Chikuma* at 1701, when they were already over *Hiryu*, but both the carrier and her fighters had reacted earlier. For a moment, the matter of which target to attack was a moot point, because this time the Japanese had a high CAP and the dive bombers were assaulted by diving Zeros as they reached the push-over point. Gallaher's section dived just in time but, once again, Best's group had to pull up to avoid collision with friendly aircraft when Shumway pushed over in front of them, and the Zeros caught Weber, he of the fatal hit on *Akagi*, and shot him down along with two VB-3 tail-enders. They fell to experienced pilots, who made echeloned attacks from all angles and held their fire until they were close enough to dispatch their victims with short bursts from their 20mm cannon. Two others were so badly shot up that their aircraft were judged unsalvageable after returning to *Enterprise*, as was Shumway's, although the Zeros only caught up with him after he had pulled out. Such was the deadliness of this attack that, had the bombers been intercepted slightly earlier, the entire strike might have been disrupted, and it seems likely that only Gallaher's tactical flair redeemed Spruance's decision to send the dive bombers unescorted.[3]

Manoeuvring at battle speed, Captain Tomeo Kaku made the leading sections miss and Gallaher ruptured a disc in his spine while trying to correct the angle of his dive at the last moment. *Hiryu* recorded three very near misses astern before Jaccard's bomb burst below the forward elevator and blew it bodily against the bridge, obscuring Kaku's forward vision but shielding him from the blast of three more bombs that landed close together, all port forward just in front of the island. There was a perceptible pause between the first and subsequent hits and at the rear of Shumway's section, Ensign Alden Hansen reported that his own bomb and those of all of those ahead of him missed, which narrows the field (see **Appendix D**).

The dive bombers were not safe even after pushing over and Ensign Philip Cobb was amazed when one Zero managed to make two passes at him in the midst of his dive. Lieutenant Harold Bottomley reported another that kept him in its sights by performing a 'falling leaf' to match his descent. It is fair to assume that those attacked either jettisoned their bombs or were at least put off their aim, and it is pleasing to think that Best and Kroeger avenged their fallen comrade by once more delivering their ship-killing heavy ordnance on target. Two of the surviving VB-3 tail-enders dived on *Haruna*, which recorded two very near misses and strafing, with a cryptic diagram showing one aircraft passing over her in a zigzag path before bombing close alongside. This was probably Ensign Charles Lane, one of those who had lost their bombs to electrical malfunction before the first strike, on *Soryu*, and who was almost suicidally determined to deliver his second bomb on target.

On board *Nagara*, combat photographer Teiichi Makishima could not bring himself to photograph the burning *Hiryu*, 'running at high speed like a mad bull', the forced draught driving the flames back along her hull. Kaku could not heave to and give his damage-control parties a chance to tackle the blaze because no sooner had the dive bombers made off than it began to rain bombs again. These came from a flight of six B-17s, under Major George Blakey, which had been diverted while on its way to Midway from Oahu. Blakey calculated that the additional 400-mile round trip precluded climbing to normal bombing altitude, so the flight proceeded at 3,600 feet, where it was hit by both flak and fighters. Battle damage prevented two B-17s from bombing altogether, while half of the remaining bombs hung up, but the group optimistically reported a straddle and a hit on *Hiryu*, and a destroyer sunk.

Arriving at about the same time and judging the carrier doomed, Stebbins and his fourteen *Hornet* dive bombers (two had turned back) went after the

Hiryu **photographed by a Japanese aircraft on 5 June. Note gutted bow section and elevator obscuring the bridge.**

nearest substantial target. Now the magic mantle of the *Tone* #4 floatplane extended over its parent too. At 1705, *Tone* was hove to in order to recover the aircraft when, with its usual blithe imprecision, it radioed 'sight enemy planes' just as the ship's lookouts spotted them and the main armament opened fire. *Tone* recorded planes flying over her at 1707, presumably those retiring from the attacks on *Hiryu* and *Haruna*, evasive manoeuvres as she regained battle speed at 1710, an attack by three dive bombers at 1720, four more plus three from level bombers at 1728 and a last salvo from three level bombers at 1732, for a total of thirteen bombs landing within splashing range of her in what must have been an invigorating twelve minutes.

The additional reports of level-bombing attacks are difficult to attribute, but coincide approximately with the attack made by Sweeney and four of his remaining six Midway B-17s, which arrived over the target at 20,000 feet slightly ahead of Blakey, while another two, delayed by engine trouble, bombed some considerable time later. Sweeney's group was not interfered with, dropped twenty-eight bombs on a cruiser and believed they had crippled her. Between forty minutes and an hour later, the last two high-level Midway B-17s believed they had hit the burning carrier and a battleship.

Some of these were dropped on *Tone*, but *Chikuma* reported five bombs off her port bow at 1732, three close astern and four off her port bow at 1745, and four off her starboard bow at 1810. The much-bombed *Haruna* recorded a last three at 1826, in a diagram showing that, had she not turned violently to starboard, at least one would have hit her bow. Although they were again deceived by the huge splashes that seemed to envelop their targets, the B-17s kept the Mobile Force under almost continuous attack for over an hour. Not only did this prevent *Hiryu*'s crew from containing the fire in her bow, it also kept other ships from coming to her rescue opportunely, so it seems fair to award VII Army Air Force an 'assist' on this one.

Possibly the most famous photograph of the Pacific War: *Hornet* Dauntlesses flying towards the smoking *Mikuma*

Night then came to give the battered Mobile Force some respite, but this was only because two further attacks from Midway did not prosper. At 1915, six Dauntlesses, under Captain Marshall Tyler and six Vindicators, under Norris flew out to the location of a burning carrier reported by a PBY, but found nothing – it was probably *Kaga*, which sank at 1925. On the way back, Norris, who was unfamiliar with night flying and disoriented, dived into the ocean from 10,000 feet, his flight following him down until his aircraft disappeared. Simard also sent the eleven PT boats based at Midway and Kure against the same target, but they too found nothing. At dawn the next day, two of them saw a column of smoke to the west and raced towards it, only to find a large oil slick and debris – presumably from *Akagi*, finally scuttled at 0500.

It would be otiose to list the orders and counterorders that emanated from Yamamoto following the wrecking of *Hiryu* – they reveal nothing that we have not discussed already. Spruance steamed east during the night, a decision that has been much celebrated by historians although he himself, in the light of both Nimitz's instructions and the IJN's known capabilities, regarded it as what we would today call a 'no-brainer', and left the bridge to get some sleep. But there was no sleep for anyone on *Yamato* or the lesser

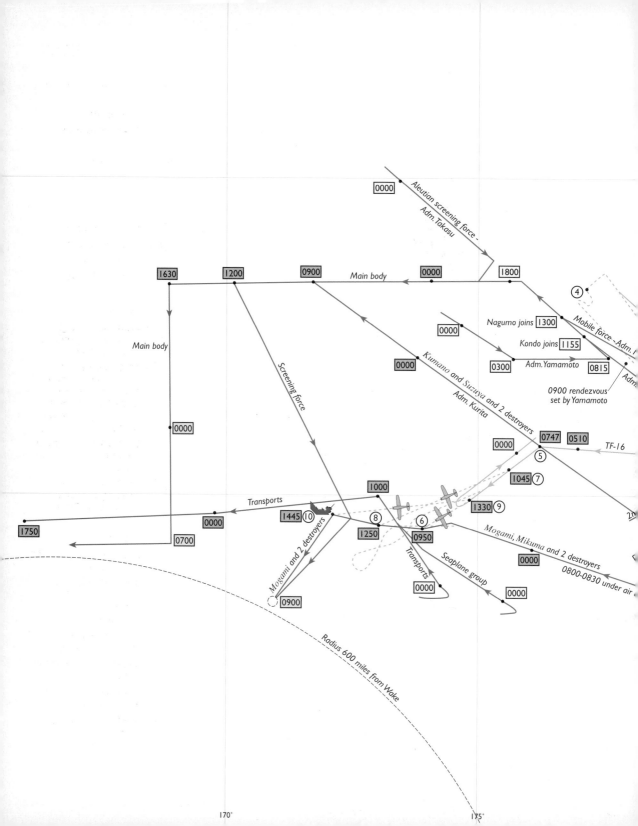

0000

Aleutian screening force -
Adm. Takasu

1630   1200   0900   *Main body*   0000   1800

4

Main body

0000   *Nagumo joins* 1300   Mobile force - Adm. I
Kondo joins 1155
Kumano and Suzuya and 2 destroyers   0000   0300   *Adm. Yamamoto*   0815   Adm

Screening force   Adm. Kurita   0800 *rendezvous*
set by Yamamoto

0000   0747   0510   TF-16

5

1045   7

0000   1000   1330   9

1750   0000   1445   10   8   6   *Mogami, Mikuma and 2 destroyers*

0700   1250   0950   0800-0830 *under air*

Mogami and 2 destroyers   *Transports*   *Transports*   *Seaplane group*   0000   0000

0900   0000

Radius 600 miles from Wake

170°   175°

Map 16
Action on 5–6 June

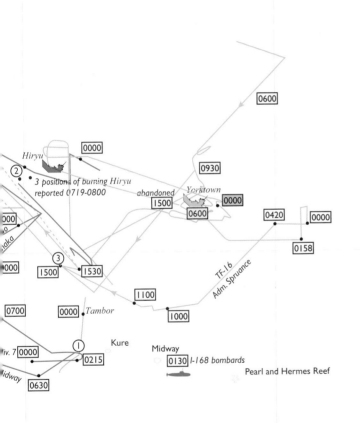

35°

0000	Action on 4 June
0000	Action on 5 June
0000	Action on 6 June
0000	Action on 7 June

June 5

① **0215**: *Tambor* sights Crudiv. 7; *Mogami* and *Mikuna* collide.

② **0719**: Midway patrol planes report burning carrier (*Hiryu*), two battleships, cruisers and destroyers in this position.

③ **1500-1530**: *Enterprise* and *Hornet* launch strikes.

④ **1830**: *Enterprise-Hornet* group attack destroyer *Tanikaze*.

June 6

⑤ **0757**: *Hornet* launches attack group.

⑥ **0950**: *Hornet* group attacks *Mogami*, *Mikuma* and two destroyers.

⑦ **1045**: *Enterprise* launches attack group.

⑧ **1250**: *Enterprise* group attacks.

⑨ **1330**: *Hornet* launches attack group.

⑩ **1445**: *Hornet* group attacks.

30°

180°   175°

flagships, where staff officers clutched at straws, as men in shock will. Fuchida reported the following telling dialogue.

> ... one of the officers protested to Ugaki, 'But how can we apologize to His Majesty for this defeat?' Admiral Yamamoto, who had remained silent during the discussions, spoke up now. 'Leave that to me,' he said abruptly. I am the only one who must apologize to His Majesty.'

Ugaki recorded that Yamamoto was wracked by severe intestinal spasms, attributed to worms, but the more likely diagnosis is that the pain was psychosomatic.

Hours after everybody else had abandoned ship, Captain Kosaku Ariga, commander of Destroyer Division 4, climbed on board *Akagi* and ordered Captain Taijiro Aoki to untie himself from her anchor. Aoki obeyed, but was a broken man for the rest of his life. On *Hiryu*, Yamaguchi and Kaku chose to die together, making grim jokes about how they would use the ship's payroll to obtain preferential treatment in hell, having formally ordered their reluctant officers to leave them. The *Bushido* code indicated that Nagumo should also have committed suicide but, possibly mindful that he would be honour-bound to follow him, Kusaka dissuaded him. Kuroshima, who perhaps should have disembowelled himself, did not.[4]

Back at Pearl, Nimitz's war diarist cautiously noted that if the outcome of this 'greatest sea battle since Jutland' was as unfavourable to the Japanese as reports indicated, it 'would virtually end their expansion'. But, he added, 'we lost a large percentage of highly trained pilots who will be difficult to replace.' Difficult, but not impossible, whereas the IJN simply did not have the reserves of men or equipment to recover from the blow. As well as the four carriers, over two hundred and fifty front-line aircraft were lost, and although about half of the aircrew survived, irreplaceable cadres and inspirational leaders had died. Skill levels dropped precipitously thereafter, as the best flyers were retained in action instead of returning home to train new pilots, until at last youngsters who were barely able to fly solo were sent on Kamikaze missions

in the cynical recognition that they would not be coming back anyway, while the last of the carriers were sacrificed as bait in the Leyte Gulf battle. This would have happened anyway, for contrary to the basic premise of Operation MI the enemy did indeed have the stomach to fight. But while damning the fecklessness of their leaders, we can still honour the unflagging bravery of the young men whose lives they threw away.

There is a Colombian proverb that says when things are not going your way even dogs pee on you, and the Japanese equivalent must have passed through Yamamoto's mind early in the morning of 5 June. He cancelled the shore-bombardment mission of Kurita's heavy cruisers at 0020, when they were 60 miles from Midway, but forgot that he had ordered *I-168* to shell the islands as well, with the result that at about 0125 Lieutenant Commander Yahachi

Crew abandoning the sinking *Mikuma* in the evening of 6 June

**Another view
of the shattered
*Mikuma***

Tanabe fired eight rounds, all into the lagoon. The reaction on shore was such as to leave no doubt that the US defences were intact, and the submarine submerged amid a hail of shells.

Kurita, on *Kumano*, led *Suzuya*, *Mikuma* and *Mogami* away in close order at 28 knots, but at 0215 sighted a USN submarine on the surface (*Tambor*, with Spruance's son among her officers) and ordered an emergency 45° turn to port. *Mogami* miscalculated the distance and rammed *Mikuma*, tearing a hole in her sister ship's fuel tank and losing 40 feet of her own bow, the mangled remains twisted almost flat. She could make 12 knots shortly afterwards, but was now deprived of the 35-knot battle speed that had served *Tone* and *Chikuma* so well.

With a US submarine in the vicinity and Midway only 100 miles away, Kurita could not afford to risk his two undamaged cruisers and therefore sped away, ordering *Mikuma*, which would not have slowed him down greatly, to remain with *Mogami* along with the destroyers *Arashio* and *Asashio*. *Tambor* never achieved a firing resolution, but had signalled 'many unidentified ships' after the sighting that caused the collision, and on Midway the ground crews swarmed to arm and refuel their remaining aircraft. 45,000 gallons of fuel were pumped by hand from 55-gallon drums and eight B-17s, six Dauntlesses and six Vindicators were prepared for a morning strike. Sweeney flew back to Oahu with some damaged B-17s and the Army detachment remained under the command of Lieutenant Colonel Brooke Allen, while Tyler became the third CO of VMSB-241 within twenty-four hours and Fleming took over the Vindicator division.

Simard ordered the B-17s into the air at dawn, but early morning mist shrouded the Japanese ships and the Forts were circling Kure Island despondently when, at 0630, a PBY signalled 'two battleships bearing 264 distant 125 miles course 268 speed 15', the first report that was accurate as to location, if not ship identification, since the battle began. At 0700 the two divisions of VMSB-241 took off, the 40-mile oil slick from *Mikuma* soon leading them directly to their target. At about 0810 Tyler's Dauntlesses dived on *Mogami* from 10,000 feet and straddled her, one bomb bursting close alongside and riddling the bridge and funnel.

Fleming's slower division turned aside to investigate a submarine that did not linger on the surface and so arrived at around 0830 to make a glide-bombing attack on *Mikuma* from 4,000 feet. None of its bombs hit the ship but Fleming's aircraft, which was seen to be on fire even before he released, did not pull out. His Vindicator crashed into *Mikuma*'s 'X' turret, and flames drawn through the air intakes swept through one of her engine rooms. Ten minutes later the B-17s arrived and dropped forty bombs, claiming one hit but obtaining none.

To Spruance, who had reversed course during the night and was now heading back towards *Yorktown*, the early morning signal from *Tambor* indicated a possible assault on Midway, so at 0420 he ordered Task Force 16 to sail at full speed towards the islands. At 0930 he turned west-north-west after PBYs confirmed that there were only the two damaged cruisers to the south-west, but falsely reported damaged carriers withdrawing to the north-west.

It was while preparing to launch a full-force strike against the latter that the airmen on *Enterprise* rebelled against Browning's intention to launch them at maximum range with 1,000-pound bombs. Shumway and Lieutenant Wallace Short, now the commanders of the combined *Yorktown* and *Enterprise* scouting and bombing squadrons, enlisted the support of the injured Gallaher and McLusky. These two confronted Browning on the bridge and requested that the launch should be postponed for an hour and the aircraft rearmed with 500-pound bombs. A shouting match between McClusky and Browning ended when Spruance said, 'I will do whatever you pilots want'. Browning stormed off to his cabin in a rage, the aircraft were rearmed and the launch was postponed until after 1500.

Starting at 1512, *Enterprise* launched thirty-two dive bombers, flying together under Shumway, but *Hornet* was once again wrong-footed and launched separate strikes, ten under Ring at 1530 and seventeen under Rodee at 1543. Although post-war comparison of charts confirmed that they came very close to finding the retreating Japanese, it was probably as well that they did not, for by now Nagumo and Kondo had joined Yamamoto and the likely damage the dive bombers could have done with their light loads on armoured vessels would not have been worth the casualties.

On their way back, first Ring's division and then Shumway's group attacked the destroyer *Tanikaze*, which had been sent back to ensure that *Hiryu* had sunk. *Tanikaze* had earlier been attacked by four B-17s out of Midway and would be attacked by another three before the day ended. In return for one Dauntless shot down (Adams of VS-5, whose sighting had doomed *Hiryu* the day before), two B-17s that failed to return and one hundred and twenty-two bombs, a fragment caused an explosion in one of the destroyer's gun mounts and six men were killed.

It was therefore a very angry and frustrated group of aviators who were turned loose on *Mogami* and *Mikuma* the next day. Ring at last got to lead what he regarded as a proper strike, eight dive bombers with 500-pound bombs and seventeen with 1,000-pound bombs, escorted by eight fighters, and they savaged the enemy stragglers. *Mogami* took two heavy hits, one that destroyed her after turret and another amidships that started a fire in her torpedo room. *Mikuma* was also hit, as was the destroyer *Asashio*, but by a lighter bomb that did not disable her. Despite determined strafing by the fighters, AA fire was sufficiently accurate to down two dive bombers, with the loss of both crews.

After the *Hornet* group returned, *Enterprise* launched thirty-one dive bombers led by Short, followed by the three remaining torpedo bombers under the command of Lieutenant Robert Laub, with orders from Spruance to attack only if the bombers completely silenced the Japanese guns. They did

Hughes **stands by** *Yorktown* **after recovering two wounded men**

The face of defeat: *Hiryu* survivors rescued by *Ballard*. Man in foreground may be Chief Engineer Elso, whom the others considered throwing overboard for monopolizing the water supply

Hammann sinks after being broken in half by the salvo of torpedoes from _I-168_ that also doomed _Yorktown_

not and Laub took his torpedoes home, but it was not for want of trying. The need for radio silence gone, the pilots broadcast a running commentary:

> This is Wally pushing over on the rear ship now, close up on me.
>
> Hey, any of you fellows got any bombs? There's a Mogi-class cruiser in the rear.
>
> Oh Baby, did we put that goddamn can on fire!
>
> Get the sons-of-bitches again. OK, that's fine.
>
> That one blew up too, good hit, good hit.
>
> Tojo, you son-of-a-bitch, you'll not get your laundry this week.

They hit _Mogami_ twice more but concentrated on _Mikuma_, scoring at least five heavy hits that destroyed her 'C' turret, mortally wounded her captain and completed the destruction of her engine rooms. _Mogami_ had prudently jettisoned her torpedoes, but *Mikuma* had not and a further hit set off a massive secondary explosion.

At about this time, B-17s from Midway failed to find the cruisers, but spotted another vessel, which they attacked employing simultaneous bombing from a tight formation, the only time the technique was employed during the battle. The target vanished amid mountainous sea-bursts, and the army pilots jubilantly reported sinking a cruiser within fifteen minutes. We can be sure USS *Grayling* crash-dived a great deal faster than that, and when she surfaced again the signal sent by her shaken captain was not such as to promote inter-service harmony.

The saga of *Yorktown* now drew to a close. With only one destroyer standing by to scuttle her if necessary, early on 5 June 1942 a mortally wounded sailor still on board attracted attention by firing a machine-gun, he and another man, who survived, being brought off in a whaleboat. The little tug *Vireo* arrived next from her station at Pearl and Hermes Reef and took the carrier under tow, barely able to keep her head into the wind, and later two destroyers from Task Force 16 joined the group. Three more arrived the next day, carrying a party of key *Yorktown* personnel under the command of Buckmaster, who had prevailed upon Spruance to let him try to save his ship.

Approaching at the same time, *I-168* was not daunted by the array of destroyers and by 1334 had achieved a firing resolution off the carrier's starboard side, where the destroyer *Hammann* was lending assistance to Buckmaster's salvage party. Tanabe fired four torpedoes in a close spread and only one missed. One broke *Hammann* in half and she sank rapidly, the death toll multiplied in grisly fashion when her own depth charges exploded not far below the surface. Two more hit *Yorktown*, and although the immediate result of this drastic counter-flooding was to correct her list somewhat, Buckmaster evacuated his men to *Vireo*, gallantly held alongside the grinding wreck for forty minutes. *Yorktown* settled slowly, doing honour to her constructors to the last, only rolling over and sinking at dawn the next day. Tanabe audaciously took *I-168* under *Yorktown* and, although jolted by depth charges from *Balch* and *Benham*, managed to get away, the air on board foul and the batteries nearly exhausted. Forced to surface sooner than was prudent, his engine exhaust was seen on the horizon and he was pursued by *Monaghan* and *Hughes*. Tanabe was lucky as well as skilled and not only escaped but also survived the war.

Three-hundred miles to the south-west the crew of *Mikuma* began to abandon ship, and *Arashio* was crowded with survivors when Ring and twenty-three *Hornet* dive bombers returned at 1445. This was the closest that any surface units came to each other during this battle, with Task Force 16 visible astern when Ring's men dived on the cruisers and completed the destruction of *Mikuma*. *Mogami* was also hit at least once more, while a bomb burst with devastating effect on the crowded stern of *Arashio*. Later still, two dive bombers were launched to photograph the results, obtaining evidence of just how much punishment a Japanese heavy cruiser could take before succumbing, as *Mikuma* finally did two hours later.

Lieutenant Cleo Dobson, flying one of the photo-reconnaissance aircraft, intended to strafe in revenge for a similar action taken by the Japanese reported after the sinking of *Langley* in the Java Sea. But 'after flying over those [hundreds of] poor devils in the water I was chicken hearted and couldn't make myself open up on them'. It might have been more merciful if he had, because US forces recovered only two *Mikuma* survivors three days later. The remaining three ships limped off to gain air cover from Wake and to report more than a thousand men killed and missing, while *Mogami* would be out of action for over a year.

12

CODA

Yamamoto sailed south during the night of 6/7 June 1942, hoping that the US carriers would be foolish enough to close, but after pounding the two cruisers there was nothing Spruance could certainly gain that outweighed what he might lose, so he turned Task Force 16 away once more and sailed back to Pearl. In the Aleutians operation, Attu and Kiska were occupied on 5 and 7 June, and Yamamoto heavily reinforced Admiral Moshiro Hosagaya's Fifth Fleet. But Theobald refused to be drawn and the capture of the two undefended, barren islands was the sole achievement of the whole enterprise. One last notable casualty was Major General Clarence Tinker, commander of VII Army Air Force, who insisted on leading a flight of four long-distance Liberator bombers from Midway in an attack on Wake. They did not find the island and Tinker's aircraft did not return. The battle was over bar the shouting, but there was a lot of that, particularly by the Army, and although Nimitz diplomatically left its claims unchallenged, there were inter-service brawls when the fleet returned to port.

Hopelessly belated improvizations could not conceal that Yamamoto was mentally defeated when he still had the means to salvage the operation. With his splendid command in flames around him, Nagumo's numbness and command paralysis is understandable. But the reason why the chapter on Midway is the fulcrum of this account is that Yamamoto decided to withdraw his still vastly superior force not so much because he had lost his fleet carriers, but because it had become apparent that the atoll could not be captured. Although Nimitz certainly did not underestimate the importance of the islands, he saw them as an adjunct to the fleet engagement, whereas they were the *sine qua non* of Operation MI. With plenty of time in which to do so, the best minds of the IJN had thought themselves into a no-win situation. I believe a belated realization that this was the case, as well as the collapse of whatever wider ambition he entertained, was what unmanned Yamamoto during the long night of 4/5 June.

When the Combined Fleet returned to Japan, the survivors of the First Air Fleet were quarantined lest they should contradict the official version that a great victory had been won. We began by considering Miyamoto Musashi's view that the field of battle is in the mind and, according to that premise, to force one's enemy into a denial of reality is surely the greatest victory of all. Thus while the USN immediately introduced new procedures and set in motion programmes to correct the many errors that Nimitz had identified in the conduct of the battle, the IJN was locked into a false version of events, not only *vis-à-vis* the Army and the public, but even internally. Among the few lessons drawn was the false tactical conclusion that fighters should be held back to defend the carriers in preference to escorting the bombers when, as we have seen, the Vals and Kates were impossibly vulnerable without the presence of the Zeros in the role for which they were designed. At the operational level, the folly of dispersion was not addressed, communications security was not radically improved and the installation of radar was not accelerated, making further, similar defeats inevitable.

Lest we should overestimate how much is resolved by battle at the deepest mental levels, during the first-ever imperial radio broadcast on 15 August 1945, Hirohito made the seemingly breathtaking understatement that events had 'not necessarily' developed in the national interest. But even a disastrously lost war might seem like a mere incident to one thinking in terms of thousands of years. In the 'Monologue', Hirohito revealingly commented (my emphasis) that 'should we continue to fight, it would not only result in the ultimate collapse and disappearance of the Japanese nation, *but it would also lead to the total destruction of civilisation.* Such being the case, how are We to save the millions of Our subjects, or to atone Ourselves before the hallowed spirits of Our Imperial Ancestors?' As Musashi would have put it, this should be given thorough and thoughtful reflection.

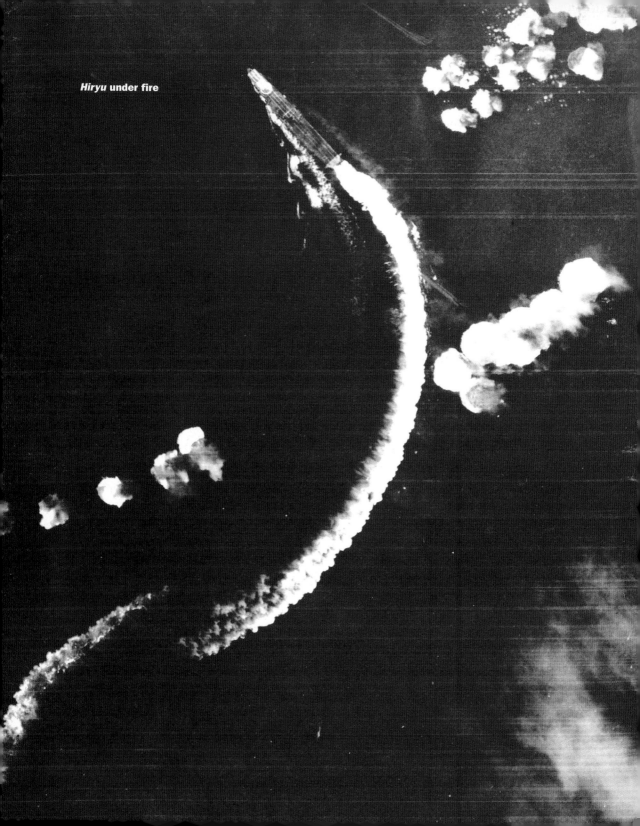
Hiryu under fire

ORDER OF BATTLE – IMPERIAL JAPANESE NAVY

Navy Ministry	
Minister	Admiral Shigetaro Shimada
Vice Minister	Vice Admiral Teijiro Toyoda
Naval Affairs	Rear Admiral Takazumi Oka
Mobilization	Rear Admiral Zenshiro Hoshina
Aviation	Rear Admiral Takijiro Onishi
Personnel	Rear Admiral Giichi Nakahara

Naval General Staff	
Chief of General Staff	Admiral Osami Nagano
Vice Chief of Staff	Vice Admiral Seiichi Ito
First Bureau (operations)	Rear Admiral Shigeru Fukudome
Plans Officer	Captain Baron Sadatoshi Tomioka
Air Officer	Commander Tatsukichi Miyo
Second Bureau (A/S warfare, logistics)	Rear Admiral Yoshio Suzuki
Third Bureau (intelligence)	Rear Admiral Kanji Ogawa
American Section	Captain Bunjiro Yamaguchi
Fourth Bureau (communications)	Rear Admiral Shigeharu Kaneko

Naval General Staff	
Commander in Chief	Admiral Isoroku Yamamoto
Chief of Staff	Rear Admiral Matome Ugaki
Senior Staff Officer	Captain Kameto Kuroshima
Operations/Administration	Commander Yasuji Watanabe
Military policy	Commander Shigeru Fujii
Submarines	Commander Takayasu Arima
Navigation	Commander Shigeru Nagata
Communications	Commander Yujiro Wada
Meteorology	Commander Kanai Ota
Air Officer	Captain Yoshitake Miwa
Air Operations	Commander Akira Sasaki

Notes Submerged displacements given for submarines, nominal (not fully laden) for surface vessels. See Jentschura for full details. Only main armament given for most ships, AA for those that had need of it at Midway. Aircraft numbers are those operational morning of 4 June 1942. The Japanese put the family name first (thus Yamamoto Isoroku), but for clarity the western style is used here and diacritical marks omitted.

Sources
Jentschura, H, Jung, D and Mickel, P, *Warships of the Imperial Japanese Navy, 1869–1945*, London, 1977.
Dull, P, *A Battle History of the Imperial Japanese Navy, 1941–1945*, Annapolis, 1978.
Fuchida, M and Okumiya, M, *Midway, the Battle that Doomed Japan*, Annapolis, 1955.

MIDWAY OPERATION
ADVANCE SUBMARINE FORCE

Unit	Name (date completed)	Commander	Normal displacement, Speed, Armament
SIXTH FLEET: Vice Admiral Teruhisa Komatsu – Chief of Staff, Rear Admiral Hisashi Mito (at Kwajalein)			
Flagship (light cruiser)	*Katori* (1940) ℞	Capt Owada	6,280 tons, 18 kts, 4 x 5.5" guns, 1 floatplane
Submarine Squadron 3	*Yasukuni Maru* (1930)		11,933 GRT requisitioned passenger liner
(RAdm Chimaki Kono)	*I-168* (1934)	LCdr Tanabe	
	I-169 (1935)		2,440 tons, 23/ 8 kts, 1 x 4" gun, 6 x 21" TT,
	I-171 (1935)		
	I-174 (1938)		2,564 tons, 23/ 8 kts
	I-175 (1938)		1 x 5" gun, 6 x 21" TT
Submarine Squadron 5	*Rio de Janeiro Maru* (1930) ℞		9,627 GRT requisitioned passenger liner
(RAdm Tadashige	*I-156* (1929)	LCdr Ohashi	
Daigo)	*I-157* (1929)	LCdr Nakajima	
	I-158 (1928)	LCdr Kitamura	2,300 tons, 20/ 8 kts, 1 x 4.7" gun, 8 x 21" TT
	I-159 (1929)	LCdr Yoshimatsu	
	I-162 (1930)	LCdr Kinashi	
	I-165 (1932)	LCdr Harada	2,330 tons, 20/ 8 kts,
	I-166 (1932)	LCdr Tanaka	1 x 3.9" gun, 6 x 21" TT
Submarine Division 13	*I-121* (1927)	LCdr Fujimori	
(Capt Takeharu	*I-122* (1927)	LCdr Norita	1,768 tons, 14/ 7 kts, 1 x 5.5" gun, 4 x 21" TT
Miyazaki)	*I-123* (1928)	LCdr Ueno	

FIRST FLEET
MAIN FORCE (Sortied from Hiroshima 29 May)

Admiral Isokoru Yamamoto – Chief of Staff, Rear Admiral Matome Ugaki			
Battleship	*Yamato* (1941) ℞	Capt Takayanagi	67,123 tons, 27 kts, 9 x 18.11" guns, 7 floatplanes
Division 1	*Nagato* (1920)	Capt Yano	Modernized 1936: 39,130 tons, 25 kts,
(Adm Yamamoto)	*Mutsu* (1921)	Capt Yamazumi	8 x 16.14" guns, 3 floatplanes
Carrier Force	*Hosho* (1922)	Capt Umetani	9,630 tons, 25 kts, could carry 20 aircraft
(Capt Kaoru Umetani)	Air Unit	Lt Irikiin	9 Mitsubishi A5M4 (type 96) 'Claude' fighters
			9 Nakajima B5N2 (type 97) 'Kate' attack bombers
	Yukaze (1921) Rescue ship	LCdr Kajimoto	Rebuilt as fast transport 1936: 1,552 tons, 36 kts
Special Duty Force	*Chiyoda* (1938	Capt Harada	12,500 tons, 28kts, 6 x 5" guns, 12 midget subs
(Capt Kaku Harada)	*Nisshin* (1942)	Capt Komazawa	12,500 tons, 28kts, 6 x 5" guns, 5 MTBs
SCREEN: Rear Admiral Shintaro Hashimoto			
Destroyer Squadron 3	*Sendai* (1924) ℞	Capt Morishita	5,595 tons, 35 kts, 7 x 5.5" guns, 8 x 24" TT
Destroyer Division 11	*Fubuki* (1928)	Capt Yamashita	
(Capt Kiichiro Shoji)	*Shirayuki* (1928)	Cdr Sugahara	2,090 tons, 38 kts, 6 x 5" guns, 9 x 24" TTs
	Hatsuyuki (1929)	LCdrKamiura	
	Murakumo (1929)	Cdr Higashi	
Destroyer Division 19	*Isonami* (1928)	Cdr Sugama	
(Capt Ranji Oe)	*Uranami* (1929)	Cdr Hagio	2,090 tons, 38 kts, 6 x 5" guns, 9 x 24" TTs
	Shikinami (1929)	Cdr Kawahashi	
	Ayanami (1930)	Cdr Sakuma	
Supply Unit 1	*Naruto* (1923)	Capt Nishioka	15,450 tons, 14 kts, 2 x 5.5" guns
(oilers)	*Toei Maru* (1938)	–	10,000 GRT requisitioned tanker

Comments	Sunk
	Air attack 17 Feb 1944
	Submarine 31 Jan 1944
Cordon A	Submarine 27 Jul 1943
Lat. 19°30' N to 23°30' N	Air attack 4 Apr 1944
on long. 167° W	Destroyers 1 Feb 1944
I-68 shelled Midway 5 June, sank	Air attack 12 Apr 1944
Hammann and Yorktown 6 June	Destroyers 4 Feb 1944
	Air attack 17 Feb 1944
	Later converted to Kaiten
Cordon B	(suicide mini-subs) carriers.
Lat. 29°30' N, long. 164°30' W	All scuttled 1946
to	
Lat. 26°10' N, long. 167° W	
	Air attack 27 Jun 1945
	Submarine 17 Jul 1944
	Scrapped 1945
Supposed to refuel aircraft at French Frigate Shoals,	Submarine 10 jun 1945
Laysan and Lisianski Is. in aborted Operation K	Destroyer 29 Aug 1942

Comments	Sunk
Largest battleship class ever built	Air attack 7 Apr 1945
First 16" gun super-Dreadnoughts ever built.	Bikini nuclear test 1946
Nagato fleet flagship to 1942	Accident 8 Jun 1943
	Scrapped 1947
Most orbats give either 'Claudes' or 'Kates', but Zuiho with Second Fleet	
carried both and Hosho would surely have been similarly equipped	
	Scrapped 1947
Originally seaplane carriers, later converted to light aircraft carriers	Air attack 25 Oct 1944
	Air attack 22 Jul 1943
	Air attack 2 Nov 1943
	Surface 11 Oct 1942
	Air attack 3 Mar 1943
	Air attack 17 Jul 1943
	Air attack 12 Oct 1942
	Submarine 9 Apr 1943
	Air attack 26 Oct 1944
	Submarine 12 Sep 1944
	Surface 15 Nov 1942
	Air attack 4 Mar 1944
	Submarine 18 Jan 1943

MOBILE FORCE
(Sortied from Hiroshima 27 May)

Unit	Name (date completed)	Commander	Normal displacement, Speed, Armament
FIRST CARRIER STRIKE FORCE: Vice Admiral Chuichi Nagumo – Chief of Staff, Rear Admiral Ryunosuke Kusaka			
Carrier Division 1	*Akagi* (1927) ⚑	Capt Aoki	Modernized 1936: 41,300 tons, 31 kts
(VAdm Nagumo)	Air Unit	Cdr Fuchida*	6 x 8", 12 x 4.7", 28 x 25mm guns
Air Operations	Fighter Wing	LCdr Itaya*	18 Mitsubishi A6M2 (type 0) 'Zero' fighters
(Cdr Minoru Genda)	Dive Bomber Wing	LCdr Chihaya*	18 Aichi D3A1 (type 99) 'Val' dive bombers
	Attack Bomber Wing	LCdr Murata *	18 Nakajima B5N2 (type 97) 'Kate' Attack bombers
	Kaga (1928)	Capt Okada (K)	Modernized 1935: 42,500 tons, 28 kts
	Air Unit	LCdr Kusumi (K)*	10 x 8", 16 x 5", 22 x 25mm guns
	Fighter Wing	Lt Sato	18 'Zeros'
	Dive Bomber Wing	Lt Ogawa (K)*	18 'Vals'
	Attack Bomber Wing	Lt Kitajima*	27 'Kates'
NB Each carrier had three spare aircraft of each type and they were ferrying 33 Zeros of the sixth Air Group intended for the future Midway air base (LCdr Kokufuda commanding) for a total of 294. Nominal aircraft complement for *Akagi* was 91, *Kaga* 90, *Hiryu* 73 and *Soryu* 71 for a total of 325, so the First Air Fleet was significantly under strength.			
Carrier Division 2	*Hiryu* (1939) ⚑	Capt Kaku (K)	20,250 tons, 34 kts
(RAdm Tamon Yamaguchi)	Air Unit	Lt Tomonaga (K)	12 x 5", 31 x 25mm guns
Air Operations	Fighter Wing	Lt Mori (K)	18 'Zeros'
(Cdr Takashi Hashiguchi)	Dive Bomber Wing	Lt Kobayashi (K)	18 'Vals'
	Attack Bomber Wing	Lt Kikuchi (K)	18 'Kates'
	Soryu (1937)	Capt Yanagimoto (K)	18,800 tons, 34 kts
	Air Unit	LCdr Egusa*	12 x 5" guns, 28 x 25mm guns
	Fighter Wing	Lt Suganami*	18 'Zeros'
	Dive Bomber Wing	Lt Ikeda	18 'Vals'
	Attack Bomber Wing	Lt Abe*	18 'Kates'
SUPPORT FORCE: Rear Admiral Hiroaki Abe			
Cruiser Division 8	*Tone* (1938) ⚑	Capt Okada	13,320 tons, 35 kts, 5 floatplanes
(RAdm Abe)	*Chikuma* (1939)	Capt Komura	8 x 8", 12 x 25mm guns,
Battleship Division 3.2	*Haruna* (1915)	Capt Koma	Modernized 1934: 34,500 tons, 30 kts, 3 floatplanes
(Capt Tamotsu Koma)	*Kirishima* (1915)	Capt Iwabuchi	8 x 14", 14 x 6", 8 x 5", 4 x 40mm, 8 x 25 mm guns
SCREEN: Rear Admiral Susumu Kimura			
Destroyer Squadron 10	*Nagara* (1922) ⚑	Capt Naoi	5,570 tons, 36 kts, 7 x 5.5", 2 x 3" guns, 8 x 24" TT
Destroyer Division 4	*Nowaki* (1941)	Cdr Koga	2,490 tons, 35 kts,
(Capt Kosaku Ariga)	*Arashi* (1941)	Cdr Watanabe	
	Hagikaze (1941)	Cdr Iwagami	6 x 5", 4 x 25mm guns, 8 x 24" TT
	Maikaze (1941)	Cdr Nakasugi	
Destroyer	*Kazegumo* (1942)	Cdr Yoshida	2,520 tons, 35 kts,
Division 10	*Yugumo* (1941)	Cdr Semba	6 x 5", 4 x 25mm guns, 8 x 24" TT
(Capt Toshio Abe)	*Makigumo* (1942)	Cdr Fujita	
Destroyer Division 17	*Urakaze* (1940)	Cdr Siraishi	
(Capt Masayuki Kitamura)	*Isokaze* (1940)	Cdr Toshima	2,490 tons, 35 kts,
	Tanikaze (1941)	Cdr Katsumi	6 x 5", 4 x 25mm guns, 8 x 24" TT
	Hamakaze (1941)	Cdr Orita	
Supply Unit	5 oilers	Capt Oto	10,000 GRT requisitioned tankers
Escort Destroyer	*Akigumo* (1941)	Cdr Soma	See *Kazegumo* above

Comments	Sunk
221 of 1,630 killed	5 June 1942
Appendectomy on 1 June	
* see **Appendix D**	
Midway 18 (0), all lost in hangar	
17 destroyed on deck, 1 to Hiryu	
c.800 of 1,708 killed	4 June 1942
Leader of second strike, destroyed on deck	
* see **Appendix D**	
Led 'Vals' Midway 18 (1), 17 lost in hangar	
second strike – destroyed on deck	
381 of c.1,100 killed, 35 captured	5 June 1942
Led Midway & second Yorktown strikes	
* see **Appendix D**	
first *Yorktown* strike 18 (13)	
Midway 18 (4), second *Yorktown* strike 9 (5)	
718 of 1,103 killed	4 June 1942
Yokosuka D4Y1 'Judy' scout to *Hiryu*	
* see **Appendix D**	
Destroyed on deck	
Midway 18 (1), 17 lost in hangar	
Attacked 4 June	Air attack 24 Jul 1945
Attacked 4 June	Air attack 25 Oct 1944
Attacked 4 June	Air attack 28 Jul 1945
Attacked 4 June	Surface 15 Nov 1942
Nagumo's flagship after loss of *Akagi*	Submarine 7 Aug 1944
	Surface 26 Oct 1944
Arashi depth charged *Nautilus* on 4 June. Later picked up VT-3 Ens Osmus,	Surface 7 Aug 1943
murdered after interrogation	Surface 7 Aug 1943
	Surface 17 Feb 1944
Makigumo picked up VS-6 Ens O'Flaherty & AMM Gaido,	Submarine 8 Jun 1944
murdered after interrogation	Surface 7 Oct 1943
	Mine 1 Feb 1943
	Submarine 21 Nov 1944
Attacked 4 June	Air attack 7 Apr 1945
5 June: attacked by 12 B-17s, 42 SBDs	Submarine 9 Jun 1944
	Air attack 7 Apr 1945
	All sunk 1943-44
	Submarine 11 Apr 1944

SECOND FLEET
MAIN FORCE (sortied from Hiroshima 29 May 1942)

Unit	Name (date completed)	Commander	Normal displacement, Speed, Armament
Vice Admiral Nobutake Kondo – Chief of Staff, Rear Admiral Kazutaka Shiraishi			
Cruiser Division 4	*Atago* (1932) ℞	Capt Ijuin	12,986 tons, 35 kts,
(VAdm Kondo)	*Chokai* (1932)	Capt Hayakawa	10 x 8" guns, 3 floatplanes
Cruiser Division 5	*Myoko* (1929)	Capt Miyoshi	12,374 tons, 35 kts,
(VAdm Takeo Takagi)	*Haguro* (1929)	Capt Mori	10 x 8" guns, 2 floatplanes
Battleship Division 3.2	*Kongo* (1913)	Capt Koyanagi	Modernized 1934: 34,500 tons, 30 kts, 3 floatplanes
(RAdm Gunichi Mikawa)	*Hiei* (1914)	Capt Nishida	8 x 14", 14 x 6", 8 x 5", 4 x 40mm, 8 x 25 mm guns
Carrier Force	*Zuiho* (1940)	Capt Obayashi	13,950 tons, 28 kts, 8 x 5", 38 x 25mm guns
(Capt Sueo Obayashi)	Fighter Wing	Lt Hidaka	12 'Claudes'
	Attack Bomber Wing	Lt Matsuo	12 'Kates'
	Mikazuki (1927) Rescue ship	LCdr Maeda	Rebuilt as fast transport 1936: 1,913 tons, 37 kts
SCREEN: Rear Admiral Shoji Nishimura			
Destroyer Squadron 4	*Yura* (1923) ℞	Capt S. Sato	5,570 tons, 36 kts, 7 x 5.5" guns, 8 x 24" TT
Destroyer Division 2	*Murasame* (1937)	Cdr Suenaga	
(Capt Masao Tachibana)	*Samidare* (1937)	Cdr Matsubara	1,980 tons, 34 kts,
	Harusame (1937)	Cdr Kamiyama	5 x 5" guns, 8 x 24" TT
	Yudachi (1937)	Cdr Kikkawa	
Destroyer	*Asagumo* (1938)	Cdr Iwahashi	
Division 9	*Minegumo* (1938)	Cdr Suzuki	2,370 tons, 35 kts, 6 x 5" guns, 8 x 24" TT
(Capt Yasuo Sato)	*Natsugumo* (1938)	Cdr Tsukamoto	
Supply Unit	*Sata* (1920)	Capt Murao	15,450 tons, 14 kts,
(oilers)	*Tsurumi* (1921)	Capt Fujita	2 x 5.5" guns
	Gen'Yo Maru (1937)	–	10,000 GRT
	Ken'Yo Maru (1939)	–	requisitioned tankers
Repair ship	*Akashi* (1939)	Capt Fukizawa	10,550 tons, 19 kts, 2 x 5" guns

SHORE BASED AIR SUPPORT

ELEVENTH AIR FLEET: Vice Admiral Nishizo Tsukahara – Chief of Staff, Rear Admiral Munetaka Sakamaki (at Tinian)			
Midway Expeditionary	'Betty' land-based bombers	From Wake	
Force (Capt Chisato Morita)	6 'Emily' flying boats	From Jaluit	
Twenty-fourth Air Flotilla	36 'Zeros'	Kwajalein	
(Radm Minoru Maeda)	36 'Bettys'	Kwajalein	
First Air Group	18 'Zeros', 18 'Betttys'	Aur	
(Capt Samaji Inouye)	18 'Zeros', 18 'Bettys'	Wotje	
Fourteenth Air Group	8 'Emily' flying boats	Jaluit	Intended for aborted Operation K
(Capt Daizo Nakajima)	10 'Mavis' flying boats	Wotje	

Comments	Sunk
	Submarine 23 Oct 1944
	Air attack 25 Oct 1944
	Scuttled 1946
	Surface 16 May 1945
	Submarine 21 Nov 1944
	Combined 13 Nov 1942
Could carry thirty-one aircraft	Air attack 25 Oct 1944
	–
	–
	Air attack 28 Jul 1943
	Air attack 25 Oct 1942
	Surface 6 Mar 1943
	Submarine 25 Aug 1944
	Air attack 8 Jun 1944
	Surface 13 Nov 1942
	Surface 25 Oct 1944
	Surface 6 Mar 1943
	Air attack 12 Oct 1942
	Air attack 30 Mar 1944
	Submarine 5 Aug 1942
	Air attack 20 Jun 1944
	Submarine 14 Jan 1944
	Air attack 30 Mar 1944

The 'Emilys' are probably double-counted from fourteenth Air Group (see below). Morita travelled on board Akagi to take up a command that was not to be. See also the 'Zeros' of Lt Cdr Kokufuda's Sixth Air Group embarked with the mobile force.

Two bombed Pearl Harbor, 3/4 March 1942. One shot down near Midway, 10 March 1942.

OCCUPATION FORCE
(sortied from Saipan/Guam 29 May 1942)

Unit	Name (date completed)	Commander	Normal displacement, Speed, Armament
CLOSE SUPPORT FORCE: Vice Admiral Takeo Kurita			
Cruiser Division 7	*Kumano* (1937) ℞	Capt Tanaka	Re-armed 1940: 13,887 tons, 35 kts, 3 floatplanes
(VAdm Kurita)	*Suzuya* (1937)	Capt Kimura M.	10 x 8", 8 x 5", 8 x 25mm guns, 12 x 24" TT
	Mikuma (1935)	Capt Sakiyama (K)	Re-armed 1940: 13,440 tons, 35 kts, 3 floatplanes
	Mogami (1935)	Capt Soji	10 x 8", 8 x 5", 8 x 25mm guns, 12 x 24" TT
Destroyer Division 8	*Asashio* (1937)	Cdr Yoshii	2,370 tons, 35 kts,
(Cdr Nobuki Ogawa) (W)	*Arashio* (1937)	Cdr Kuboki	6 x 5", 4 x 25mm guns, 8 x 24" TT
Oiler	*Nichiei Maru* (1938)	–	10,000 GRT requisitioned tanker
TRANSPORT FORCE: Rear Admiral Raizo Tanaka			
Destroyer Squadron 2	*Jintsu* (1925) ℞	Cdr Kozai	5,195 tons, 35 kts, 7 x 5.5" guns, 8 x 24" TT
Destroyer Division 15	*Kuroshio* (1940)	Cdr Ugaki	2,490 tons, 35 kts,
(Capt Shiro Sato)	*Oyashio* (1940)	Cdr Arima	6 x 5" guns, 8 x 24" TT
Destroyer Division 16	*Yukikaze* (1940)	Cdr Tobita	
(Capt Siro Shibuya)	*Amatsukaze* (1940)	Cdr Hara	2,490 tons, 35 kts,
	Tokitsukaze (1940)	Cdr Nakahara	6 x 5" guns, 8 x 24" TT
	Hatsukaze (1940)	Cdr Takahashi	
Destroyer Division 18	*Shiranui* (1939)	Cdr Akasawa	2,490 tons, 35 kts,
(Capt Yoshito Miyasaka)	*Kagero* (1939)	Cdr Yokoi	6 x 5" guns, 8 x 24" TT
	Kasumi (1939)	Cdr Tomura	2,370 tons, 35 kts,
	Arare (1939)	Cdr Ogata	6 x 5" guns, 8 x 24" TT
Transports	12 Marus	–	Details not known
	Patrol Boat 1 (1920)	Old destroyers converted to	1,390 tons, 20 kts, 2 x 4.7" guns
	Patrol Boat 2 (1921)	troop transports, 1939–41	two Daihatsu landing craft
	Patrol Boat 34 (1921)		935 tons, 14 kts, one Daihatsu landing craft
Oiler	*Akebono Maru* (1939)	–	10,000 GRT requisitioned tanker
KURE ISLAND FORCE: Rear Admiral Ruitaro Fujita			
Seaplane	*Chitose* (1936) ℞	Capt Furukawa	12,250 tons, 29 kts, 23 floatplanes
carriers	*Kamikawa Maru* (1937)	Capt Shinoda	6,853 GRT, 17 kts, 12 floatplanes
Rescue destroyer	*Hayashio* (1940)	Capt Kaneda	2,490 tons, 35 kts, 6 x 5" guns, 8 x 24" TT
MINESWEEPING FORCE (via Wake Island)			
Minesweeper Force	4 Minesweepers		250–300 GRT converted whalecatchers
(Capt Sadatomo Miyamoto)	Subchaser *Ch 16* (1940)		
	Subchaser *Ch 17* (1941)	–	460 tons, 16 kts, 136 depth charges
	Subchaser *Ch 18* (1941)	–	
Supply	*Soya* (1940)	Cdr Kubota	2,224 GRT ammunition ship, 12 kts
Unit	2 Marus	–	Details not known

Comments	Sunk
	Air attack 25 Nov 1944
	Air attack 25 Oct 1944
Collided night 4/5 June, many air attacks 5–6 June, c.1,000 killed	6 June 1942
	Surface 25 Oct 1944
Both hit once 6 June, *Arashio* with great loss among *Mikuma*.survivors	Air attack 4 Mar 1943
	Air attack 4 Mar 1943
	Submarine 6 Jan 1945
	Surface 13 Jul 1943
	Mines and aircraft
	8 May 1943
	Given to China post war
	Air attack 6 Apr 1945
	Air attack 3 Mar 1943
	Collision 2 Nov 1943
	Air attack 27 Oct 1944
	With *Kuroshio* (above)
	Air attack 7 Apr 1945
	Submarine 5 Jul 1942
Second Special Naval Landing Force under Capt Minoru Ota, plus Col Ichiki's army detachment and two construction battalions (total 5,000 men).	Fate unknown
	Submarine 13 Jan 1943
	Submarine 25 Jul 1945
	Air attack 3 Jul 1944
Torpedoed by PBY on 3 June 1942	Air attack 30 Mar 1944
Converted to aircraft carrier 1943	Air attack 25 Oct 1944
Requisitioned freighter	Submarine 28 Apr 1943
	Air attack 24 Nov 1942
	Fate unknown
	Air attack 4 Jul 1944
	Submarine 29 Apr 1945
	Air attack 30 Dec 1944
	In service after war
	Fate unknown

ALEUTIANS OPERATION
ADVANCED SUBMARINE DETACHMENT

Unit	Name (date completed)	Commander	Normal displacement, Speed, Armament
Rear Admiral Shigeaki Yamazaki			
Submarine Squadron 1	I-9 (1935)	Cdr Fujii	4,140 tons, 23/ 8 kts, 1 x 5.5" gun, 6 x 21" TT
	I-15 (1940)	Cdr Ishikawa	
Submarine Division 2	I-17 (1940)	Cdr Nishino	
(Capt Hiroshilmazato)	I-19 (1940)	Cdr Narahara	3, 654 tons, 23/ 8 kts, 1 x 5.5" gun, 6 x 21" TT
Submarine Division 4	I-25 (1941)	Cdr Togami	
(Capt Mitsuru Nagai)	I- 26 (1941)	Cdr Yokota	

DISTANT COVERING FORCE (detached from First Fleet 3 June 1942)

Vice Admiral Shiro Takasu – Chief of Staff, Rear Admiral Kengo Kobayashi			
Battleship Division 2	Hyuga (1918)	Capt Matsuda	Modernized 1937: 36,000 tons, 25 kts,
(VAdm Takasu)	Ise (1917	Capt Takeda	12 x 14" guns, 3 floatplanes
	Fuso (1915)	Capt Kinoshita	Modernized 1935: 34,700 tons, 23 kts,
	Yamashiro (1917)	Capt Kogure	12 x 14" guns, 3 floatplanes
SCREEN – Rear Admiral Fukuji Kishi			
Cruiser Division 9	Kitakami (1921)	Capt Norimitsu	Rebuilt as torpedo cruisers 1941
(RAdm Fukiji Kishi)	Oi (1921)	Capt Narita	5,500 tons, 36 kts, 7 x 5.5" guns, 40 x 24" TT
Destroyer Division 20	Asagiri (1930)	Cdr Maekawa	
(Capt Yuji Yamada)	Yugiri (1930)	Cdr Motokura	2,090 tons, 38 kts,
	Shirakumo (1928)	Cdr Hitomi	6 x 5" guns, 9 x 24" TT
	Amagiri (1930)	Capt Ashida	
Destroyer Division 24	Umikaze (1937)	Cdr Sugitani	
(Capt Yasuji Hirai)	Yamakaze (1937)	Cdr Hamanaka	1,980 tons, 34 kts,
	Kawakaze (1937)	Cdr Wakabayashi	5 x 5" guns, 8 x 24" TT
	Suzukaze (1937)	Cdr Shibayama	
Destroyer Division 27	Shigure (1936)	Cdr Seo	1,980 tons, 34 kts,
(Capt Matake Yoshimura)	Shiratsuyu (1936)	LCdr Hashimoto	5 x 5" guns, 8 x 24" TT
	Ariake (1935)	Cdr Yoshida	1,680 tons, 36 kts,
	Yugure (1935)	Cdr Kamo	5 x 5" guns, 9 x 24" TT
Supply Unit 2	San Clemente Maru (1937)	Capt Eguchi	7,335 GRT requisitioned tanker
(oilers)	Toa Maru (1934)	–	10,000 GRT requisitioned tanker

Comments	Sunk
Scouted Kiska late May 1942. Cordon C	Destroyer 13 Jun 1944
Scouted Adak late May 1942. Cordon C	Destroyer 2 Nov 1942
Scouted Attu late May 1942. Cordon C	Air/surface 19 Aug 1943
Patrolled Unimak Pass, Dutch Harbor	Destroyer 25 Nov 1943
Patrolled Seattle, shelled Astoria	Missing 20 Sep 1943
Patrolled Seattle, shelled Vancouver	Destroyer 28 Oct 1944

1943-44: two rear turrets replaced	Air attack 24 Jul 1945
with flight deck, 22 aircraft	Air attack 28 Jul 1945
	Surface 25 Oct 1944
	Surface 25 Oct 1944
	Scrapped 1947
	Submarine 19 Jul 1944
	Air attack 28 Aug 1942
	Surface 25 Nov 1943
	Submarine 16 Mar 1944
	Mine, 23 Apr 1944
	Submarine 1 Feb 1944
	Submarine 25 Jun 1942
	Surface 6 Aug 1943
	Submarine 26 Jan 1944
	Submarine 24 Jan 1945
	Collision 15 Jun 1944
	Air attack 28 Jul 1943
	Air attack 21 Jul 1943
	Submarine 4 May 1943
	Submarine 25 Nov 1943

FIFTH FLEET
MAIN FORCE (sortied from Ominato 26 May1942)

Unit	Name (date completed)	Commander	Normal displacement, Speed, Armament
Vice Admiral Moshiro Hosogaya – Chief of Staff, Capt Tasuku Nakazawa			
Cruiser Division 4.1 (VAdm Hosogaya)	Nachi (1928) ♄	Capt Kiyota	Modernized 1941: 14,980 tons, 34 kts, 10 x 8" guns, 8 x 24" TT, 3 floatplanes
Screen (Cdr Hajime Takeuchi)	Inazuma (1932)	Cdr Takeuchi	1,980 tons, 38 kts,
	Ikazuchi (1932)	LCdr Kudo	6 x 5" guns, 9 x 24" TT
Supply Unit	Fujisan Maru (1931) Tanker		9,524 GRT
	Nissan Maru (1938) Tanker		6,800 GRT
	Three cargo ships		Details not known
SECOND CARRIER STRIKING FORCE:　Rear Admiral Kakuji Kakuta			
Carrier Force (RAdm Kakuta)	Ryujo (1933) ♄	Capt Kato	Modernized 1936: 12,732 tons, 29 kts, 1 x 5" guns
	Air Unit	Lt Yamagami	–
	Fighter Wing	Lt Kobayashi	16 'Zeros'
	Attack Bomber Wing	Lt Yamagami	21 'Kates'
	Junyo (1942)	Capt Ishii	26,949 tons, 25 kts, 8 x 5" guns
	Air Unit	Lt Shiga	–
	Fighter wing	Lt Shiga	22 'Zeros'
	Dive Bomber Wing	Lt Abe	21 'Vals'
SCREEN			
Cruiser Division 4.2 (Capt Shunsaku Nabeshima)	Maya (1932)	Capt Nabeshima	Modernized 1941 and 1939
	Takao (1932)	Capt Asakura	14,838 tons, 10 x 8" guns, 3 floatplanes
Destroyer Division 7 (Capt Kaname Konishi)	Akebono (1931)	LCdr Nakagawa	2,090 tons, 38 kts, 6 x 5" guns, 9 x 24" TT
	Ushio (1931)	Cdr Uesugi	
	Sazanami (1932)	LCdr Uwai	
Oiler	Teiyo Maru (1931)	–	9,849 GRT requisitioned tanker

OCCUPATION FORCES

Unit	Name (date completed)	Commander	Normal displacement, Speed, Armament
ATTU – ADAK INVASION FORCE: Rear Admiral Sentaro Omori (sortied from Ominato 29 May 1942)			
Flagship (light cruiser)	Abukuma (1925) ♄	Capt Murayama	5,570 tons, 36 kts, 7 x 5.5" guns
Destroyer Division 21 (Capt Toshio Shimizu)	Wakaba (1934)	LCdr Kuroki	
	Nenohi (1933)	LCdr Terauchi	1,680 tons, 36 kts,
	Hatsuharu (1933)	Cdr Makino	5 x 5" guns, 9 x 24" TT
	Hatsushimo (1934)	LCdr Migihama	
Seaplane tender?	Kimikawa Maru (1937)	–	Details not known, carried eight floatplanes
Minelayer	Magane Maru (1940)	–	3,120 GRT requisitioned freighter
Transport	Kinugasa Maru (1936)	–	8,407 GRT, 17 kts requisitioned freighter
KISKA INVASION FORCE: Capt Takeji Ono (sortied from Ominato 27 May 1942)			
Cruiser Division 21 (Capt Ono)	Kiso (1921)	Capt Ono	5,500 tons, 36 kts,
	Tama (1921)	Capt Kawabata	7 x 5.5" guns, 8 x 21" TT, 1 floatplane
Destroyer Division 6 (Capt Yusuke Yamada)	Hibiki (1933)	LCdr Ishii	1,980 tons, 38 kts,
	Akatsuki (1932)	Cdr Takasuka	6 x 5" guns, 9 x 24" TT
	Hokaze (1921)	LCdr Tanaka	1,200 tons, 34 kts, 4 x 4.7" guns, 6 tubes
Armed merchant ship	Asaka Maru (1937)	Capt Ban	7,399 GRT, 19 kts, 4 x 6" guns
Minesweeper Division 13 (Capt Toshio Mitsuka)	Kaiho Maru (1941)	–	1,093 GRT requisitioned freighter
	Two Marus	–	Details not known
Transports (LCdr Hifumi Mukai)	Hakusan Maru (1928)	–	89 GRT requisitioned trawler
	Kumagawa Maru	–	Details not known

Comments	Sunk
	Air attack 5 Nov 1944
	Submarine 14 May 1944
	Submarine 14 Apr 1944
	Aircraft 17 Fen 1944
Sunk in Kiska Harbor by AAF bombers	19 June 1942
	Fate unknown
	Air attack 24 Aug 1942
Nominal aircraft complement fourty-eight.	
Laid down in 1939 as liner Kashiwara Maru, conversion completed 5 May 1942.	Damaged by submarines in 1944, scrapped 1947
Nominal aircraft complement fifty-three.	
	Submarine 23 Oct 1944
	Scuttled 1946
	Air attack 13 Nov 1944
	Scrapped 1948
	Submarine 14 Jan 1944
	Submarine 19 Aug 1944

Comments	Sunk
	PT boat and air 26 Oct 1944
	Air attack 24 Oct 1944
	Submarine 4 Jul 1942
	Air attack 13 Nov 1944
	Mine 30 Jul 1945
	Submarine 23 Oct 1944
	Submarine 24 Jan 1944
Maj Hozumi and 1,200 army detachment	Submarine 7 Oct 1944
	Air attack 13 Nov 1944
	Submarine 25 Oct 1944
	Given to USSR after war
	Surface 13 Nov 1942
	Submarine 6 Jul 1944
	Air attack 12 Oct 1944
	Submarine 19 Apr 1945
	Fate unknown
550-man Special Naval Force	Air attack 5 Jun 1944
700 construction troops and equipment	Fate unknown

Devastators aboard USS *Enterprise* prior to take-off on June 1942

Department of the Navy	
Secretary of the Navy	Frank Knox
Under Secretary	James Forrestal
Bureau of Naval Personnel	Rear Admiral Randall Jacobs
Bureau of Ships	Rear Admiral Edward Cochrane
Bureau of Aeronautics	Rear Admiral John McCain
Bureau of Ordnance	Rear Admiral William Blandy

United States Fleet	
Commander in Chief and Chief of Naval Operations (CominCh)	Admiral Ernest King (*see note*)
Deputy Chief of Naval Operations	Vice Admiral Frederick Horne
Chief of Staff (COS)	Rear Admiral Russell Willson
Deputy COS (operations)	Rear Admiral Richard Edwards
King's planning officer	Captain Charles 'Savvy' Cooke
King's intelligence officer	Captain George Dyer
Office of War Plans (until late May)	Rear Admiral Richmond Turner
Office of Naval Intelligence (ONI)	Rear Admiral Alan Kirk
Office of Communications (Op 20)	Rear Admiral Joseph Redman
Comms. Security (Op-20-G)	Captain John Redman

Pacific Fleet	
Commander in Chief (CinCPac)	Admiral Chester Nimitz
Chief of Staff	Rear Admiral Milo Draemel
War Plans Officer	Captain Charles 'Soc' McMorris
Assistants	Captain Lynde McCormick and Colonel
	Omar Pfeiffer, USMC (Fleet Marine Officer)
Intelligence Officer	Commander Edwin Layton
Station Hypo	Lieutenant Commander Joseph Rochefort
	('Devil's Advocate' Captain James Steele)
Communications Officer	Commander Maurice Curts
Commander Carriers	Vice Admiral William 'Bull' Halsey (hospitalized)
Shore representative, carriers	Rear Admiral Leigh Noyes

Notes Prior to Executive Order 9096 of 12 March 1942, the offices of Fleet commander-in-chief and chief of naval operations were separate. Fleet bureaucracy was in flux at the time of the battle of Midway because King was putting his own men (Edwards, Cooke and Dyer) in place alongside the senior office chiefs of the old CNO structure. Aircraft numbers are those operational – that is, with crews available and mechanically functional – on the morning of 4 June 1942.

Sources
Silverstone, P, *U.S. Warships of World War II*, London, 1965.
Morison, S, *History of United States Naval Operations in World War II*, Boston, 1975.
Lundstrom, J, *The First Team*, Annapolis, 1984.

MIDWAY OPERATION

Unit	Name (date completed)	Commander	Normal displacement, Speed, Armament
SUBMARINE FORCE PEARL HARBOR: Rear Admiral Robert English			
TG 7.1	Dolphin (1932) unique	LCdr Rutter	2,240 tons, 17/8 kts, 6 x 21" TT, 1 x 3"gun
	Gato (1941) name class (204)	LCdr Myers	See Growler
	Grenadier (1940) T class (12)	LCdr Lent	See Tambor
	Tambor (1939) T class	LCdr Murphy	2,370 tons, 20/8.7kts, 85 crew
	Trout (1940) T class	LCdr Fenno	10 x 21" TT
	Grayling (1940) T class	LCdr Olsen	1 x 5", 1 x 40mm guns
	Nautilus (1930) class of 2	LCdr Brockman	4,050 tons, 17/8 kts, 6 x 21" TT, 2 x 6" guns
	Grouper (1941) Gato class	LCdr Duke	See Growler
	Gudgeon (1941) T class	LCdr Lyon	See Tambor
	Flying Fish (1941) Gato class	LCdr Donaho	See Growler
	Cachalot (1933) name class (2)	LCdr Lewis	1,680 tons, 17/8 kts, 6 x 21" TT, 1 x 3" gun
TG 7.3	Growler (1941) Gato class	LCdr Gilmore	2,415 tons, 20.25/10 kts, 80 crew
	Finback (1941) Gato class	LCdr Hull	10 x 21" TT, 1 x 5", 1 x 40mm guns
	Pike (1935) P1 class (2)	LCdr New	1,960 tons, 19/8 kts, 6 x 21" TT, 1 x 3" gun
	Tarpon (1935) P2 class (2)	LCdr Wallace	1,968 tons, 19/8 kts, 6 x 21" TT, 1 x 4" gun

HAWAIIAN SEA FRONTIER: Rear Admiral David Bagley (Pearl Harbor)
VII Army Air Corps (Oahu): Major General Clarence Tinker (killed in LB-30 raid on Wake, 7 June 1942)

Naval Air Station Midway: Captain Cyril Simard. Air Operations: Commander Logan Ramsey			
Sixth & part Third Marine Defense Batts, Coast Artillery Group and part Second Raider Batt (Col Harold Shannon, Sand Island)	Maj William Benson i/c Eastern Island		3,652 USMC, USN and AAF plus 5 light tanks 4 x 7", 6 x 5", 28 x 3", 8 x 37mm, 24 x 20mm guns
Sea Force	MTB Squadron 1	Lt McKellar	11 PT boats arrived Midway with Ballard 29 May
Naval aircraft	VP 23	Cdr Hughes	11 PBY-5 'Catalina' flying boats at Sand Is.
Patrol group	VP 44	LCdr Brixner	15 PBY-5A (amphibian) on Eastern Is.
(Cdr Massie Hughes)	VT-8 Detachment	Lt Fieberling (K)	6 TBF-1 'Avenger'
Marine Aircraft Group 22	VMF 221	Maj Parks (K)	20 F2A-3 'Buffalo'
(LCol Ira Kimes)		Capt Armistead	6 F4F-3 'Wildcat'
	VMSB 241*	Maj Henderson (K)	16 SBD-2 'Dauntless'
		Maj Norris (K)	16 SB2U-3 'Vindicator' (5 kept back 4 June)
VII Army Air Force	Local command Capt Simard	Capt Collins	4 B-26 'Marauder'
Detachment (Maj Gen Willis		LCol Sweeney	16 B-17E 'Flying Fortress'
Hale until 2 June)			4 LB-30 'Liberator' (B-24) arrived 6 June
Patrol/PBY refuelling duty at other reefs and islands			
Tender	Thornton (1919)	LCdr Kline	Converted destroyers
Tender	Ballard (1918)	Cdr Gilbert	1,190 tons, 25 kts, 2 x 3" guns
Destroyer	Clark (1935)	Cdr Richardson	1,850 tons, 37 kts, 8 x 21" TT, 8 x 5" guns
Converted yacht/tender	Crystal (1929) Acq. Jan 1942	LCdr Drotning	1,030 GRT
Converted tuna boats	YP 284, 290, 345, 350		Emergency requisitions
Midway relief refuelling			
Gasoline tanker	Kaloli (1941) Acq. Apr 1942	LCdr Chapman	1,729 GRT
Minesweeper/tug	Vireo (1919)	Lt Legg	840 tons, 14 kts, 2 x 3" guns
Oiler	Guadalupe (1940)	Cdr Thurber	7,256 tons, 18.3 kts, 1 x 5", 4 x 3", 8 x 40mm guns
Destroyer	Blue (1937)	Cdr Williams	1,500 tons, 36.5 kts,
Destroyer	Ralph Talbot (1936)	Cdr Earle	16 x 21" TT, 4 x 5", 4 x 1.1" guns

*Lofton Henderson's name was given to the much fought-over airstrip on Guadalcanal. Capt Richard Fleming was awarded the only Midway Medal of Honor, posthumously, for attacking Mikuma in an SB2U-3.

Comments	Sunk
	Scrapped 1946
Outer screen west of Midway	Discarded 1960
	Aircraft 22 Apr 1943
Inner screen west of Midway.	Scrapped 1960
On 6 June 1942 *Grayling* bombed by B-17s, which reported sinking a cruiser.	Destroyer 29 Feb 1944
	Rammed 9 Sep 1943
Outer screen NW. On 4 June 1942. *Grouper* and *Nautilus* close on Mobile Force	Scrapped 1945
and are attacked. Latter fires torpedoes at *Kaga*	Scrapped 1960
	Missing Apr 1944
Inner screen	Scrapped 1960
northwest of Midway	Scrapped 1957
	Destroyer 8 Nov 1944
Patrol line north of Oahu, had taken up station by 1000 hrs, 28 May 1942	Scrapped 1959
	Scrapped 1957
	Sank en route to scrap 1957

Comments	Sunk
4 June 1942: downed 2 'Kates', 1 'Val',	Maj Benson, 6 Marines, 2 AAF killed,
1 'Zero', damaged 4 'Vals', 1 'Zero'	20 wounded
9 Midway, 2 Kure, sortied 4/5 June	PT 25 strafed 4 June
2 spot Mobile Force morning 4 June	4 June: 1 shot down, 2 lost to fuel exhaustion
4 make torpedo attack night 3/4 June	
Attacked Mobile Force morning 4 June	5 lost, 1 crippled
4 June: shot down 3 'Kates', 2 'Zeros',	14 F2A-3 lost, 5 crippled
damaged 18 'Kates', 2 'Zeros'	2 F4F-3 lost, 3 crippled
4 June: 27 (10) attack Mobile Force	6 SBD lost, 2 crippled
5 June: 24 (1) attack cruisers*	6 SB2U lost, 2 crippled
Attacked Mobile Force morning 4 June	2 lost, 2 crippled
Attacked repeatedly 4–5 June	2 lost, 7 damaged
Abortive raid on Wake 7 June	1 lost

Comments	Sunk
29 May *Thornton* and *Clark* at French Frigate Shoals seen by	Collision 5 Apr 1945
I-123, aborted Operation K, relieved by *Ballard* 4 June	Sold 1946
	Scrapped 1946
Pearl and Hermes Reef, Lisianski, Laysan, Gardner Pinnacles and Necker	Sold 1947
	Probably returned to owner

Comments	Sunk
Delivered avgas Midway 2 June, then to P and H Reef. *Vireo* to *Yorktown* 5 June	Returned Dec 1945
	Sold 1947
	Unknown
Pearl Harbor to Midway 3–6 June	Destroyer 22 Aug 1942
	Target, Bikini Atoll, 1947

CARRIER STRIKING FORCE

Unit	Name (date completed)	Commander	Normal displacement, Speed, Armament
Acting Commander, Carriers: Rear Admiral Frank Fletcher – Air Officer Task Force 17: Commander Murr Arnold			
TG 17.5	Yorktown (1936) ⚓	Capt Buckmaster	19,900 tons, 34 kts, 8 x 5", 16 x 1.1", 20 x 20mm guns
Carrier Group	Air Group	LCdr Pederson	(79 aircraft, 71 operational)
(Capt Elliott Buckmaster)	VF-3	LCdr Thach	25 F4F-4 'Wildcat'
	VB-3	LCdr Leslie	17 SBD-3 'Dauntless'
	VS-5	Lt Short	17 SBD-3 'Dauntless'
	VT-3	LCdr Massey (K)	12 TBD-1 'Devastator'
TG 17.2 Cruiser Group	Astoria (1933) ⚓	Capt Scanland	9,950/9,800 tons, 32.7 kts, 4 floatplanes
(RAdm William Smith)	Portland (1932)	Capt Du Bose	9 x 8', 8 x 5" guns
TG 17.4	Hammann (1939) ⚓	Cdr True	
Destroyer Screen	Hughes (1939)	LCdr Ramsey	
(Capt Gilbert Hoover)	Morris (1939)	Cdr Jarrett	1,570 tons, 38 kts,
Comdesron 2	Anderson (1939)	LCdr Ginder	12 x 21" TT, 5 x 5" guns
	Russell (1938)	LCdr Hartwig	
	Gwin (1940)	Cdr Higgins	1,630 tons, 37 kts, 5 x 21" TT, 4 x 5" guns
Task Force 16: Rear Admiral Raymond Spruance – Chief of Staff, Commander Miles Browning			
TG 16.5	Enterprise (1936) ⚓	Capt Murray	19,900 tons, 34 kts, 8 x 5", 16 x 1.1", 20 x 20mm guns
Carrier Group	Air Group	LCdr McClusky	(78 aircraft, 74 operational)
(RAdm Spruance)	VF-6	Lt Gray	27 F4F-4
	VB-6	Lt Best	18 SBD-2 & 3
	VS-6	Lt Gallaher	15 SBD-3
	VT-6	LCdr Lindsey (K)	14 TDB-1
	Hornet (1940)	RAdm Mitscher	20,000 tons, 34 kts, 8 x 5", 16 x 1.1", 20 x 20mm guns
	Air Group	Cdr Ring	(77 aircraft, 76 operational)
	VF-8	LCdr Mitchell	27 F4F-4
	VB-8	LCdr Johnson	19 SBD-3
	VS-8	LCdr Rodee	15 SBD-3
	VT-8	LCdr Waldron (K)	15 TDB-1
TG 16.2	New Orleans (1933) ⚓	Capt Good	
Cruiser Group	Minneapolis (1933)	Capt Lowry	
(RAdm Thomas Kincaid)	Vincennes (1936)	Capt Riefkohl	9,950 tons, 32,7 kts, 9 x 8"guns, 4 floatplanes
Comcrudiv 6	Northampton (1929)	Capt Chandler	9,050 tons, 32.7 kts, 9 x 8" guns, 3 floatplanes
	Pensacola (1929)	Capt Lowe	9,100 tons, 32.7 kts, 10 x 8" guns, 2 floatplanes
	Atlanta (1941)	Capt Jenkins	6,000 tons, 32 kts, 16 x 5" guns, 8 x 21" TT
TG 16.4	Phelps (1935)	LCdr Beck	1,850 tons, 37 kts, 8 x 5"guns, 8 x 21" TT
Destroyer Screen	Worden (1934)	LCdr Pogue	
(Capt, Alexander Early)	Monaghan (1935)	LCdr Burford	1,395 tons, 36.5 kts, 5 x 5" guns, 8 x 21" TT
Comdesron 1	Aylwin (1934)	LCdr Phelan	
Desron 6	Balch (1936)	LCdr Tiemroth	1,850 tons, 37 kts, 8 x 5" guns, 8 x 21" TT
(Capt Edward Sauer)	Conyngham (1935)	LCdr Daniel	1,500 tons, 36.5 kts, 5 x 5" guns, 12 x 21" TT
	Benham (1938)	LCdr Worthington	
	Ellet (1938)	LCdr Gardner	1,500 tons, 36.5 kts, 4 x 5" guns, 16 x 21" TT
	Maury (1938)	LCdr Sims	
Oiler group	Cimarron (1939) oiler	Cdr Ihrig	Fleet oilers: 7,256 tons, 18.3 kts,
	Platte (1939) oiler	Capt Henkle	4 x 5", 8 x 40mm guns
	Dewey (1934) destroyer	LCdr Chillingworth	1,395 tons, 36.5 kts, 5 x 5" guns, 8 x 21" TT
	Monssen (1940) destroyer	Cdr Smoot	1,630 tons, 37 kts, 5 x 5" guns, 10 x 21" TT

*Things got too complicated for this limited format after the two strikes on 4 June – see 'Finish'.

Comments	Sunk
65 of 2,000+ killed	Sunk by *I-168*, 7 June 1942
Directed air operations on board	
First strike 6 (1), CAP 12 (0), 11 (4). Two killed	
See **Appendix D** and * below	
See * below	
Firststrike 12 (12). 20 killed, 1 captured and murdered	
Fletcher transferred to 4 June	Guns 9 Aug 1942
	Scrapped 1959
Yorktown salvage, 81 of 241 killed	Sunk by *I-168*, 6 June 1942
Left to guard Yorktown 4–5 June	Target, Bikini Atoll, 1946
	Scrapped 1947
	Target, Bikini Atoll, 1946
	Scrapped 1947
Joined Yorktown guard 5 June	Torpedo 13 July 1943
	Scrapped 1958
Wounded leading first strike	
First strike 10 (0), CAP 8 (0), 10 (1)	
See **Appendix D** and * below	
See **Appendix D** and * below	
First strike 14 (10). 18 killed, 2 captured and murdered	
	Aircraft 26 Oct 1942
Did not have a good battle	
First strike 10 (10), CAP 8 (1), 8 (0). 3 killed	
First strike 19 (4). See * below.	
First strike 15 (0). See * below	
First strike 15 (15). 29 killed	
	Scrapped 1959
	Scrapped 1960
	Torpedo 9 Aug 1942
	Torpedo 1 Dec 1942
	Target, Bikini Atoll, 1946
	Torpedo 13 Nov 1942
	Scrapped 1947
	Aground 12 Jan 1943
Joined *Yorktown* guard 5 June	Storm 18 Dec 1944
	Scrapped 1947
Yorktown salvage party 6 June	Scrapped 1946
	Sunk as target 1948
Yorktown salvage party 6 June	Torpedo 15 Nov 1942
	Scrapped 1947
	Scrapped 1946
	Unknown. Sisters to Neosho sunk
	Coral Sea 11 Apr 1942
	Scrapped 1947
	Gunfire 13 Nov 1942

ALEUTIANS OPERATION
SURFACE ELEMENT

Unit	Name (date completed)	Commander	Normal displacement, Speed, Armament
Task Force 8: Rear Admiral Robert Theobald – Chief of Staff, Captain Frank Fahrion			
TG 8.6	*Nashville*(1937) Fb	Capt Craven	9,475 tons, 34 kts, 15 x 6", 8 x 5" guns, 4 floatplanes
Main Body	*Indianapolis* (1931)	Capt Hanson	9,950 tons, 32.7 kts, 9 x 8", 8 x 5" guns, 4 floatplanes
(RAdm Theobald)	*Louisville* (1930)	Capt Nixon	9,050 tons, 32.7 kts, 9 x 8", 8 x 5" guns, 4 floatplanes
	St. Louis (1938)	Capt Rood	10,000 tons, 34 kts, 15 x 6", 8 x 5" guns, 4 floatplanes
	Honolulu (1937)	Capt Dodd	9,650 tons, 34 kts, 15 x 6", 8 x 5" guns, 4 floatplanes
Desdiv 11	Gridley (1936)	LCdr Strickney	1,500 tons, 36.5 kts
(Cdr Frederick	*McCall* (1937)	LCdr Veeder	4 x 5" guns, 16 x 21" TT
Moosbrugger)	*Gilmer* (1919)	LCdr Parish	1,190 tons, 35 kts
	Humphreys (1919)	LCdr Wells	4 x 4" guns, 12 x 21" TT
Destroyer Striking Group: Commander Wyatt Craig			
Desdiv 6	*Case* (1935)	Cdr Bedilion	1,500 tons, 36.5 kts
(Cdr Craig)	*Reid* (1936)	Cdr Pullen	5 x 5" guns, 12 x 21" TT
	Brooks (1919)	LCdr Singleton	
	Sands (1919)	LCdr Bowers	
	Kane (1919)	LCdr Greytak	1,190 tons, 35 kts
	Dent (1918)	LCdr Tobelman	4 x 4" guns, 12 x 21" TT
	Talbot (1918)	LCdr McFall	
	King (1920)	LCdr Gentry	
	Waters (1918)	LCdr Armstrong	
Submarine Group: Commander Burton Lake			
TG 8.5	*S-18* (1920)	Lt Newsome	
(Cdr Lake)	*S-23* (1920)	Lt Duryea	
	S-27 (1922)	Lt Jukes	1,090 tons, 14.5/11 kts
	S-28 (1922)	Lt Crowley	4 x 21" TT, 1 x 4" gun
	S-34 (1919)	Lt Wogan	
	S-35 (1919)	Lt Stevens	
Tanker Group: Captain Houston Maples			
TG 8.9	*Sabine* (1940) Tanker	Capt Maples	7,256 tons, 18.3 kts, 4 x 5", 8 x 40mm guns
(Capt Maples)	*Brazos* (1919) Tanker	Cdr Kelly	5,950 tons, 14 kts, 2 x 5", 8 x 40mm guns
	SS *Comet* (1942) Transport	Irvin Larkin, Master	6,221 tons, 17(?) kts

Comments	Sunk
	Sold to Chile 1951
	Torpedo 29 Jul 1945
	Scrapped 1960
	Sold to Brazil 1951
	Scrapped 1960
	Scrapped 1947
	Scrapped 1947
	Scrapped 1947
	Scrapped 1946
	Scrapped 1948
	Kamikaze 11 Dec 1944
	Kamikaze 6 Jan 1945
	Scrapped 1946
	Scrapped 1946
	Scrapped 1946
	Scrapped 1946
	Scrapped 1946
	Scrapped 1947
	Scrapped 1946
	Scrapped 1946
	Grounding 19 Jun 1942
	Accident 4 Jul 1944
	Scrapped 1946
	Sunk as target 1946
	Not known
	Scrapped 1947
	Returned 1948

COAST GUARD GROUP

Unit	Name (date completed)	Commander	Normal displacement, Speed, Armament
TG 8.2 Surface Search/Scouting Group: Captain Ralph Parker (Kodiak)			
Gunboat	*Charleston* (1936)	Cdr Sherwood	1,900 tons, 20 kts, 4 x 6", 16 x 40mm guns
Oiler (conv. minesweeper)	*Oriole* (1918)	LCdr Lindsay	840 tons, 14 kts, 2 x 3" guns
Coast Guard cutters	*Haida* (1921)	Cdr Leslie	1,780 tons, 16 kts, 2 x 5", 2 x 3", 4 x 20mm guns
	Onondaga (1934)	LCdr Mehlman	1,005 tons, 13 kts, 2 x 3", 3 x 20mm guns
	Cyane (1934)	LCdr Tollaksen	337 tons, 16 kts
	Aurora (1931)	Lt (jg) McCabe	2 x 3", 2 x 20mm guns
	Bonham (1926)	Lt (jg) Gill	220 tons, 11 kts, 1 x 3" gun

AIR ELEMENT

Unit	Name	Commander	Armament
TG 8.1 Air Search Group (based on USN seaplane tenders): USN Captain Leslie Gehres (Kodiak)			
Sand Point group	*Williamson* (1919)	LCdr Kivette	20 PBY-5 'Catalina'
Dutch Harbor group	*Gillis* (1919)	LCdr Garton	of Patrol Wing 4
Cold Bay group	*Casco* (1941)	Cdr Combs	and one air force B-17
Kodiak group	No tender	Capt Gehres	3 VSO, 1 B-17, 2 LB-30 (B-24)
Kodiak group	No tender	Capt Gehres	
TG 8.3 Air Striking Group: AAC Brigadier General William Butler (Anchorage)			
Fort Randall, Cold Bay			25 P-40, 12 B-26, 5 B-17, 1 LB-30
Fort Glenn, Umnak			12 P-40
Kodiak			15 P-39, 17 P-40, 5 B-17, 2 LB-30
Mainland			25 P-38, 17 P-39, 4 P-36,
(Anchorage)			7 B-17, 5 B-18, 12 B-26, 2 LB-30

DISTANT FORCES

Unit	Name	Commander	Normal displacement, Speed, Armament
Battleships: Vice Admiral William Pye (San Francisco)			
TF 1	*Pennsylvania* (1915)* ℞		
(RAdm Walter Anderson)	*New Mexico* (1917)		33,000 – 33,400 tons, 22 kts
	Mississippi (1917)		12 x 14", 24 x 5" guns, 3 seaplanes
	Idaho (1917)		
	Tennessee (1919)*		31,500 – 32,600 tons, 21 kts
	Maryland (1920)* ℞		12 x 14", 24 x 5" guns, 3 seaplanes
	Colorado (1921)		
Light aircraft carrier	*Long Island* (conv. 1941)		11,300 tons, 18 kts, 21 aircraft
Destroyer group	8 destroyers		
Saratoga Group: Rear Admiral Aubrey Fitch (en route from San Diego)			
TF 11	*Saratoga* (1925)		33,000 tons, 34 kts, 20 x 5" guns, 90 aircraft
	San Diego (1941)		6,000 tons, 32 kts, 16 x 5" guns, 8 x 21" TT
	4 destroyers		

*Damaged at Pearl Harbor

Comments	Sunk
	Became training ship 1948
	Sold 1947
	Sold 1948
	Sold 1954
	Sold 1954
	Sold 1954
	Sold 1959

	Scrapped 1946
	Scrapped 1946
	Coast Guard 1949

Comments	Sunk
	Target, Bikini Atoll, 1946
On 31 May 1942, Pye sent *Maryland*, *Colorado* and three destroyers 650 miles NW to investigate a reported Japanese converted carrier. On 5 June he took out the rest of the force to rendezvous with Anderson 260 miles west of San Francisco, then returned to port	Scrapped 1947
	Scrapped 1956
	Scrapped 1947
	Scrapped 1959
	Scrapped 1959
	Scrapped 1959
Converted SS *Mormacmail*	Returned 1949
Sailed from San Diego 31 May 1942, arrived Pearl Harbor 6 June. Took thirty-four replacement aircraft to TF 16	Target, Bikini Atoll 1946
	Scrapped 1960

PART OF COMMANDER-IN-CHIEF ATLANTIC FLEET CIRCULAR
OF 21 JANUARY 1941

1. I have been concerned for many years over the increasing tendency – now grown almost to 'standard practice' – of flag officers and other group commanders to issue orders and instructions in which their subordinates are told 'how' as well as 'what' to do to such an extent that the 'Custom of the service' has virtually become the antithesis of that essential element of command – 'initiative of the subordinate.'

2. We are preparing for – and are now close to – those active operations (commonly called war) which require the exercise and utilization of the full powers and capabilities of every officer in command status. There will be neither time nor opportunity to do more than prescribe the several tasks of the several subordinates (to say 'what,' perhaps 'when' and 'where,' and usually for their intelligent co-operation, 'why'); leaving to them – expecting and requiring of them – the capacity to perform the assigned tasks (to do the 'how').

3. If the subordinates are deprived – as they now are – of that training and experience which will enable them to act 'on their own' – if they do not know, by constant practice, how to exercise 'initiative of the subordinates' – if they are reluctant (afraid) to act because they are accustomed to detailed orders and instructions – if they are not habituated to think, to judge, to decide and to act for themselves in their several echelons of command – we shall be in sorry case when the time for 'active operations' arrives.

The memorandum continues in this vein, concluding with five admirably pragmatic points of guidance for senior commanders that amount to one: stop fussing and prepare for fighting.

PART OF MEMORANDUM TO PRESIDENT ROOSEVELT
OF 5 MARCH 1942

1. The delineation of general areas of responsibility for operations in the Pacific is now taking place, in which it appears that we will take full charge of all operations eastward of the Malay Peninsula and Sumatra.

2. You have expressed the view – concurred in by all your chief military advisers – that we should concentrate on a <u>very few</u> lines of military endeavour and concentrate our efforts on these lines. It is to be recognized that the <u>very few</u> lines of U.S. military effort may require to be shifted in accordance with developments but the total number should be kept at a <u>very few</u>.

Paragraphs three to six concern the world-wide picture, with the emphasis on holding 'the citadel and arsenal of Britain itself by means of the supply of munitions, raw materials and food – and to some extent by troops, when they will release British troops to other British military areas', and supporting British military commitments in the Middle East and the India-Burma-China line.

7. Australia – and New Zealand – are 'white man's countries' which it is essential that we shall not allow to be overrun by Japanese because of the repercussions among the non-white races of the world.

8. Reverting to the premise of paragraph 2 – a <u>very few</u> lines of military endeavour – the general area that needs immediate attention – and is in our sphere of responsibility – is Australasia, which term is intended to include the Australian continent, it approaches from the northwest east – modified ABDA area – and its approaches from the northeast and east – ANZAC area. These approaches need to actively used – continuously – to hamper the enemy advance and/or consolidation of his advance bases.

9. Our primary concern in the Pacific is to hold Hawaii and its approaches (via Midway) from the westward and to maintain its communications with the West Coast. Our next care in the Pacific is to preserve Australasia (par. 8 above) which requires that it communications be maintained – via eastward of Samoa, Fiji and southward of New Caledonia.

10. We have now – or will have soon – 'strong points' at Samoa, Suva (Fiji) and New Caledonia (also a defended fueling base at Bora Bora, Society Islands). A naval operating base is shortly to be set up in Tongatabu (Tonga Islands) to service our naval forces operating in the South Pacific. Efate (New Hebrides) and Funafuti (Ellice Islands) are projected additional 'strong points.'

11. When the foregoing 6 'strong points' are made reasonably secure, we shall not only be able to cover the lines of communications – to Australia (and New Zealand) but – given the naval forces, air units and amphibious troops – we can drive northwest from the New Hebrides into the Solomons and the Bismarck Archipelago after the same fashion of step-by-step advances that the Japanese used in the South China Sea. Such a line of operations will be offensive rather than passive – and will draw Japanese forces there to oppose it, thus relieving pressure elsewhere, whether in Hawaii, ABDA area, Alaska or even India.

NB This memorandum does not mention the strategy of by-passing enemy strong points that featured in the pre-war War Plan Orange and which was later adopted, or indeed the fully amphibious drive through the mid Pacific that the USN was to undertake. King, no less than Yamamoto, was still thinking in terms of capturing islands for use as air bases in support of fleet activities, to make aggressive use of the limited resources available to him.

ENTERPRISE AIR GROUP

Commander Air Group Section (500lb SAP)

LCdr Clarence McClusky	Missed *Kaga* to port, wounded by 'Zero', returned, aircraft inoperative	
Ens William Pittman	Missed *Kaga* to starboard, damaged by 'Zero', returned, aircraft inoperative	
Ens Richard Jaccard	Missed *Kaga* to port	Hit *Hiryu* forward elevator

Scouting Squadron Six (VS-6)

First Division (500lb SAP + 2 x 100lb frag on first strike)

Lt Wilmer Gallaher (CO)	Hit *Kaga* aft among 'Kates'	Led second strike, missed *Hiryu* astern
Ens Reid Stone	Missed *Kaga* to port	Missed *Hiryu* astern
Ens John Roberts (K)	Hit by AA, missed *Kaga* to starboard, never pulled out	
Lt Norman Kleiss	Hit *Kaga* opposite forward elevator	Missed *Hiryu* astern
Ens James Dexter	Hit *Kaga* refuelling cart opposite island	Attacked *Hiryu*, result unknown

Second Division (500lb SAP + 2 x 100lb frag on first strike)

Lt Clarence Dickinson	Hit *Kaga* amidships, fuel exhausted, ditched near *Phelps*, crew recovered	
Ens John McCarthy	Attacked *Kaga*, encounter with *Hiryu* fighters, fuel exhausted, ditched near *Hammann*, crew recovered	
Ens Carl Pfeiffer (K)	Attacked *Kaga*, lost during return flight after encounter with *Hiryu* fighters	
Lt Norman West	Attacked *Kaga*	Turned back with mechanical trouble
Ens Vernon Micheel	Attacked *Kaga*	Attacked *Hiryu*, result unknown
Ens John Lough (K)	Attacked *Kaga*, lost during return flight after encounter with *Hiryu* fighters	

Third Division (500lb SAP)

Lt Charles Ware (K)	Attacked *Kaga*, lost during return flight after encounter with *Hiryu* fighters	
Ens Frank O'Flaherty (K)	Attacked *Kaga*, AA damage, ditched, crew recovered by *Makigumo*, interrogated, murdered	
Ens James Shelton (K)	Attacked *Kaga*, lost during return flight after encounter with *Hiryu* fighters	
Ens Eldor Rodenburg	Turned back early with engine trouble	
NB	There were several more hits on *Kaga*	Possibly one more hit on *Hiryu*

Bombing Squadron Six (VB-6)

First Division (1,000lb SAP)

Lt Richard Best (CO)	Hit *Akagi* midships elevator	Forced to abort first dive when VB-3 crossed in front of them, they were the last to attack *Hiryu*
Lt Edwin Kroeger	Bomb through *Akagi* deck exploded alongside	
Ens Frederick Weber (K)	Hit *Akagi* aft among 'Kates'	Forced to abort by VB-3, killed by 'Zeros' before diving
Lt Wilbur Roberts	Attacked *Kaga*, landed *Yorktown*, aircraft lost with ship	
Ens Delbert Halsey (K)	Attacked *Kaga*, fuel exhausted, ditched, crew lost	

Second Division (1,000lb SAP)

Lt Joe Penland	Attacked *Kaga*, damaged by 'Zeros', ditched, crew recovered 5 June 1942	
Ens Tony Schneider	Fuel exhausted, ditched before bombing within sight of target, crew recovered 6 June 1942	
Ens Eugene Greene (K)	Attacked *Kaga*, fuel exhausted, ditched, crew lost	
Ens Thomas Ramsey	Attacked *Kaga*, fuel exhausted ditched, crew recovered 10 June 1942	
Ens Lewis Hopkins	Attacked *Kaga*, damaged by 'Zeros', returned to *Enterprise*, aircraft inoperative	

Third Division (1,000lb SAP)

Lt John Van Buren (K)	Attacked *Kaga*, fuel exhausted, ditched, crew lost	
Ens Norman Vandivier (K)	Attacked *Kaga*, fuel exhausted, ditched, crew lost	
Ens George Goldsmith	Hit *Kaga* amidships, damaged by 'Zero', landed *Yorktown*, aircraft lost with ship	
Lt Edward Anderson	Attacked *Kaga*, damaged by 'Zeros', returned to *Enterprise*, aircraft inoperative	
Ens Bertram Varian (K)	Attacked *Kaga*, damaged by 'Zeros', ditched, crew lost	
NB	Large number of unattributed hits on *Kaga*	One, possibly two, hits on *Hiryu*

YORKTOWN AIR GROUP (to Enterprise after first strike)

Bombing Squadron Three (VB-3) – first strike all, second strike seven of fifteen carried 1,000lb SAP

First Division

LCdr Maxwell Leslie (CO)	Lost bomb, strafed *Soryu*, fuel exhausted, ditched near *Astoria*	
Lt Paul Holmberg	Hit *Soryu* amidships, damaged by AA, ditched near *Astoria*	
Ens Paul Schlegel	Attacked *Soryu*	Attacked *Hiryu*, missed
Ens Robert Campbell	Attacked *Soryu*	Attacked *Hiryu*, missed
Ens Alden Hanson	Attacked *Soryu*	Attacked *Hiryu*, missed
Ens R Benson	Attacked *Soryu*	Attacked *Hiryu*, result unknown

Second Division

Lt Gordon Sherwood	Attacked *Soryu*	Attacked *Hiryu*, result unknown, shot up after pulling out
Ens Roy Isaman	Lost bomb, strafed *Soryu*	Attacked *Hiryu*, result unknown
Ens Philip Cobb	Attacked *Soryu*	Shot up during dive, probably missed
Lt Harold Bottomley	Hit *Soryu* aft among 'Vals'	Shot up during dive, probably missed
Ens Charles Lane	Lost bomb, strafed *Soryu*	Very near miss on *Haruna*
Ens John Butler (K)	Attacked *Haruna*	Killed by 'Zeros' before diving

Third Division

Lt DeWitt Shumway (XO)	Attacked *Soryu*	Led VB-3 dive on *Hiryu*, missed, shot up on pulling out
Ens Robert Elder	Attacked *Isokaze*	Very near miss on *Haruna*
Ens Bunyan Cooner	Attacked *Isokaze*	Shot up before dive, probably jettisoned
Lt Osborne Wiseman (K)	Attacked *Haruna*	Killed by 'Zeros' before diving
Ens Milford Merrill	Lost bomb, strafed *Isokaze*	Shot up before dive, probably jettisoned
N.B.	Several more hits on *Soryu*	One, possibly two hits on *Hiryu*

HIRYU AIR GROUP (all attacks on *Yorktown*)

Dive bombers
First Division – most with 532lb land bombs

*Lt Michio Kobayashi (K)	Jettisoned. Stayed behind to report	By Lt Provost & Ens Halford (VF-6)
PO1 Kihichiro Yamada (K)	Jettisoned	VF-3 claims included:
PO3 Hideo Sakai (K)	Jettisoned	Lt Brassfield – 4
*Lt Takenori Kondo (K)	Jettisoned	Lt McCuskey –3
PO2 Nobumichi Nakao (K)	Jettisoned	Ens Gibbs – 2
Sea1 Masao Seki (K)	Jettisoned	Lts Woollen, Barnes – 1 each
*PO1 Tamotsu Imaizumi (K)	Hit island AA batteries	By AA fire as he released bomb
PO2 Takayoshi Tsuchiya	Missed astern (SAP), returned to *Hiryu*	
PO3 Naoshi Koizumi (K)	Very near miss astern	By AA fire as he released bomb

Second Division – most with 551lb SAP

WO Toshikatsu Nishihara (K)	*Lt Michiji Yamashita flying as observer. Jettisoned	By Lt Mattson (VF-3)
PO1 Sadao Matsumoto	Missed astern (land bomb), returned to *Hiryu*	
PO3 Junichi Kuroki (K)	Downed with bomb	*See note above*
WO Iwao Nakazawa	Hit amidships. *Ens Shimematsu Nakayama flying as observer, returned to *Hiryu*	
PO1 Tetsuo Seo	Very near miss to starboard, returned to *Hiryu*	
PO2 Sumio Kondo (K)	Downed with bomb	*See note above*
*WO Shizuo Nakagawa	Hit forward elevator after 'glide bombing' approach, returned to *Hiryu*	
PO2 Takazo Ikeda (K)	Downed with bomb	Possibly by Ens Stephen Groves (K, maybe by AA)
Sea1 Issei Fuchigami (K)	Downed with bomb	and Ens Formanek (VF-8), but also 5" AA fire

Fighter escort

*Lt Yasihiro Shigematsu	Only escort to reach *Yorktown*, returned to *Hiryu*. KIA 1944 with 10 confirmed kills	
PO2 Noboru Totaka (K)		By Ens Bain (VF-3)
Sea1 Sueyoshi Yoshimoto (K)		By Lt Crommelin (VF-3)
*WOYoshijiro Minegishi	Damaged while attacking returning *Enterprise* SDBs, returned to *Hiryu*, escorted second strike	
PO1 Hitoshi Sasaki	Damaged while attacking returning *Enterprise* SDBs, ditched	
PO3 Minoru Chiyoshima (K)		By Lt Bass (VF-3)

Torpedo bombers
First Division

*Lt Joichi Tomonaga (K)	Attacked starboard side when on fire, missed	By LCdr Thach (VF-3)
PO1 Zenkichi Ishii (K)	Attacked starboard side, missed, killed going away	By Lt Rawie's Division (VF-6)
PO1 Hachiro Sugimoto (K)	Intercepted, jettisoned near <u>Balch</u>	By Lt Leonard (VF-3)
*WO Yukio Obayashi (K)	Attacked port side, missed	By AA, Ens Adams (VF-3) close behind
Sea1 Takeshi Suzuki (K)	Shot down before attacking	By Lt Woollen (VF-3)

Second Division

PO1 Toshio Takahashi	*Lt Toshio Hashimoto flying as observer. Wide right from port side, returned to *Hiryu*, survived the war	
PO2 Takuro Yanagimoto	Probable hit probable (centre element of port side attack), returned to *Hiryu*	
PO3 Yoshimitsu Nagayama	Probable hit probable (centre element of port side attack), returned to *Hiryu*	
*WO Shigeo Suzuki (*Akagi*)	Third aircraft in centre element of port side attack, torpedo hung up, took it back to *Hiryu*	
Sea1 Harumi Nakao	Left-hand aircraft of port side attack, badly shot up, returned to *Hiryu*	

Fighter escort

*Lt Shigeru Mori (K)	Attacked Mach Barnes	By Lt McCuskey (VF-3)
PO2 Toshi Yamamoto (K)	Also attacked Barnes	By Ens Roach (VF-6)
*WO Yoshijiro Minegishi	Shot down Lt Woollen, killed Ens George Hopper (both VF-3), returned to *Hiryu*. KIA 1944	
PO2 Keji Kotani	Shot down Ens Gibbs (VF-3), returned to *Hiryu*.	
*PO1 Akira Yamamoto (*Kaga*)	Attacked AP1 Packard (VF-6), Barnes and Thach, returned to *Hiryu*. KIA 1944 with 13 confirmed kills	
PO3 Makoto Bando (*Kaga*)	Damaged by McCuskey, returned to *Hiryu*. Survived the war	
NB Mori, Yamamoto and Minegishi all flew brand new Sixth (Midway) Air Group 'Zeroes' on this sortie		

*Division (*chutai*) or section (*shotai*) leaders

Notes
Japanese ranks   WO – Warrant Officer. PO1, 2, 3 – Petty Officer First, Second, Third Class. Sea1 – Seaman First Class.
US ranks   AP1 – Aviation Pilot First Class. Mach – Machinist

Sources
Lundstrom, John, *The First Team*, Annapolis, 1984   Cressman, Robert (ed.), *A Glorious Page In Our History*, Missoula, 1990

REFERENCES

CHAPTER 1 **START**

1. Fuchida Mitsuo and Okumiya Masatake, *Midway: The Battle that Doomed Japan*, Annapolis, 1955, p. 247.
2. Goldstein, Donald and Dillon, Katherine, *Fading Victory: the Diary of Admiral Matome Ugaki 1941-1945*, Pittsburgh, 1991, p. 122.
3. Marder, Arthur, *Old Friends, New Enemies*, Oxford, 1981, p. 177.
4. Hirohito became Emperor Showa in 1926, just as his father, Yoshihito (b. 1879), had become Taisho in 1912 and his grandfather, Mutsihito (b. 1852), became Meiji in 1867.
5. Willmott, H. P., *Empires in the Balance*, London, 1982, p. 12.
6. Slim, William, *Defeat into Victory*, London, 1957, p. 526.

CHAPTER 2 **MIND**

1. Disrespect intended only for those who employ the term. The works in question are Wetzler, Peter, *Hirohito and War*, Honolulu, 1998 and Bix, Herbert, *Hirohito and the Making of Modern Japan*, London, 2000.
2. Dower, John, *War Without Mercy*, New York, 1976.
3. Ikegami Eiko, *The Taming of the Samurai*, London, 1995.
4. Miller, Edward, *War Plan Orange*, Annapolis, 1991, p. 29.
5. KIA November 1943. Chicago airport, the world's busiest, was named in O'Hare's honour.

CHAPTER 3 **MACHINERY**

1. Holmes, W. J., *Double-Edged Secrets*, Annapolis, 1979.
2. Campbell, John, *Naval Weapons of World War Two*, London, 1985.
3. Francillon, R. J., *Japanese Aircraft of the Pacific War*, London, 1979. In the absence of a similar 'bible' for USN aircraft, performance data was averaged from several Internet sites.
4. Japanese records are clear on this, but the negligible damage done by a 532-pound bomb to the runway at Midway led some to believe that the lighter bombs had also been employed. After the battle, Nimitz complained about the ineffectiveness of the semi armour-piercing bombs dropped by his aviators, but they proved devastatingly effective against the wooden decks of the carriers.
5. Brown, Captain Eric M., *Duels in the Sky*, Shrewsbury, 1989, contains comparative assessments of the various types by one who flew many of them.

6. For a full discussion, see Lundstrom, John, *The First Team*, Annapolis, 1984, Chapter 18. The six-gun configuration responded to a British requirement for their version (Martlet), intended for convoy protection against the robust Focke-Wulf 200 Kurier (Condor).

CHAPTER 5 **INTELLIGENCE**

1. This chapter is based primarily on Parker, Frederick, 'A Priceless Advantage: US Navy CI and the battles of Coral Sea, Midway and the Aleutians', from the *United States Criptologic History* posted at www.CENTURYinter.net/midway by permission of the National Security Agency.
2. Prange, Gordon, *Miracle at Midway*, p 99.
3. Not to be confused with Lieutenant Commander Thomas Dyer, second only to Rochefort as a 'Hypo' cryptanalyst. George Dyer is only mentioned once in John Prados's omnibus work *Combined Fleet Decoded*, New York, 1995. Nonetheless, this intelligence summary, which identified what might have been a fatal oversight, was produced during the brief period when he was King's personal intelligence officer.
4. Layton, Rear Admiral Edwin, *And I Was There*, New York, 1985.

CHAPTER 7 **POINT LUCK**

1. Reynolds, Clark, 'The Truth About Miles Browning', Appendix 5 in Cressman, Robert (ed.), *A Glorious Page in Our History*, Missoula, 1990.
2. US servicemen traditionally hate the Rear Echelon Mother-Esteemers (REMFs) with a rare passion. REMF-in-chief for the battle of Midway was Rear Admiral Leigh Noyes.
3. Before the men of *Yorktown* joined him Thach's command had consisted of the experienced Machinists Barnes and Cheek, as well as the rookie Ensign Dibb, whom he kept under his wing.

CHAPTER 8 **SACRIFICE**

1. Ferrier had lied about his age to join up and persisted in the deceit until he left the US Navy following service in the Korean and Vietnam wars. He was with the expedition that found the sunken *Yorktown* in 1998, see Ballard, Robert, *Return to Midway*, London, 1999.
2. Details and map from Lundstrom, John, *The First Team*, Annapolis, 1984, in turn based on unpublished research by Bowen Weisheit for the Ensign C. Markland Kelly Jr. Foundation of Baltimore, Maryland. Kelly was one of the two VF-8 pilots who was never found.

CHAPTER 9 **KILLING STROKE**

1. Approximately fourteen Zeros were lost in the battle over the carriers (four, *Kaga*; four, *Hiryu*; three, *Akagi*; three, *Soryu*). Six from *Hiryu* (four lost, one damaged) escorted the

first *Yorktown* strike; four from *Hiryu* (two lost) and two from *Kaga* the second. Six from *Soryu*, four from *Kaga*, three from *Hiryu* and one from *Akagi* were flying CAP when *Hiryu* was wrecked, suggesting that six from *Akagi* and five from *Kaga* were caught on board. Only two of *Hiryu*'s Midway-damaged Zeros were unserviceable, and her air unit put three of the 6th Air Group fighters that she was ferrying into service.

2. Stafford, Commander (R) Edward P, *The Big E*, New York, 1962, p. 94.

3. Lundstrom, John, *The First Team*, p. 359.

CHAPTER 10 **DEATH THROES**

1. Gaido had received a promotion and a Distinguished Flying Cross for remaining at his post to fire at the 'body-crashing' Nell that had clipped the tail off his Dauntless during Halsey's raid of 1 February 1942 raid on the Gilbert Islands. O'Flaherty and Osmus were posthumously awarded the Navy Cross and had destroyers (D 340 and DE 701) named for them in 1943.

2. *Yorktown* had eight spare aircraft on board, *Enterprise* had four and *Hornet* had only one.

CHAPTER 11 **FINISH**

1. Fletcher awaits a good biographer, and it is my understanding that John Lundstrom will shortly, or may have already, filled the void.

2. Only five of each, some damaged, returned from the first strikes, but *Hiryu* carried spare aircraft. Earlier signals also mentioned nine or ten Zeros for escort duty.

3. In *Miracle at Midway*, New York, 1982, (p. 290), Gordon Prange declared that 'Gallaher was much more fortunate than he deserved to be', but we really have only Shumway's word that the results obtained by his disobedience justified the disorder into which it threw the VS/VB-6 attack.

4. Nagumo killed himself after unsuccessfully defending Saipan against US assault in June 1944. Kusaka rose to the rank of vice admiral and survived the war. Kuroshima served out the war on the NGS, where we may be sure he was not permitted to forget his earlier arrogance. Genda rose to the post-war rank of general in the Japanese Self-Defence Force and went on to pursue a career in politics. Fuchida became a Christian evangelist. Ariga and Toshio Abe, the destroyer-division commanders who would have been hanged for the torture and murder of the US aviators, respectively died in command of *Yamato*, in a Kamikaze mission in April 1945, and of her sister ship, *Shinano*, which was completed as an aircraft carrier and sunk on her maiden voyage by U.S.S. *Archerfish* in November 1944.

ANNOTATED BIBLIOGRAPHY

I owe a particular debt and credit throughout to:

Cressman, Robert (ed.), *A Glorious Page in Our History*, Missoula, 1990.

Lundstrom, John, *The First Team*, Annapolis, 1984.

Office of Naval Intelligence, *The Japanese Story of the Battle of Midway*, Washington DC, 1947.

USN Action Reports at *www.history.navy.mil/docs/wwii/mid1.htm*

Thematic inspiration came from:

Barde, Robert, 'Midway: Tarnished Victory', *Military Affairs*, Vol. XLVII, No. 4, December 1983.

Musashi Miyamoto (trans. Thomas Cleary), *The Book of Five Rings*, Boston, 1994.

Deep background came from:

Marder, Arthur, *Old Friends, New Enemies*, Oxford, 1981.

Warner, Denis and Peggy, *The Tide at Sunrise*, London, 1974.

Willmott, H. P., *Empires in the Balance*, London, 1982.

Other important narratives are:

Lord, Walter, *Incredible Victory*, New York, 1967.

Morison, Samuel Eliot, *Coral Sea, Midway and Submarine Actions, May 1942 – August 1942*, Boston, 1975.

Prange, Gordon, *Miracle at Midway*, New York, 1982

For the Japanese read:

Agawa Hiroyuki, *The Reluctant Admiral*, Tokyo, 1979.

Chihaya Masataka, 'An Intimate Look at the Japanese Navy', in Goldstein, Donald and Dillon, Katherine (eds.), *The Pearl Harbor Papers*, New York, 1993.

Dull, Paul, *A Battle History of the Imperial Japanese Navy 1941–1945*, Annapolis, 1978.

Evans, David and Peattie, Mark, *Kaigun*, Annapolis, 1997.

Fuchida Mitsuo and Okumiya Masatake, *Midway: The Battle That Doomed Japan*, Annapolis, 1955.

Goldstein, Donald and Dillon, Katherine (eds.), *Fading Victory: the Diary of Admiral Matome Ugaki, 1941–1945*, Pittsburgh, 1991.

For the Americans read:

Buell, Thomas, *Master of Sea Power*, Boston, 1980. [Biography of Admiral King.]

Ferrier, Harry, 'Torpedo Squadron Eight: The Other Chapter', *US Naval Institute Proceedings*, October 1964.

Gay, George, *Sole Survivor*, Naples, Florida, 1979.

Heinl, Lieutenant Colonel Robert, *The Defense of Wake*, Washington DC, 1947, and *Marines at Midway*, Washington DC, 1948.

Miller, Edward, *War Plan Orange*, Annapolis, 1991.

Parker, Frederick, 'A Priceless Advantage: US Navy CI and the Battles of Coral Sea, Midway and the Aleutians', from the *United States Cryptologic History*, posted at *www.CENTURYinter.net/midway* by permission of the National Security Agency.

Potter, E. B., *Nimitz*, Annapolis, 1976.

INDEX

PICTURE CREDITS